The Bounded Field

New Directions in Anthropology

General Editor: **Jacqueline Waldren**, *Institute of Social Anthropology, University of Oxford*

THE BOUNDED FIELD

Localism and Local Identity in an Italian Alpine Valley

Jaro Stacul

Berghahn Books
New York • Oxford

First published in 2003 by

Berghahn Books

www.berghahnbooks.com

Copyright © 2003 Jaro Stacul

Library of Congress Cataloging-in-Publication Data

Stacul, Jaro.
  The bounded field: localism and local identity in an Italian Alpine valley / Jaro Stacul.
    p. cm. -- (New directions in anthropology; v. 18)
  Includes bibliographical references and index.
  ISBN 1-57181-463-9 (alk. paper)
    1. Ethnicity--Italy--Trentino--Alto Adige. 2. Villages--Italy--Trentino--Alto Adige.
  3. Trentino-Alto Adige (Italy)--History. 4. Trentino-Alto Adige (Italy)--Social life and customs. I. Title. II. Series.

  DG975.T792S67 2004
  307.72'0945'38--dc21   2003052309

British Library Cataloguing in Publication Data

A catalogue record for this book is available from the British Library.

Printed in the United States on acid-free paper.

ISBN 1-57181-463-9 hardback

Contents

LIST OF ILLUSTRATIONS

Photographs by the author unless otherwise stated.

NOTE ON LANGUAGE

Most villagers speak Italian as well as their own dialect, a variant of Venetic, and this book contains words and phrases in both, accompanied by English translation. As far as the transcription of the dialect terms is concerned, I have availed myself of the dictionary of the local dialect, '*Dizionario Primierotto*', by Livio Tissot (1996).

In order to distinguish the languages used in the valley, words in the local dialect are printed in ***bold italics*** while Italian words are printed in *ordinary italics*. *Ordinary italics* are also used for other non-English words and for emphasis.

PREFACE AND ACKNOWLEDGEMENTS

No academic work is purely the result of individual endeavour: rather, it is the outcome of the efforts of the researcher aided by those who have contributed with advice and constructive criticism. I have accumulated several debts, both in Cambridge and in my fieldsite, in the preparation of this work which represents a revised and expanded version of my doctoral dissertation in Social Anthropology at the University of Cambridge. These debts can hardly be fully acknowledged.

With much gratitude I wish to thank the granting bodies whose financial support made possible both my stay in Cambridge as a research student and the writing up of the dissertation on which this book is based. A one-year scholarship to study abroad from the University of Trieste enabled me to undertake my postgraduate studies. Funds from the Accademia Nazionale dei Lincei and a TMR Grant from the European Commission enabled me to complete my studies at the University of Cambridge. Additional funding from Churchill College, the William Wyse Fund of Trinity College, and the Audrey Richards Fund of the Department of Social Anthropology of Cambridge University helped with the costs of my fieldwork in the Italian Alps. As a postdoctoral Research Associate I have been provided financial support throughout the various stages of writing this book. I am grateful to the University of Trieste for giving me a Young Researcher Grant, and to the British Academy for a Small Research Grant which enabled me to spend some time in Italy at the European University Institute in Florence and in Trent to collect much needed bibliographical and archival material.

I owe a special intellectual debt to my Ph.D. supervisor, Ray Abrahams, and to Patrick Heady. They patiently read the drafts of this work, and made several important suggestions during my fieldwork, when I was writing up the results of my research, and when I turned my dissertation into a book. Their comments and comparative readings that they suggested were crucial in helping me to make sense of the information I collected in the field. Their constructive criticism helped strengthen arguments, and I learned a great deal from them about localism and local politics during the course of my work. Susan Drucker-Brown and Davide Però read an earlier draft of the manuscript when it was close to completion, shared their ideas, and gave important suggestions that improved the quality of this book. An anonymous reader provided insightful comments that became the basis for the final revisions of this work. However, I take every responsibility for the views expressed herein.

My grateful thanks go to my examiners, Alan MacFarlane and Paul Sant Cassia, for a stimulating viva, and to Maria Arioti, Gil Daryn, Hildegard Diemberger, Paola Filippucci, Christina Moutsou, David Sutton and Jacqueline Waldren for their feedback on parts of the manuscript, either as a draft of this book, or in the form of a doctoral dissertation. I also benefited greatly from discussions with Donatella Della Porta, Sarah Green, Helen Kopnina, Luca Libertini, Maryon McDonald and Cesare Poppi on some of the issues explored in this work. I had other chances to discuss some of the findings of my research, particularly when I delivered a paper at the conference 'Roots and Rituals: Managing Ethnicity', which took place in Amsterdam in the spring of 1998, and when I presented another paper at the workshop 'Neo-nationalism in the EU: Anthropological Perspectives', held in Brussels in early 2002. I am indebted to the Department of Social Anthropology of the University of Cambridge for providing a desk space and the infrastructure, not to mention a stimulating intellectual environment, which enhanced the completion of this book. In Cambridge my thanks are also due to Paul Caldwell and to Vince Woodley for technical support. The final revisions for this work were completed after I was elected into a Lectureship at the School of Social Sciences and International Development at the University of Wales Swansea. I would like to thank Felicia Hughes-Freeland, Margaret Kenna, and the other colleagues of the School for their welcome, and for their encouragement in my completion of this manuscript.

It goes without saying that one of my main debts is to the people in the field. My greatest thanks are due to Agata ('Aghetina') Boso for her hospitality, and especially for helping me to establish contacts in Caoria. She made me familiar with the mores of her native community, and played a decisive role in the success of my fieldwork. Without her help this research would not have been possible, and these acknowledgements cannot fully express how much I owe to her. I also wish to express my gratitude to don Diego Mengarda for giving me accommodation while I was conducting fieldwork in Ronco, and for allowing me to search the parish records of Caoria and Ronco.

In Caoria my thanks are also due to Federico Loss 'Schenèla', who took some of his time to introduce me to the world of the hunters. He gave me a real sense of what going hunting is like. However, I cannot measure the contribution offered by Antonia ('Antonietta') Corona to my understanding of Caoria and its people. In Ronco I wish to thank Bortolo Rattin for giving me detailed information about his village and its recent history, and my neighbours, the Fontana families. Obviously it would not be possible to thank all the people in Caoria and Ronco (not to mention the other villages) to whom I owe almost as much.

I am very grateful to Renzo Grosselli, Diego Leoni and the late Corrado Trotter (1914–97) for their patience and kind help, and particularly for making me familiar with Trentine history and for stimulating discussions. I also owe a debt to the Municipality (*Comune*) of Canal San Bovo for allowing me to search their historical archives, and especially to Maria-Wanda Sperandio and Bruno Zortea for their invaluable help. It is thanks to them that I managed to find most of the unpublished historical information necessary for this book.

Various other people and institutions, both inside and outside the valley, contributed to the collection of historical information and quantitative data. Among them I wish to thank the Land Registry Office (*Ufficio del Catasto*) of Fiera di Primiero and the Emigration Office of the Autonomous Province of Trent for giving me access to their records, and the librarians of the public libraries of Canal San Bovo and Fiera di Primiero. Finally, my thanks are due to the Museo degli Usi e Costumi della Gente Trentina of San Michele all'Adige and the Ente Parco Paneveggio-Pale di San Martino for funding exploratory research in the Vanoi valley in the early 1990s.

J.S.
Cambridge/Swansea, May 2002

1
INTRODUCING LOCALISM

Back to the 'Local'?

This book is an analysis of localism and local identity in an Italian Alpine valley in the late twentieth century. For the anthropologists studying peoples and their cultures and places no concept seems as central to anthropological fieldwork as the notion of localism. But how is it defined? Localism may be defined as a 'set of ideas about the significance of place' (Strathern 1984a: 44) or as the 'continuing reference to "place" in assertion of a political or cultural will to distinctiveness' (Nadel-Klein 1991: 501); in its pejorative meaning it also connotes the 'tendency to see communities as different from each other and to prefer one's own' (Reed 1982: 136), and in Italy the term refers to the tendency to give one's loyalty and allegiance to one's locality rather than to the state (Cento Bull 2000: 99). In exploring this issue this book partly follows a long tradition in anthropological studies in the Mediterranean area, which flourished particularly between the 1950s and the 1980s, but became less popular as a consequence of the shift of focus from 'local' issues to 'global' ones. However, the renewed emphasis on the 'local' in the social sciences suggests that there is no automatic contradiction between such interests, and the present work attempts in fact to examine some connections between them.

The recent reemergence of the 'local' in the social sciences is the consequence of the decline of a political discourse overlooking the local itself and its particularisms (Mabileau 1993: 22), and especially of the redefinition of the concept of homogeneous national culture (see for example Bhabha 1994: 5). Underlying this renewed emphasis is the fact that the state no longer imposes (or is not willing to impose) an organising principle on society: it is no longer expected to perform certain functions that used to legitimate its existence (Bauman 1998: 65), and does not necessarily represent an uncontested form of political allegiance and cultural belonging. During the last few years the 'local' came to the fore as a result of the decoupling of nation and space (Delanty 1999: 57): in this sense, the 'local' assumed a political dimension, which rests on its potential 'to support the central values of late modernity, and thus make the national seem like a relic of an older authoritarian society' (Frykman 1999: 17). Geographers and sociologists have acknowledged the political dimension of the 'local' (Keith and Pile 1993), and in particular the role of place as the ideal basis for political action (Harvey 1989: 302–3). Especially at a time when everything is in motion, changing and shifting, and nothing is certain, humans look for a community to which they can belong (Hobsbawm 1996: 40), and opting for a territorial community may give them the sense of safety that a rapidly changing world can hardly provide (Löfgren 1996: 165). Yet this attachment to place, to the 'local', may imply increasing suspicion against those who do not belong to the community; it may be expressed by intolerance of difference, or by what Bauman (1995: 251) has called a 'reparochialization' of politics, which goes hand in hand with a politics of culture aimed at reinforcing exclusion (Wright 1998). Holmes (2000: 3) aptly describes this phenomenon as 'integralism', which is expressed by a renewed commitment to a distinct regional culture, and very often to the routines and intimacies of family life: it may represent a consciousness of belonging linked to a specific cultural (and geographical) milieu. This commitment, the author notes, is not mere nostalgia, but is a way of coping with changes: 'integralist' is also the political form such attitudes may take on, and may be expressed by an exclusionary political economy which recasts society (and, I would add, the 'local') as a domain of political engagement (Holmes 2000: 5).

In Social Anthropology, too, locality features as a relevant theme of debate. Yet the debate surrounding it in recent years hardly tackled its political dimension, but rather centred on the elusiveness of the concept (Smith 1999: 136), and on the view that in a globalising world localities are not necessarily actual social forms, but represent instead structures of feeling (Appadurai 1995: 222). Such a view also led some scholars to postulate the unsustainability of the concept of the 'local' for an understanding of culture, to challenge the equation between culture itself and community (Baumann 1996) and particular places, and to stress the significance of deterritorialisation and displacement (see, for example, Gupta and Ferguson 1997 and Rapport and Dawson 1998). Rapport and Dawson (1998: 27), for instance, went so far as to suggest that one's identity is not formed in a locality, but 'on the move'. Likewise Lovell (1998: 5) argued that what characterises locality is multivocality, and suggested that boundedness of localities is instead a reflection of a modernist theoretical analysis.[1] But how far do multivocality and movement inform the constructions and representations of locality as the context for political action nowadays?

Anthropology and the 'Local'

This study sets out to go back to the idea of boundedness by exploring how it is expressed, in the era of late modernity, in two villages. Yet anthropology's interest in the 'local' is not novel, and this study is part of a tradition: anthropological scholarship has addressed the issue of European localism in ways reflecting the changes of theoretical perspective within the discipline. It concentrated on diversity within nation-states, and particularly on the importance of locality and of localised cultural idioms. Earlier European case studies focused on small-scale, face-to-face and relatively bounded social units in the Mediterranean and, following the structural-functionalist tradition, highlighted the conception of community based upon locality as typical of southern Europe (see, for example, Pitt-Rivers 1954; Campbell 1964). The notion of 'locality' acquired a different dimension in the 1970s, when the discipline's theoretical focus shifted to change and structuring factors such as state formation, national integration, and bureaucratisation (Boissevain 1975: 5–11; Davis 1977: 18; Grillo 1980: 5–7), and especially to the relationship between the national and the local, the macro and the micro or the 'whole' and its 'parts': social change at the local level chiefly emerged as the outcome of external forces (Goddard 1994: 58). What united those studies was an emphasis on state processes, and on the way urban values affect the lives of people even in small villages (see, for example, Cole and Wolf 1974; Silverman 1975). The debate on 'locality' that went on in that period was characterised by stress on the economic, social, and political forces which hold together 'locality' itself and shape local identity. Village identity, for instance, was considered determined by the economic and political systems that encompass rural communities (Cole and Wolf 1974: 285). Overall Mediterranean anthropology between the 1970s and the 1980s focused on the issue of the link and gaps between locality and the nation-state (Goddard 1994: 85), and the relationship between these two was interpreted as the replication of that between tradition and modernity. The ascription of tradition to locality, in particular, was predicated upon the existence of 'localistic' attitudes, among which strong subnational identities, and preference for personalistic forms of political action loom largest.[2]

While locality and the state (and the countryside and the city) were treated as synonyms respectively of tradition and modernity (Davis 1969: 173–4), it was also agreed that urban values play a crucial role in affecting the social actors' conceptualisations of locality as a frame of identification: localistic sentiment was associated with a rhetoric of 'urbanness' and 'urbanity', and expressed by the idiom of 'civilisation' (Silverman 1975; see also Corbin and Corbin 1987). According to Silverman (1975), this idiom is an ideology about town life used in villages to discriminate between insiders and outsiders, and is promoted by local notables who act as mediators between locality and the nation. This notion of 'civilisation' was looked upon as an integral part of the cultural dominance of Mediterranean agro-towns over the rural hinterlands (Blok and Driessen 1984).

This rhetoric of urbanness is particularly important to understanding localism in Italy, because it was regarded as evidence that the social order propagated by the élites is widely accepted: in this regard, Cole and Wolf (1974: 281) argued in their work on ethnicity in an Alpine valley that one aspect distinguishing the Italian-speaking village from the neighbouring German-speaking one is that for the former's inhabitants the ideal life is not on the land, but in the city. In sum, central to this notion of 'locality' is the role of political and economic pressure and ideology, and the idea of a 'local' society, just like national economy and people, chiefly emerged against the background (or as the construction) of an encompassing and homogenising national entity or in opposition to it.

In the 1980s Anthony Cohen questioned the view that locality is shaped by external forces only, and tackled the issue in a rather different way by introducing a Barthian notion of boundaries, and by arguing that local identities are formed primarily from within: according to him, 'locality' is not formed by factors such as 'isolation', but by a self-willed process of active identity maintenance, and acquires its significance from the meaning that actors attach to it (1982: 9). Cohen (1985: 16–20; 1986: 10–13) conceptualised 'locality' as a 'symbolic construction', and suggested that with industrialisation the 'structural' boundaries of locality are replaced by 'symbolic' ones. In his analysis the nation-state exists mainly as an impersonal force which plays little or no part in the formulation of identity. His theories have been criticised on the grounds that while he set out to dereify the nation in the name of the local, in fact he reified the local at the expense of the nation (Knight 1994: 216).[3]

The growing interest in Europe, the popularity of the concept of the 'invention of tradition' (Hobsbawm 1983) in the 1980s, along with a critique of the notion of the Mediterranean as a culture area (Llobera 1986; Herzfeld 1987; Pina-Cabral 1989), resulted in a shift of interest from local communities to ethnic differences within Europe, especially in the groups of people who chose to identify with nationalist movements or strong linguistic minorities (such as, for example, the Basques and the Bretons) that did not achieve statehood. Although the notion of locality hardly came into play, these studies proved useful for understanding local identity too: most of them introduced an instrumentalist view of ethnic identity based on Ardener's notion of 'hollow categories' (1989a: 69–71), i.e. groups that are not biologically distinct populations, yet are needed by other groups (or by the larger society) for classificatory purposes (see for example Chapman 1978 and McDonald 1989).

What unites most of the studies of European localities until the 1980s and from the late 1980s onwards is an attempt to answer the question of who creates local or ethnic identities. On the one hand local and ethnic identities are deemed to reflect the social order propagated by the élites (i.e. politicians or intellectuals), and individual social actors hardly play an active role; on the other hand local identity emerges as a subjective construction (see for example Cohen 1985). This polarisation has resulted in a reification of either official discourse or subjectivities, but the articulation between the constructions of the élites and the individuals' readings of them hardly became an object of enquiry. Perhaps it may be postulated that it is not so much the idea of local identity as a construction that needs to be rediscussed, as the theoretical framework within which such an idea has been formulated: most of the existing studies reflect a conceptualisation of the nation (and, implicitly, the region or the political party) as an entity existing over and above social relations. In other words, they hold on to a view of the nation (and national identity) as an important component of how social actors conceptualise the social order. Yet recent shifts in theory and historical developments suggest that both this conceptualisation and an analysis of identities, whether political or territorial, as mere 'inventions' are rather reductive. Although the role individuals play in making sense of the nation has been noted by various authors, attempts at finding out how this process works are rare. This is rather striking: as Bourdieu (1977) and de Certeau (1984) have shown, social agents never simply enact culture, but reinterpret and reappropriate it in their own ways.

The little interest of social scientists in individual agency in the study of nationalisms and micro-nationalisms largely stems from an image of politics as a 'formulation, achievement and sustained organisation of collective interests', which implies that forms of expression that do not meet such criteria are outside politics, or simply irrelevant (Lüdtke 1985: 303–5). Gavin Smith (1999: 44–45) relates this to the influence of Marxism, and particularly of Gramsci: although Gramsci was very attentive to working people's perceptions of the world, for him a particular set of perceptions could only be interpreted as they occurred within specific political projects, and nationalism is no exception. Despite Gramsci's attempt to shift his focus from organisations, discipline, and propaganda to individual agency, in fact he continued to understand collective expression in terms of the institutions that made this expression possible, and his interest in perception remained purely theoretical. So, despite his emphasis on agency, politics remained to be understood chiefly as a collective fact, with the result that political expression ended up being referred to practices, legitimation, or representation made by the state or by political parties. This conceptualisation of politics implies that social actors do not express ideas of their own, and that their views replicate those propagated by the political establishment (the state, political parties, etc.). By contrast, now it is agreed that nationalist ideologies, i.e. those that refer to the production of conceptions of peoplehood (Fox 1990: 5), often achieve their appeal when they are accommodated to local-level discourses.[4] States or political parties do not simply impose their values on local society, but local society itself may be a motive force in the consolidation of the nation-state and in forging a national or political identity (Sahlins 1989: 8). In other words, ideologies find fertile ground when they 'mobilise' themes already existing in local culture, and the associations individuals make between themselves and nationalist or party ideologies may be decisive for the ideologies' achievement of their appeal. Anthony Cohen (1996: 803–4) aptly made this point when he suggested that we need to identify the difference between official representations of the nation (or locality) and the individuals' interpretations of those representations: while the politician 'collectivises' nationalism or regionalism, the individual 'personalises' it (Cohen 1996: 805), so the politician must formulate political messages in ways which enable individuals to appropriate such messages for their own requirements. This means that a theory of regional or national identity has to allow for human agency, and so it has to put people back into regions or nations. If we take on board this idea we can no longer assume that the nation or the political party are powerful concepts, and if they are we should ask why. Knowledge has become more available and more contested, and these days societies are no longer defined by a dominant actor or institution: neither the élites nor collective actors have the power to define the 'situation' (Delanty 1999: 9), so questions of human agency become problematic.

Linked to the issue of human agency is that of European integration: European integration and 'globalisation' have posed the problem of the relationships between local societies and global processes and transnational units (such as the European Union) encompassing the nation-state and 'locality'. While the idea of European economic integration is associated with the common market and the removal of trade barriers, it also raises the issue of how a 'European' identity relates to a local one (Macdonald 1993). Although it seems unlikely that a European identity will replace a national or regional one (Passerini 2000; Shore 2000: 18), the fact remains that the European Union's policy aimed at promoting local identities and European regions can also bring about renewed stress on regional identity and the erosion of national consensus (Shore and Black 1994: 291–4) and further integralist political engagements. In some parts of Europe this erosion is engendered by the transfer of national powers to local and regional bodies, and by the demands for devolution facilitated by the European Union (Kroes 2000: 40). So, while the 'old' national boundaries are blurred, new ones may be created not only vis-à-vis non-Europeans (see for example Stolcke 1995), but also within Europe itself, given that the construction of a European unity has to contend with divisions (McDonald 1996: 48; Stråth 2000) and can lead to separation, hatred and parochialism (Tilly 1992: 716–7). While the dynamics of territorial development is increasingly 'placeless' from the viewpoint of the dominant organisations, the defence of specific interests or of autonomous identities may take the form of irreducible local experience (Castells and Henderson 1987: 7; Revelli 1995: 211).

The reemergence of locality is also expressed by the reappraisal and idealisation of customs and rituals of the 'traditional' community-centred way of life abandoned in the quest for modernisation (Boissevain 1994: 51). This goes hand in hand with people's tendency to understand themselves genealogically and to be interpreted by others in genealogical terms (Frykman 1999: 14), which may have the effect of casting the region and locality as foci of attachment at the expense of larger entities. On top of this, the advent of regionalist movements in various parts of Western Europe between the 1980s and the 1990s revealed that region-alism has assumed a new dimension in relation to globalisation, as such move-ments make competing claims to 'European-ness', and have a programme of European federalism on the basis of regions rather than states. More importantly, their sense of distinctiveness is often predicated upon affluence (Harvie 1994; De Winter and Türsan 1998).

While anthropology has been sensitive to the expansion of economic and political scale, it has not yet paid much attention to the new regional Europe. On the one hand, this little interest stems from the assumption that the new region-alism raises the same theoretical issues that the invention of tradition did in the 1980s, and so it is not new; on the other hand, region building did not attract leading intellectuals: rather, it is planners, entrepreneurs or local artists who are the main active participants in this process (Frykman 1999: 16). The other prob-lem, as I hinted earlier in this chapter, is that while there have been attempts to problematise 'locality' (e.g. Gupta and Ferguson 1997: 6–7), the outcome has often been an increasing emphasis on mobility and displacement at the expense of 'locality' itself as a context for political action. Although the significance of mobility and displacement is undeniable for an understanding of 'locality', the fact remains that mobility of actors does not necessarily inform the ways 'locality' itself is constructed by politicians and by those who live in a certain place. This does not entail taking for granted the rootedness of peoples in their own territo-ries, but rather means looking at 'locality' as it is represented and described by individual social actors, and as the context for observing how encompassing 'global', national and regional systems interact with local meanings at the most intimate levels. Central to the definition of locality is also the idea of collective identity, an idea which, paradoxically, is being deconstructed. Yet in order to achieve consensus regionalist movements have necessarily to construct an 'imag-ined community' (Anderson 1991); but what kind of 'imagined community' do actors or political leaders appeal to? How can social actors conceptualise a local or regional identity at a time when the idea of collective identity is being decon-structed? The study of localism in Italy raises very similar issues, as will be seen in the next section.

Localism in the Anthropology of Italy

The anthropological study of 'locality' in Italy reflects a concern with the same issues that have been explored by the literature on localism in Europe more gen-erally. In the case of Italy, however, localism is considered tantamount to opposi-tion to the state or to a feeling of not being part of the state itself (Romanelli 1991: 171). 'Locality' emerges in the analysis of the interconnections between state and civil society, particularly in relation to the weakness of the state at the local level (Schneider 1971). Two works figure centrally in the anthropological analysis of Italian localism: Silverman's *'Three Bells of Civilisation'* (1975), and Pratt's *'The Walled City'* (1986). In Silverman's analysis the notion of locality is seen as a reflection of the ideas propagated by the élites, who are also the main proponents of community identity (1975: 142), and of the town-centred organisation of central Italian society. The notion of locality is expressed by the idiom of 'civilisation' or *civiltà* as an ideology about town life that justifies local inequalities. For Silverman (1975: 228–9) 'locality' is a 'replication of an "urban" structure, including certain political, social, and cultural patterns' which is related to the Italian administrative system that assigns uniform status to all municipalities. In her analysis Italian rural villages are assumed to repeat certain patterns of urban life. Pratt reaches similar conclusions in his exploration of localism in Tuscany: he too argues that a city-centric idiom is used as a political ideology (1986: 144), which is symbolised by the metaphor of the 'walled city' as an expression of territorially-defined interests. According to him, this is a construction of political leaders, particularly in local administration by the Christian Democratic Party whose power rested on strong local bases, and drew on an ideology of class harmony as opposed to that of class conflict.

What unites such studies is an interest in the élites holding political power, the nation-state, or political parties as the 'structures' that affect, not to say determine, human action and beliefs. Most anthropologists ended up concentrating on official discourse or 'objective' factors in forging local identity, and 'locality', just like 'national identity', emerged chiefly as a political construction. Locality and nation were the ends of a continuum that leads from tradition to modernity, from *gemeinschaft* to *gesellschaft*; the nation, in turn, has been regarded as an encompassing unit, as a 'roof over a culture' (Gellner 1983: 99). Implicit in this conceptualisation of locality is the view that 'high cultures' pervade entire populations (Gellner 1983: 55, but see also Smith 1991: 16–17) including the 'peripheries'. But to what extent do people adhere to this hegemonic representation of locality?

Italy in the late 1990s lends itself very well to an exploration of this issue, especially in light of the political changes that occurred in that period. The rise of regionalist political movements in northern Italy, in particular, has shown that the source of cultural identity and political legitimacy remains at the local level, and that politics is inextricably linked with territory (Diamanti 1994a: 409). The ascendancy of the Lega Nord/Northern League and of other autonomist parties (hereafter referred to as *leghe*) in northern Italy and in the national political arena in the 1990s posed the issue of northern Italian identity very dramatically in a nation-state in which language and dialect were not as important for the development of autonomist or separatist movements as in other parts of Europe in the same period (Strassoldo 1996: 82).[5]

The economic and political crisis that followed the collapse of the Berlin Wall, along with European economic and political integration, altered the Italian political situation. The years between the aftermath of the Second World War and the early 1990s were characterised by tension between 'Comrades' and 'Christians' (i.e. Communists and Catholics), in Kertzer's terms (1980). Then, the fall of Communism and the dissolution of the Italian Communist Party on the one hand, and the corruption scandals which led to the demise of the Christian Democratic Party on the other brought about a political situation of confusion and uncertainty. This paved the way for the rise of autonomist political movements in northern Italy that contested the idea of national identity and the legitimacy of a nation-state seen as corrupted (Ginsborg 1998: 332); such parties had in their agenda the transformation of Italy into a federal state and, for some time, were even planning the territorial division between the North and the South of the country. Central to these movements' rhetoric was stress on local history and traditions and opposition to state influence, and the idea that northern Italy partakes of a 'central European' culture as opposed to a 'Mediterranean' one (Ruzza and Schmidtke 1996: 182; Dematteo 2001: 147), even though a 'northern Italian' ethnic identity is not built on linguistic differences. These political movements presented themselves as 'populist' in that they purported to recreate a lost 'authenticity' against the centralised nation-state, and especially to maintain a traditional *gemeinschaft* (Ginsborg 1998: 332).

In Italy the emergence of regionalist movements in the early 1990s was a new phenomenon, both because this did not happen in economically disadvantaged areas, but in the most affluent (Ginsborg 1998: 333), and because the issue of a northern Italian identity had never come to the fore until then. Their rise coincided with the apparent decline of the Italian state as the dominant framework controlling the national economy, with several privatisation initiatives that were taking place all over the country, and with the state's function shifting from being a provider of goods to a regulator. As a result, the 'localism' focused on in this work contrasts with the anthropological accounts of the 1970s–1980s: while earlier ideas of communities emerged as replications of urban structures, in the rhetoric of regionalist movements 'community' and everyday culture and values became a banner to fly proudly as opposed to the 'civilisation' symbolised by the nation-state (Destro 1997: 371). The state, in turn, was not pointed to as an agent of modernity, but as the main cause for pervasive corruption. The researchers who have so far focused on the advent of autonomist political movements in northern Italy seem to agree that the economic crisis of the late 1980s and immigration to Italy from the non-european countries have been decisive factors, and agree that the development of a small-scale, kin-based industry with minimal or no state intervention enhanced to a significant extent the rise of the *leghe* (Diamanti 1994a; Cento Bull 1996). What the *leghe* undermined was the idea of national identity itself in a country in which local and regional identities remain very strong (Diamanti 1999). However, while the ascendancy of the *leghe* was a new phenomenon in the country, in fact it reflected a situation of fragmentation and 'antipolitics' which was (and still is) spreading all over western Europe, and particularly an endeavour to affirm the autonomy of society against the state. If we were to define such regionalist groups by reference to the concept of ideology we would be led to assume that their emergence represents an assertion of a right-wing ideology. Yet the agendas of such groups do not necessarily encompass fidelity to the idea of the nation, but are characterised instead by political orientations that can hardly be placed along a single axis (Holmes 2000: 13).

The case of Trentino, an Alpine region in northern Italy where this research has been conducted, both reflects and contrasts with the situation so far described: the electoral success of the *leghe* in that area in the 1990s went hand in hand with the region's being geographically at the 'margins' of northern Italy and with the fact that it is one of the most affluent Italian regions because of state subsidies. Trentino has been recalcitrant to conventional anthropological analysis, and despite the presence of linguistic minorities[6] it has never been considered as problematic as other regions claiming to have a language of their own. Yet although Italian and Italian dialects are the main languages spoken there, the region was subjected to Germanic and Austrian sovereignty for about 800 years until 1918. Trentino shares a common history with the nearby German-speaking South Tyrol, and common language and dialects with the surrounding Italian-speaking regions, plus several identity traits that have been redistributed in the course of the consolidation of the Italian and Austrian states. In the social sciences Alpine communities have been largely focused on as 'folklore', as the ideal settings for observing dying ways of life, and Trentino is no exception. However, the Alps are also patriotic symbols (Berthoud 2001: 89), and have been a 'myth' in the building of national identity. In the late twentieth century, by contrast, Alpine regions were increasingly turning into sites of resistance to the power of nation-states. In a sense, the Alps may be the ideal settings to assess how ways of life, beliefs and values, which apparently have nothing to do with social and political transformations, are in fact integral parts of them.

What makes the region intriguing also is its division into many valleys, each of which forms an administrative unit or municipality representing itself as different from all the others (Sanguanini 1992: 146). As a mountainous province, Trentino enjoys a considerable degree of autonomy[7] from the central government and, as part of an autonomous region (together with South Tyrol) it has a wider latitude in implementing European Union decisions than do the other ordinary Italian regions (Levy 1996: 17). In Trentino the advent of regionalist movements in the 1990s was followed by a rereading of regional history with significant stress on the cultural traits distinguishing Trentino from the Italian nation-state which encompasses it. Paradoxically, the political and cultural distinctiveness of Trentino vis-à-vis the nation-state was not so much predicated upon the existence on a putative 'authentic regional culture', as on common culture and an almost unbroken history with the neighbouring German-speaking South Tyrol. This was all the more unusual, allowing for the fact that from the late nineteenth century until recently Trentino presented itself as an 'Italian region' as opposed to the 'German' one of

South Tyrol (Poppi 1991; Sanguanini 1992: 149). By contrast, in the 1990s the idea of a province partaking of a 'central European' culture was appropriated by some political formations to legitimate differentiation vis-à-vis the nation-state. Thus, in late modernity the region, with its own history and culture, became the new economic and political actor. Yet its meanings may be defined by more than one political actor: the idea of a 'Europe of the regions', for example, was central to the agendas of the new Right. This brings us back to the issue raised earlier in this section: while allegiance to regionalist parties may be expressed by figures and by the number of votes that gain them electoral success, little is known about the meanings that political ideas have for the people who receive them, how individuals 'personalise' party ideologies, and what localism is about for the people involved in a changing political situation.

Fieldwork in the Italian Alps

Fieldwork in Trentino was conducted to explore these issues, particularly to find out why locality, instead of the nation-state, is and remains a compelling formulation of selfhood in spite of (or in response to) social and economic changes. The main focus of this research is on how individual social actors organise and account for ideas of local and regional identity, and what they understand of the political ideas and ideological messages emanating from national, regional and other centres. This book represents an analysis of the social context within which certain political ideas found fertile ground: it is meant as an attempt to explore the complex ways in which a political transformation interweaves with political practices, culture and discourse. The province of Trent, as already noted, lends itself to this very well, not only because of its history, but also because it is divided into several valleys, each with its own identity. The Vanoi valley, where this research has been carried out, is a place where issues of both village and ethnic identity came to the fore particularly after the electoral success of autonomist movements. The valley's location at the eastern end of the province, on the border with the Veneto region, also made it particularly suitable for research on localism because, as a border area, it has a special relationship to the state surrounding (or encompassing) it (Donnan and Wilson 1994: 2), and it represents the kind of setting wherein ideas of distinctiveness are very likely to inform local discourse. The fact that it was the arena where the Italian and the Austro-Hungarian army faced each other during the First World War also provided much food for thought, as it led me to investigate how narratives of the conflict interweave with attachment to place. However, studying a post-peasant society also involved finding out how a political transformation, which is deemed the product of late modernity, relates to the values and beliefs ascribed to a post-peasant society.

If we were to look for a dominant external construction of local identity we would not find it, because there is more than one. The several war memorials that dot the valley's landscape, for example, cast the area as a field or remembrance and an integral part of the Italian state. By contrast, both the Christian Democratic Party and the Northern League used to cast locality as outside and in opposition to the Italian state, and the Trentine-Tyrolean Autonomist Party used to stress the Tyrolean or Austrian character of local identity. So, different external constructions of local identity coexist. The political situation of the region in 1995, at the beginning of my research, seemed favourable to an exploration of this coexistence: the regional government had just proposed the establishment of a European Region of Tyrol, and the municipal elections were drawing near. Soon after I started my fieldwork I realised that local identity figured prominently in discussions: there was a shared feeling that it was under threat, as more than 50 percent of the houses there were owned by people who do not normally reside there. This, as I noted, was described as a loss of autonomy. Aside from this emphasis, the idea of autonomy (*autonomia*) did not inform local identity only: although villagers think and talk a great deal about it, the concept was (and still is) central to Trentino's self-definition.[8] Local newspapers are replete with articles about the *autonomia* of the province; the province of Trent itself is known as the *Provincia Autonoma*; the news of the local television station often centres on the issue of *autonomia*; political leaders, too, draw upon the idiom of *autonomia* to propagate their ideas; several historical publications about the province of Trent outline the history of the *autonomia*. At the time of this research the idea of *autonomia* permeated much of local discourse, but it was not entirely clear how far this represented a set of ideas propagated by the urban élites only, and one of the issues that emerged was how official discourses and local-level understandings and beliefs coexist and relate to each other. This did not involve an analysis confined to individuals interpreting and handling meanings only: rather, it entailed assessing how far handling meanings can make sense of action, and particularly how practices and beliefs which apparently have nothing to do with political processes can instead form the background against which such processes are debated and understood.

I conducted the bulk of my fieldwork in two villages, Caoria and Ronco, in the Vanoi valley in eastern Trentino from the spring of 1995 until the early autumn of 1996, and then in several spells until 2001. My choice of the valley as the location for my field research was not accidental, as I had carried out exploratory fieldwork there in the early 1990s. Although its population continues to decline, the valley persists as a viable community mainly because its residents have reinforced ties to those who leave at the same time as they keep their children on the land. A substantial part of the inhabitants who left still own land and houses in the valley, and come back for weekends or holidays, or for special occasions such as weddings, funerals, or the patron saint day. It is chiefly through these kinship ties that local identity is handed down from generation to generation. I spent most of my time in Caoria, and I moved to Ronco during the second half of my fieldwork for comparative purposes. In Caoria I lived in a house that I shared with the landlady, who introduced me to her covillagers and made me familiar with the mores of her village, while in Ronco I lived in a house owned by the local parish. In the course of my fieldwork I had contact with both men and women, and I worked alone. Most of my contacts were with people who are either retired or manual workers who were born in the village, and have spent most of their lives there.

Most of the information analysed in this book has been collected through intensive participant observation and through unstructured interviews and casual conversations in private homes, in bars, and in various collective venues. So, the ethnographic information contained in this work is based chiefly on field notes. This study also included a search of local and national archives, though such sources have been relied upon mainly to corroborate or to assess the validity of oral accounts. I drew upon oral histories about the past as long as they could serve to make sense of the present, and the tape recorder was used only a few times towards the end of field research, after obtaining the informants' consent. Occasionally I participated in the local people's lives through helping with a few farm chores. My participation in public events, such as attendance of the sessions of the municipal council and of the holy mass on Sunday morning, or participation in a few hunting forays or in the celebrations of the patron saint day, also provided opportunities to collect meaningful data. The names used in this work are real names, though in a few cases I used pseudonyms in order to protect the people's privacy, or I simply omitted the names.

The Structure of the Book

This book is divided into eight chapters, including the present Introduction and the Conclusions, each of which focuses on different aspects of discourse about localism. As localism is treated mainly as a set of ideas about the significance of place, this work explores a set of themes in which the idea of the 'local' emerges. Although politics does not pervade all the ethnographic information discussed, most of the views and practices discussed in this work are examined because of the political dimensions they often take on. Chapter 2 is an analysis of the setting's historical background. Although it is meant as a description of the setting and as a succession of historical events, the chapter's main foci are the material factors involved in the reproduction of a human group, and the structural conditions and changing historical circumstances that are central to the processes of identity making investigated here. I then move to an exploration of the present-day organisation of village life in chapter 3, which sets the background against which issues of identity analysed later in this book can be seen. In this chapter I pay particular heed to the ways in which the idea of a 'private space' underlies social actors' descriptions of the place they live in. By looking at social behaviour in various contexts, the chapter then focuses on the domains occupied by men and women, and highlights how ideas about differences between men and women constitute locality and affect the ways social actors conceptualise it.

In chapter 4 I extend my exploration of the idea of 'private space' a step further by focusing on the making of a 'private space': the chapter analyses hunting as one of the 'practices' through which 'territory' is symbolically turned into private property, and political discourse is filtered. Hunting is looked at as a practice that is functional to the creation of distinctiveness through the appropriation of the symbols of another ethnic group, and is analysed as an expression of the tension between the 'local' and the 'national'. The idea of 'modernity' as an ideology about town life is discussed in chapter 5, which sets out to assess how far such a notion affects the ways social actors think about otherness. It is also concerned with the significance of physical and symbolic boundaries in articulating identities. The chapter continues with an analysis of how local-level constructions of otherness inform the ways social actors relate to the outside and the state, particularly as a response to the advent of regionalist political formations. The chapter then moves to an analysis of the meanings that a 'Tyrolean identity' takes on, and of how this identity relates to a local one.

I focus on representations of history in chapter 6 in an attempt to make sense of accounts of the past that seem at odds with 'official' views. It concentrates on how social actors seek to keep control over the memory of 'local' events, and on the embedding of the 'local' in the wider, translocal context. It illustrates the complex ways cyclical readings of time enable social actors to place themselves outside the time frame of the Italian nation-state, and question its legitimacy. I move to an exploration of local politics and its practices in chapter 7, where I tackle the issue of human agency, particularly the capacity of actors to interpret political symbols and ideologies instead of taking them for granted. I explore briefly the political history of the valley from the aftermath of the Second World War to the 1990s, and then I look at some significant events which illuminate the actors' views of politics. I then illustrate the process whereby official meanings are accommodated to local-level discourses. Finally, the concluding chapter pulls together the threads of the argument, and attempts to provide at least partial answers to the questions asked in this work.

NOTES

1. See also Macdonald (1997: 4).
2. See, for instance, Bailey (1971), Blok (1974), Boissevain (1974), Silverman (1975), Gellner (1977), White (1980), and Pratt (1986).
3. Strathern (1987: 32), for example, observed that the idea that rural communities are peripheral 'blocks our understanding of the way that self-acknowledged differences draw on common British ideas about difference'. Similarly, Nadel-Klein (1991: 501–2) suggested that localism itself is a product of modern political economy, and that it is 'an integral part of the development process of the cultural construction of class'.
4. Sutton (1997: 415) convincingly made this point in his study of a Greek island. See also Macdonald (1997) and Heady (1999) for an exploration of the same idea.
5. This contrasts with the situation of the 1970s, when language and dialect played an important part in the development of autonomist movements in Italy, particularly in autonomous regions such as Friuli, Sardinia and Val d'Aosta that claim to have a language of their own.
6. It should be noted that within Trentino there are linguistic minorities such as the Ladins and the Mocheno-Cimbri who inhabit their own valleys and speak Romance and Germanic dialects respectively.
7. The autonomy that was granted to Trentino-South Tyrol in 1947 was designed 'to ensure that the cultural, economic and social development of the South Tyrolese lay in Italian hands rather than in those of the South Tyrolese…' (Alcock 1996: 73).
8. In the valley different terms are used to refer to the same thing, the most common being *indipendenza* ('independence').

2
The Setting and its
Historical Background

An Alpine Valley

The Vanoi valley is an Alpine community situated at the eastern fringes of the province of Trent, in northern Italy, at the border with the Veneto region with which it shares a common Italian dialect. It is located at the interface between Mediterranean Europe south of the Alps and continental Europe to the north. It forms both an ecological and an administrative unit in that its geographical boundaries roughly coincide with the administrative ones, its territory falling within the limits of the municipality (*comune*) of Canal San Bovo. It is the largest of the eight municipalities that form the district (*comprensorio*) of Primiero, one of the subregional units into which the province of Trent is divided. Although there were well over 4,000 inhabitants in the valley in the 1940s (Romagna 1992: 106), the resident population now is scarcely 1,700. The majority of the people living there consist mainly of retired agriculturalists and lumberjacks who earn a pension from the state, and people who work in various kinds of manual trades.

The territory of the *comune* of Canal San Bovo, whose shape is roughly that of an elongated oval, extends approximately thirteen kilometres from north to south and about six from east to west. Mount Cauriol and Mount Totoga, which can be seen from almost everywhere in the valley, mark respectively its northern and southern end. The *comune* has a total land area of 125.54 square kilometres, and numbers seven villages: Canal San Bovo (the municipal seat), Caoria, Cicona, Gobbera, Prade, Ronco and Zortea. Caoria and Ronco, where I conducted my fieldwork, have respectively 405 and 204 inhabitants.[1] Almost all settlements in the valley are nucleated; by contrast, Ronco, because it lies over a steep slope (which overlooks the village of Canal San Bovo), is scattered. This mountain valley has been formed by the waters of the stream Vanoi, which flows from north to south, and joins the stream Cismon after crossing the regional boundary between Trentino and Veneto. The significance that the stream has in local discourse is mainly related to the frequent floods (the last of which occurred in 1966), which in the past levelled several houses in the valley.

Only the two ends of the valley are inhabited; its central part, by contrast, is steep and narrow, uninhabitable, and too rocky even for pasturage. Both slopes rise sharply from the valley floor and differ greatly from each other in most respects. The western, shady side is the steeper of the two. Because of its unfavourable orientation it is uninhabitable and covered with forest for the most part, and almost all the settlements lie on the eastern side. The eastern mountain ranges separate the *comune* from the valley of Primiero, now an important tourist resort; the Lagorai mountain chain on the north divides the valley from the Val di Fiemme; finally, the mountain ranges on the west and on the south mark the boundary between the municipality and the plateau of Tesino, with whose inhabitants there has been rivalry from time immemorial.

Mountains range in elevation from 2,000 to 2,500 metres, and the average altitude of the valley floor is about 700 metres. By motor car there are three ways of access to the valley: a narrow and steep road, built by the Austro-Hungarian army at the turn of the twentieth century, which links the valley and Tesino through an Alpine pass; the old road, running from north to south across a saddle at 1,000 metres above sea level, which connects the valley and Primiero; finally, the recently built three-kilometre tunnel that goes to Primiero through Mount Totoga. The paved road, which links the villages of the valley, extends from the northern to the southern end; it winds along the eastern side of the valley and follows the course of the stream for a few kilometres, until it ends abruptly at the upper end. The valley is about fifteen minutes' drive from the market townlet of Fiera di Primiero, and roughly one hour from the provincial capital of Trent. A coach, which runs three to four times a day, links the valley and Primiero, but is seldom used by the local people who prefer to use their cars. Locations of the villages differ greatly: while Caoria and Canal San Bovo lie on the eastern bank of the stream, all the other villages are located at higher altitudes. Moreover, while all the other villages are within walking distance from each other, Caoria and Ronco are more difficult to reach because of distance, on the one hand, and because of the conditions of the roads going there, on the other.

In Trentino the valley is regarded, geographically and socially, as the most isolated municipality of the province. Sociological literature too treats the valley as 'backward' (Osti 1989: 200), and the media portray it as an 'exotic' setting. In the nearby Primiero the people of the valley are referred to as those of *la intro*, i.e. 'the interior', the inhabitants of a putative 'remote' and 'isolated' place. In fact the valley, seen from afar, looks like an isolated community, and villagers feel that it is isolated. Despite this, isolation is an illusion. Geographically, historically and economically the valley is part of a larger whole, and isolation is partly a matter of self-representation. The inhabitants of the valley are full participants in the Italian body politic: they are entitled to vote in national elections, they read the national and regional press, and watch television. When I visited my fieldsite in 2001 I found that various people had access to the internet at home. While until a few years ago the valley was hardly accessible despite the economic relevance of forestry and timber trade with the nearby Veneto region, nowadays, notwithstanding the improvement of roads, the valley is economically 'marginal', and is experiencing a process of depopulation. However, the rate of population decline is much slower than it was in the aftermath of the last world conflict, and now the valley is witnessing a period of some revitalisation, especially among younger families committed to staying there, and hoping to ensure the preservation of the social and cultural fabric of the villages.

In the Vanoi valley the climate is affected by various elements, of which elevation is the most relevant. Rainfall is as abundant as throughout the Alpine crescent, and the climate is characterised by very cold winters and warm summers. The first frost, often accompanied by a dusting of snow, may occur as early as the beginning of November, even though during the last few years heavy snowfalls did not occur until December. Nowadays the depth of snow in the valley floor rarely exceeds 30–40 centimetres. However, I heard that in the past the abundance of snowfalls caused the roads to be blocked very frequently. The weather usually becomes mild in April and May, though mountains may remain snow-capped until late May. In July and August the temperature may rise to well over 25 °C. The arrival of autumn, by contrast, is marked by sudden low temperatures and heavy rainfalls. The length of daylight, too, varies considerably from summer to winter. In June evenings linger until 9 p.m.; in December, by contrast, there is no light until 8 a.m., and it is dark shortly after 4 p.m. Like many other mountain communities, the valley under study shares many characteristics that are typical of Alpine ecosystems, particularly a diversified environment in which cultivable land is in short supply, while non-cultivable, 'marginal' areas abound (Rhoades and Thompson 1975: 543; Vincze 1980: 389).

An analysis of the relationship between the environmental characteristics and the exploitation techniques until the 1960s explains why, in local discourse, the valley is still described, to a certain extent, as clearly bounded, historically stable, and highly autonomous. Until recently the local economy was conditional on the interdependence of farming, forestry, animal husbandry and seasonal migration, and especially on the existence of communal regulations governing the use of fields and pastures. The main characteristic of the local ecosystem is its division into three distinct ecological zones: the valley floor, the high meadows and the high pastures which lie close to the mountain peaks. Three spatially distinct spheres of production coexist: fields and meadows in the valley floor and in the villages, which provide crops and hay; privately owned high meadows (hereafter referred to as *masi*) located midway between the village itself and the high pastures, used for grazing in combination with haying and agriculture; and high-altitude pastures or *malghe*, located above the timberline, where cattle and sheep still graze during the summertime. So, livestock transfer from the village to the pastures was very seldom direct (Viazzo 1989: 20) and, as in most Alpine valleys, villagers used to leave the village in March–April to move to the *masi*, a more suitable setting for agricultural activities than the valley floor. Until recently abundance of cultivable land and longer exposure to sun rays compelled most villagers to stay there up to eight months every year, and to go to the village from time to time only to work the vegetable garden or to attend the holy mass on Sunday morning. So, peasants had to face the problem of integrating two different forms of production into a functional unit.[2]

Using an expression of Robert Netting (1981: 3), it may be suggested that the territory just described is above all a 'cultural landscape', as it has been used and modelled for generations by a resident human population. This is suggested by the presence of terraced garden patches tilled and fertilised, by the extensive network of footpaths, and finally by the place names that distinguish each field and house, usually the name of the family group to which some past occupants belonged, so as to symbolise man's appropriation and domestication of the natural environment: in a sense, the valley's landscape is an 'extension' of its inhabitants. The landholding system is an integral part of this 'cultural landscape': it is characterised by the presence of privately-owned landholdings in the valley floor and in the high meadows or *masi*, and of communal land at higher altitudes. Fragmentation of landed property and its division into tiny patches is a salient feature, which was interpreted both as a sign of irrational exploitation of the natural environment, and as a device to reduce the risk of crop failures through the cultivation of many dispersed strips with differing microenvironments; this means that the fragmentation of landholdings enabled farmers to cope with the climatic fluctuations that have always undermined small-scale agriculture, especially in Alpine ecosystems (Netting 1981: 17).

This, however, was the conventional portrait of a farming community where the provision of food and shelter used to be the main task, and where farmers owned their land, animals and tools. Nowadays this image of the valley is ascribed to the 'old days': it is what researchers might expect to find in putative 'remote' settings, usually presented by the media as very 'traditional', where technological change had little or no impact.[3] In fact what the researcher or the occasional visitor may find there are the remains of a 'cultural landscape' that deteriorated after the demise of agro-pastoralism. What nowadays may at first sight look like a 'natural' environment, the result of humans' domestication of the Alpine territory, is in fact the outcome of its going wild: meadows are seldom scythed, most of the vegetable gardens are no longer cultivated, and the forest is encroaching on the villages. This is all the more surprising, allowing for the fact that photographs of the 1950s portray the villages as surrounded by a mosaic of cultivated patches, even at some distance from the inhabited area, sometimes at high altitudes.

Despite the inhabitants' emphasis on the valley's ideal 'self-sufficiency', the area has been dependent on provincial and state subsidies since as early as the aftermath of the Second World War. Unlike the nearby valley of Primiero, which experienced the growth of tourism during the last few decades thanks to the ski resort of San Martino di Castrozza, the Vanoi valley neither appealed to mountain climbers, nor became an important tourist resort. In fact the urban dwellers who spend their vacation there are those who cannot afford to stay in more expensive places, and find it more convenient to purchase land and houses there than in the adjacent valley of Primiero. Phrased differently, the valley witnessed only the development of a kind of 'poor tourism'.

Two Villages: Caoria and Ronco

Caoria and Ronco, whose inhabitants describe each other as 'similar' or 'of the same kind' (*simili* or ***de la stesa sort***), lie at the opposite ends of the valley, and are nine kilometres apart. Caoria is a nucleated settlement numbering roughly 400 inhabitants, the overwhelming majority of whom were born in the community and own land there; the village, in this respect, is talked about as a 'homogeneous unit' in that most of its inhabitants define themselves as 'true Caorians' (***veri caoriòti***). The village lies at the upper (northern) end of the valley, at an altitude of 800 metres above sea level, where the stream Valsorda joins the Vanoi and divides the village into two halves, upper or inner Caoria (***Caoria de entre***) and lower or outer Caoria (***Caoria de fora***).

The most noticeable characteristic of the village, seen from afar, is the presence of two churches, one at the centre of the community, the other one at its southern edge, which dominate the village landscape. The former was built in the 1950s, while the latter, a fine example of eighteenth-century architecture, is now closed and is falling into disrepair. One may also be struck by the coexistence of rural architecture, which consists mainly of log houses, remains of the rural past formerly acting as stables for the livestock, and modern buildings dating to the 1960s, the time when tourists started acquiring land in the valley and built their own houses for summer vacation. Other houses are closed or used in the summer for a few days, normally by the villagers who live elsewhere, whereas those which are not inhabited at all are left to crumble. Most of the houses owned by resident Caorians are inhabited by a married couple living on one floor and by one of their sons, together with his spouse and children, who live next door or on another floor. The impressive amount of firewood, piled by each house, is also very likely to be noticed, even by the casual visitor.

Aside from rural houses and churches, a rather 'imposing' monument of the past is the building that houses the old primary school, built in 1913 by the Austro-Hungarian administration, now closed by reason of the small number of children living in Caoria. A small kindergarten is still open, despite the provincial government's attempts to close it for the same reason. A sawmill, formerly the symbol of the local economy and of the village's ideal 'self-sufficiency', now employs scarcely thirty workers, most of whom reside in Caoria and have spent most of their lives there. It is the only sawmill owned by the provincial adminis-tration, and its main function nowadays is to employ local people in order to pre-vent the valley from becoming depopulated. The running of a sawmill in Caoria becomes possible chiefly thanks to the pressures exercised by the municipality on the provincial government rather than to the profits made from it. Nowadays forestry in the area is no longer a viable economic activity, and the sawmill sym-bolises what remains, in the valley, of an activity that used to be a source of local pride. The decisive stroke to forestry was given by Austria's entry into the Euro-pean Union in 1994 and by the subsequent introduction into the Italian market of Austrian timber, whose costs of processing are much lower than in Italy. Unlike the 'old days', the lumberjacks who work outside the sawmill are either self-employed or carry out their activity for private companies based outside the municipality. That forestry is no longer profitable is also shown by the huge piles of timber that lie abandoned at the very edge of the village, some of which have been there for five or six years without having been sold to anyone.

Caoria, as already noted, is an outlying village of the municipality of Canal San Bovo. The communal seat, Canal San Bovo itself, is six kilometres away. Villagers usually go there on errands such as applications to the municipal administration or for occasional visits to the chemist. Caoria has one supermarket, two inns open during the summer, three bars, one post office, one branch of the local bank (formerly a rural credit institution), and two offices of the provincial Forestry Department (whose officials are the only 'authorities' in the village entitled to carry firearms). Tourists (largely from the nearby Veneto region) usually visit the village in the summertime, and rent a house from residents. Most of them, how-ever, are either natives or descendants of villagers who live in urban centres in northern Italy or abroad.

Clearly, the image of the valley that I had clashed with the conventional one of an agro-pastoral community as depicted by most of the brochures available at the local tourist board or by anthropologists until the 1960s, that is to say a 'tra-ditional' setting that has preserved its customs since time immemorial. Most of the holdings that are scattered around the dwellings have not been tilled for years, and the same is true of the terraced fields on the steeper slopes. Nowadays only a few households own livestock, and at the time of my fieldwork there were only seven cows in the village. In fact Caoria is not a unique case, and the decline of pastoralism there reflects a development which affected the whole Alpine region: in 1992, for example, there were 289 livestock in the valley as compared to 981 in 1970. Most of the cattle grazed in the high pastures every summer come from outside the valley, and so do the herders who rear them. For those who still pur-sue agro-pastoral chores agriculture and animal husbandry represent a way of life rather than profitable activities.

In the early 1990s the provincial government created a natural park whose boundaries nearly reach the village of Caoria, which also encompasses landholdings owned by the inhabitants of Caoria itself. Its establishment was part of the development project undertaken by the provincial government whose goal was the prevention of environmental degradation in poor or 'marginal' areas such as the valley under study. Such projects involved areas where agro-pastoral chores are no longer carried out, and where a significant amount of land has been transferred to the provincial government itself. At the time of its establishment the park also undertook the project of an open-air museum under the sponsorship of the provincial administration of Trent and of the European Union, which funded other development projects in the area to encourage tourism. In spite of this, however, very few in the valley took advantage of the European funding made available in the 1990s.

Caoria also has a museum of the Great War, which narrates the events of 1916, notably the conquest of the valley by the Italian troops during the First World War. The museum is run, on a voluntary basis, by the local group of the National Alpini Association (ANA), whose members (who did their military service in the Alpine infantry) organise events of various kinds in the community ranging from commemorations to the feast of the patron saint. Another formal association in the village is that of the hunters or *Gruppo Cacciatori*, which controls hunting preserves during the hunting season, and is open only to residents and people who have kinship ties in the valley. Both groups have a significant role in forging local identity, as will be seen later on in this work.

The village of Ronco has a population of about 200 people and, like Caoria, lies at an altitude of about 800 metres above sea level. It is divided into two sides, Costa, which lies on a steep slope facing the village of Canal San Bovo, along the road to the Tesino plateau, and Chiesa, which clusters around the late eighteenth-century church. It also includes a small hamlet, Cainari, even though it falls within the boundaries of the municipality of Castello Tesino. Ronco is more 'isolated' than Caoria in that it is more difficult to reach, and because it does not offer as much as the other village does: a woman of Caoria once said that when the people of Ronco visit her village 'they come to a city', so as to stress the difference between the two settlements. Ronco has one branch of the local bank, two small shops, and two bars, plus a small factory making snow blowers. Depopulation had the same effects as in Caoria, and nowadays most of the remaining inhabitants have a job elsewhere. Unlike Caoria, Ronco does not have formal associations running festivals, and even the patron saint feast is organised by volunteers. Aside from this, most of the considerations about Caoria and the valley hold true for Ronco as well.

Like Caoria, Ronco too is surrounded by a mosaic of holdings, most of which are either abandoned or densely overgrown. Unlike Caoria, however, pastoral activities are still carried out, as there are five households that still engage in such chores, keep a considerable number of livestock, and often spend the summer in the high pastures. This is what local people call 'living the old way' (***viver a la vecia***) which, as already stressed, no longer enables them to make a livelihood. Despite being a 'traditional' local activity, animal breeding is possible only thanks to the subsidies of the provincial government aimed at keeping the local people on the land and at preventing the valley from becoming depopulated.[4]

A Brief Local History: From the Middle Ages to the Eighteenth Century

In this section I will try to outline the valley's history. Its aim is not so much to present a mere list of events accompanied by dates, as an attempt to highlight the factors that contributed to the formation of local identity. It is outside the scope of this chapter to explain local history in detail: rather it sets out to focus on the events that help make sense of the situation I found during my fieldwork. Phrased differently, in this work history functions as the 'means', and not as the 'end'. What follows is mainly an attempt to shed light on the relationship, over the years, between the valley and the larger matrix of which it forms a part. Most of the information discussed in this section draws on data collected from published material, and relies to a limited extent on archival research. Perhaps it is a bit contentious to suggest that the history of the valley is characterised by a tension between the two worlds at the boundaries of which it used to lie. That the eastern Alps act as a sort of borderland between the 'Italian' world and the 'Germanic' one is nicely illustrated by the seminal study by Cole and Wolf, '*The Hidden Frontier*' (1974). However, while their work examined ethnic differences between two adjacent villages where different languages and dialects are spoken, in the area studied a sense of distinctiveness vis-à-vis the surrounding regions is not built on 'ethnic' difference precisely because, as I will show, the role of language in shaping local identity is not as significant as it is in the politics of identity in most of contemporary Europe. As a matter of fact, one of the most interesting and, perhaps, intriguing aspects of the history of Primiero is that the area was subjected to Austrian or Germanic sovereignties for about six centuries even though Germanic languages have never been spoken by its inhabitants (Pistoia 1992: 8).

There is no evidence that the area of Primiero (which encompasses the Vanoi valley) was inhabited during Roman times. Archaeological excavations carried out between 1995 and 1996 revealed the presence of a small chapel in Fiera di Primiero as early as the sixth century AD. More reliable sources date to the late Middle Ages, and give evidence that the area was subject to the political rule of Feltre (a town in the present-day Veneto region) from the early eleventh century until 1339,[5] and that it acted as a thoroughfare between the Republic of Venice and German-speaking areas until the turn of the twentieth century (Zieger 1975). In the 1350s the district gained its independence from Feltre, and the publication of the first statutes in 1367 testifies to this. In 1373 Primiero was taken over by the dukes of Austria and by the counts of Tyrol (Grosselli 1989: 28), and remained under Austrian rule for nearly 600 years, even though the control of its territorial boundaries, especially with the nearby valleys, always remained problematic.

While the history of the valley of Primiero is fairly well documented, very little is known about the first inhabitants of the Vanoi valley itself: one of the hypotheses about their origins is that they came from the community of Imer, in the valley of Primiero, to which the valley was subjected until 1795 (Romagna 1992: 33), but there are no reliable documentary sources proving this. The valley as a territorial unit is mentioned only starting from the early modern age. Notwithstanding this historical void, the statutes of 1367 (which remained in force until 1807) give us at least a partial understanding of the social organisation of the district in the late Middle Ages. The district was divided into four subunits one of which, that of Imer, included the Vanoi valley. Such statutes granted a considerable degree of autonomy to such subunits, within which the smallest territorial unit was the village. Villages availed themselves of extensive areas of woodland and meadowland reserved to the members of the community only, whose main source of subsistence was the interweaving of pastoral and agricultural activities.

An interesting aspect of the statutes is their emphasis on the distinction between natives and outsiders: strangers (who in the Latin documents of the time are referred to as *forenses*) included timber traders or those who rented pastures, and were forbidden from buying land there. This device was intended to prevent the alienation of landed property to people who did not pay taxes to the community (Pistoia 1992: 75). This suggests that landownership acted as a marker of distinction between 'insiders' and 'outsiders', and that a strict control over land and rights served to limit membership. What characterised the landholding system was the coexistence of communal and private property: just like these days, pastures and forests were communal property, while fields and meadows were privately owned. This landholding system was not specific to the area studied, but was very widespread in the rest of Trentino and in the Alpine crescent as a whole (Capuzzo 1985: 376). In the late fourteenth century the local population mainly consisted of smallholders owning their own land (Capuzzo 1985: 390) or working landholdings belonging to a few large landowners, that is to say, the noble families and the ecclesiastical institutions that had control over forested areas and pastures.

In 1401 the district came under the rule of the Tyrolean counts of Welsperg, who maintained their jurisdiction over the area until 1827. In the early fifteenth century the district had to protect its boundaries from the attempts of outsiders, especially the community of Tesino, to seize control of the Vanoi valley, and from the bishop of Feltre who was claiming ownership of some mountains in the district itself.[6] The proximity of the Republic of Venice enhanced the development of economic relationships between the district (and Trentino) and the Republic itself (Calì 1988: 106): it is in this period that some noble Venetic families were granted use of pastures and forested areas and, from the late fifteenth century, of mines too (Zieger 1975: 47; Pistoia 1996: 14–19), both in the valley of Primiero and in that of Vanoi. It seems reasonable to believe that the Vanoi valley's appearance in the historical records coincided with the development of mining and with the large-scale immigration of Germanic peoples from Tyrol and Bohemia. Caoria is mentioned for the first time in 1565 (Pistoia 1996: 11), and probably it is no accident that the oldest house in the village dates to the sixteenth century. The occurrence of Germanic surnames in the Vanoi valley (Loss, Orsingher, Taufer) as well as in the district testifies to this. Such waves of immigration brought about a sudden demographic growth not only in the area under study, but also in the whole Alpine crescent (Viazzo 1989: 158–9). Although we can suppose that a Germanic language was spoken in the valley during that period alongside Romance dialects, documentary sources give no evidence of this; in all likelihood the Germanic settlers were quickly assimilated by the Italian-speaking population, even though their Germanic surnames have been retained. The second half of the fifteenth century was characterised by warfare between Tyrol and the Republic of Venice over the control of mining (particularly extraction of copper and silver) at the boundary between these two, especially after the production of silver and copper took a sudden leap. The conflict involved the district of Primiero too, but boundaries remained unchanged. In the same period Primiero unsuccessfully tried to question Tesino's possession of the mountains west of the Vanoi valley where mining was flourishing, and it was only around 1560 that the dispute was settled (Zieger 1975: 70).[7]

As far as the Vanoi valley is concerned, before the creation of a municipality (1795) the only governing body in the area was the parish of Canal San Bovo, established in the late sixteenth century, whose boundaries encompassed the valley in its entirety. Among the obligations that all parishioners were subject to were those of contributing towards the maintenance of the priest of Canal San Bovo, and of attending religious services and processions in that village. The exercise of the priest's authority from the centre to the periphery, however, was far from easy because of the distance between the villages. In fact the analysis of the relations between the 'centre' of the parish and its 'periphery' of the valley casts light on a history of divisions,[8] and the written sources available in the parish records of Caoria show this very clearly: although in the eighteenth century Caoria belonged to the parish of Canal San Bovo, in 1742 it was the only village in the valley (aside from Canal San Bovo) with a small chapel where the holy mass could be celebrated.[9] In 1789 a priest, subject to that of Canal San Bovo, took residence in Caoria. Quarrels between the priests of the above villages arose when the former questioned the latter's right to receive tributes from the priests (and, implicitly, from the people) of the other communities in the valley,[10] and such quarrels were eventually settled with the establishment of an independent parish in Caoria in 1813.[11] The case of Caoria highlights the role played by the village priest in heralding the separation of the parish from that of Canal San Bovo and in forging village identity; however, it is not unique, as it reflects a situation typical of areas of small-scale producers (see for example Hroch 1985: 144).[12]

From the Late Eighteenth Century to the Present: Italians or Austrians?

Towards the end of the eighteenth century (1783) Primiero separated from the Diocese of Feltre and joined that of Trent. During this period the Austrian administration introduced compulsory primary education, so that the inhabitants of the district were obliged to learn to read and write, whereas a few miles away, in Veneto, education became mandatory only in the second half of the nineteenth century. It is in the same period that a free peasantry, settled upon its own land, became the structural basis of Tyrolean society, thanks to the autonomy that Tyrol was granted from the Habsburg monarchy.[13] In the years 1796 and 1798, after the introduction of the draft, the able-bodied men of Primiero (and of Trentino) fought with the Austrian troops against Napoleon.[14] The Austrian defeat led to the annexation of the district (and of Tyrol) to the short-lived Bavarian Kingdom in 1805, which put an end to the high degree of autonomy from which each valley had so far benefited (Calì 1988: 109). The anticlerical legislation of the new government gave rise to the Tyrolean insurrection of 1809 (in which many people of Primiero took part), led by Andreas Hofer[15] in his unsuccessful attempt to establish an autonomous peasant republic in the Alps. So, under Andreas Hofer German-speaking and Italian-speaking peoples fought side by side; however, in the following years the rise of liberal nationalism, especially in the town of Trent, increased the social distance between the two ethnic groups, as a consequence of the pressures exercised by the central government in Vienna and by the regional one in Innsbruck to do away with local autonomies (Calì 1988: 111).

While in the eighteenth century there was little dispute about what part of Tyrol was Italian and what was German, as the terms were those defined in cultural linguistic terms, in the nineteenth century language began to assume political importance (Levy 1988: 13) when, with the fall of Napoleon, Trentino and the district became part of the Austro-Hungarian Empire. In spite of the fact that Trentino was under that sovereignty, there was no attempt to Germanise all aspects of life in the lands of the Empire, and the Habsburgs were quite willing to have children educated in their own language (Levy 1988: 141). It must also be noted that there was a discrepancy between linguistic identity and linguistic classification: even the Austrian census of 1910, for example, classified population by language habitually spoken, not by mother tongue. As a consequence, people with German as mother tongue could be classified as Italian, and people with Italian as mother tongue could be classified as German (Cole and Wolf 1974: 289). This had the effect of making the categories 'Italian' and 'Austrian' less fixed than might be thought, and in all likelihood affected the ways social actors perceive such categories nowadays.

One aspect worth mentioning, as far as the early nineteenth century is concerned, is the fact that Caoria remained without a resident priest for some years, and in spite of the efforts made by the Diocese of Trent to find someone, nobody was willing to stay in a place considered remote and isolated. Interestingly, it was the idea of remoteness and, more precisely, of distance to which Caorians appealed, in 1844, when they petitioned the municipality of Canal San Bovo to obtain the separation of their village from the *comune* itself. Although their request gave no concrete results, it shows, once again, that attempts at separation were not sporadic. The events of 1848 had little impact in the district, except in Canal San Bovo, where the local priest attempted to inculcate revolutionary ideas into the locals (Zieger 1975: 148). In fact Italian nationalism in Trentino found support among the educated classes in the urban centres, whereas the countryside population remained indifferent to the national question (Alcock 1970: 12). The late nineteenth century saw the development of tourism in the valley of Primiero and the arrival of mountain climbers from various parts of Europe, notably Austria, Britain[16] and Germany. It is during these years that the economic gap between the two nearby valleys widened, especially after the valley of Primiero became a tourist resort. The economic crisis of the 1870s, not to mention the frequent floods of the following decade, brought about a growth of emigration of people in search of employment (Grosselli 1987), particularly from the Vanoi valley. To reduce emigration the municipal administration of Canal San Bovo yielded several forested landholdings to villagers in order to have them cleared and turned into cultivable areas or meadowland,[17] and in that period attempts to appropriate landholdings illicitly occurred quite frequently (Pistoia 1996: 25). This transfer of landed property, however, could not prevent the increase of emigration to Vorarlberg (western Austria), Switzerland, and the territories of the Dual Monarchy, where people could spend the cold season in order to supplement the poor income earned from agro-pastoral activities (Grosselli 1989: 105). Those who engaged in migration included for the most part weavers (especially women), pedlars, lumberjacks, or sawmill operators whose main skill was physical strength, not to mention the women who emigrated to urban centres to work as domestic servants. Permanent emigration to Brazil played an important part too, given the high demand for lumberjacks in newly colonised territories, and many families of Caoria emigrated there between 1880 and 1900 (Grosselli 1989: 126).

The early years of the twentieth century were characterised by political turmoil in the Vanoi valley, notably by the unsuccessful attempt, pursued by the representatives of the villages of Caoria and Prade in the municipal government, to divide the *comune* of Canal San Bovo into four independent municipalities.[18] However, the main event which affected present-day perceptions and representations of local identity was the Great War. The eve of the conflict saw

Trentino divided between proclerical Christian Socialists, who favoured continued Austrian dominance in Tyrol, and Socialists who advocated autonomy for the province. However, especially in the towns of Trent and Rovereto, the cultural affinity with the neighbouring Italian regions and the gravitation of economic interests towards the markets of Veneto and Lombardy, coupled with the difficulty in maintaining relations with the territories of the Austro-Hungarian Empire, enhanced the advance of Italianism (Alcock 1970: 12). The district of Primiero, however, was divided between these two opposing forces; it is not purely coincidence that Cesare Battisti, the leader of Trentine Socialists, in one of his writings (1912: 29) portrayed the people of the district as 'short' and 'brown-haired', so as to throw into relief the physical characteristics that were ascribed to the 'typical Italian peoples'.

With the outbreak of the conflict in 1914 the inhabitants of the district who were doing military service were sent to fight in Galicia. Although the whole district of Primiero turned into a thoroughfare for the Italian and Austro-Hungarian armies between 1916 and 1918, it was the Vanoi valley, and particularly the village of Caoria, that directly experienced and became an arena of the fights, and found itself on the front line between the two armies. This event is vividly 'remembered' among the local people. With the temporary withdrawal of the Austro-Hungarian army in 1916, the Italian troops entered the valley, but had to leave it shortly afterwards. Caoria was deeply affected by such events, as the people who happened to be in the *masi* (about 200, who included the elderly, women and children) were taken to a camp for refugees in Mitterndorf, in Austria (Zorzi 1966: 31–32); by contrast, those who happened to be in the village were sent to camps for refugees in northern and central Italy, where they remained until 1919. It was only towards the end of the war, however, that the Italian army conquered the valley, and the event was symbolised by the seizure of Mount Cauriol. With the end of the war both the Province of Trent and the German-speaking one of Bolzano/Bozen or South Tyrol became part of the Italian Kingdom.

Trentino's formal incorporation in Italy in 1918 seems to suggest that Italian identity represented an imposition 'from above', in the same way that being labelled as 'Austrian' or 'Italian' did not necessarily imply commitment to the Italian or Austrian state, particularly among people who could hardly read and write. Especially in Trentino, there seemed to be little or no connection between village and national identity (Leoni 1995: 3). The Italian victory meant the district's annexation to the Italian Kingdom, but it was a 'forced' annexation: as Palla noted (1994: 53), those who advocated it were based in the urban centres of Trent or Rovereto; the countryside, dominated by priests and grass-roots politicians, had little or no interest in changing the status quo: in other words, the distinction between the city and the countryside was essentially a political division (Meriggi 1991: 71). By contrast, loyalty to Austria mainly meant economic privileges for the peasants, social stability, the preservation of the moral and religious values of local society (Palla 1994: 84), but not necessarily the existence of a 'national' sentiment. Therefore the legitimation of national identity in Trentino turned out to be a difficult task for the Italian state (Leoni 1995: 5). The advent of Fascism in the early 1920s and the subsequent establishment of a strong central government in Rome led to the abolition of the autonomy Trentino had enjoyed under Austro-Hungarian rule. Despite this, the events of the Second World War had little impact in the Vanoi valley and in the whole district, and Fascist ideology did not find fertile ground in the area (Piccoli 1978: 222). That the fights between Fascists and partisans in the Vanoi valley are not recounted as part of the history of some villages is a case in point.

At the end of the last world conflict the district could still be described as a 'peasant' society. The economic crisis of the 1950s brought about an increase of temporary and permanent emigration abroad, particularly to Belgium, Britain, France, Germany and Switzerland. The men who emigrated abroad found employment as manual workers, whereas for women the main option was that of domestic servants. Some of those who returned to the valley took up the option from their pre-capitalist past, and came back to agro-pastoralism, but the flood of 1966 put an end to all this. Forestry remained the main economic activity in the valley until a few years ago, as long as the price of timber rendered it profitable, and in the aftermath of the Second World War some timber companies opened branches in Caoria. While the valley remained economically dependent on forestry, Primiero experienced economic growth thanks to the renewed development of tourism from the 1960s onwards. As in most of Italian rural communities, the Christian Democratic Party (DC) dominated the political arena of the municipality from the aftermath of the Second World War until the early 1990s; a form of patronage as the dominant idiom of political life persisted (and still persists, to some extent) owing to the economic underdevelopment of the valley, which has unfolded in terms of increasing dependence on state and provincial subsidies.

The end of the war was followed, in 1947, by the creation of the autonomous region Trentino-South Tyrol, divided into two autonomous provinces, the Italian-speaking one of Trent, and the German-speaking one of Bolzano/Bozen. Although the two provinces enjoyed a considerable degree of autonomy, in fact the autonomy statute was designed to ensure that the cultural, economic and social development of South Tyrol lay in Italian hands (Alcock 1996: 73; see also Calì 1988: 113). However, while the development of industry in the region gave employment to the Italian-speaking resident population and caused depopulation of the Trentine countryside, in South Tyrol a system of impartible inheritance enhanced the development of agriculture as a viable economic activity, and enabled the overwhelming majority of the German-speaking population to remain on the land. The autonomy agreement was preceded by a short-lived protest movement all over Trentino, the Association for the Study of Regional Autonomy (or ASAR), which advocated autonomy and unity for the two provinces. So, it is especially with the rise of nationalism at the turn of the century, and all the more so with the advent of Fascism and with the creation of the autonomous region that the opposition between the provinces of Trent and Bolzano/Bozen became clear-cut (Sanguanini 1992: 150). Although the two provinces formed parts of the same regional unit, in fact they were considered expressions of two distinct traditions with different cultural traits which were redistributed during the consolidation of the Italian and Austrian states. That the two groups speak different languages and occupy distinct territorial units remained a significant element of differentiation.

The political situation of Trentino-South Tyrol suddenly changed between the late 1980s and the early 1990s as a consequence of the economic crisis, the demise of the Christian Democratic Party at the national and local level, and Austria's entry into the European Union. The economic crisis chiefly meant a crisis of the large industrial system which gave employment to the Italian-speaking population, particularly in Trentino. In South Tyrol, by contrast, an economy based on tourism and agriculture, that is to say a 'local' economy, continued to thrive in spite of the crisis (Turato 1998: 88–89). The economic gap that such transformations brought about had the effect of legitimating the view that in Trentino it was necessary to follow the example of South Tyrol and develop a 'local' economy. The economic crisis in Trentino furthered the belief that the economic system inherited from the Italian state, along with the autonomy granted from the Italian state itself, hindered, rather than enhanced, the economic potential of the province (Turato 1998: 105). This made people believe that Trentino could be better off economically by relying on its own means, and by developing economic relationships with the regions north of the national border instead of with the rest of Italy.

Such transformations went hand in hand with the ascendancy of autonomist political formations, among which the Northern League had a programme of European federalism, and the Trentine-Tyrolean Autonomist Party (PATT) which championed a revival of the ASAR, more power for the autonomous provinces, and closer links with South Tyrol. This happened when, as a consequence of the 1992 Maastricht Treaty, the European Union recognised the existence of local and regional governments, and admitted that regions had a place in the construction of Europe (Alcock 1996: 81). However, the sort of 'regional centralism' which figured prominently on the Northern League's agenda could mean the end of Trentino's provincial autonomy. So, when the PATT was in charge of the provincial government in the 1990s it stressed the coexistence of different ethnic groups in Trentino (notably the Ladins and the Mocheno-Cimbri) in order to legitimate the autonomy of the province then undermined by the Northern League's political programmes. One of the consequences of this development, at the regional level, was the PATT's project of establishment of a transnational Autonomous European Region of Tyrol (Euregio), encompassing Trentino, South Tyrol and the Austrian Tyrol, drawing on a model of European federalism

(Barozzi 1996; Luverà 1996). An intriguing aspect of this was a redefinition of Trentine regional identity, which implied stressing cultural continuity and unbroken history with South Tyrol. What these events brought about was partly an inversion of the roles that had so far been ascribed to each ethnic group in the region. The paradoxical effect was that in the 1990s forging a Trentine identity did not entail stressing a distinct 'local' culture but, as will be seen in more detail, resulted in the appropriation of the cultural symbols of the German-speaking South Tyrol.

In sum, over many generations the *dramatis personæ* had to endure the hardships which living in a mountainous area entails. Particularly, they had to negotiate the intrigues which are the result of their inhabiting a space at the economic and geographical margins of two nation-states, the Austro-Hungarian Empire until 1918, and the Italian state afterwards. Coping with this situation also meant furthering a cultural awareness, which enabled social actors to affirm their local identity in several circumstances. However, at the turn of the millennium the allures and the uncertainties which globalisation entails meant that, in order to preserve a local identity, social actors had to come to terms with a changing world. I return to these themes in the chapters that follow.

NOTES

1. Sources: Municipalities of Canal San Bovo and Castello Tesino.
2. I speak, for the sake of brevity, of the inhabitants of the valley as 'peasants' (*contadini*), rather than herders, because this is what the majority of my informants call themselves, even though agricultural tasks are no longer viable economic activities.
3. This was the case, for example, of a TV programme broadcast on the Italian first national channel (RAI 1) in March 1996.
4. This is the case of a shepherd owning about 600 sheep, who lives far away from the valley and from the Province, but remains a resident of Ronco in order to benefit from the subsidies of the Province of Trent which are not available in other regions under the same favourable conditions.
5. In fact it belonged to the Diocese of Feltre until 1783.
6. It should be noted that the Church maintained control over many estates in the area until the late nineteenth century.
7. In fact disputes between the municipality of Canal San Bovo and the *comuni* of Tesino still occur in relation to the possession of mountains, especially hunting preserves, when there are no documents stating who can claim rights over certain tracts of land.
8. This historical information draws upon the collection of writings of the late nineteenth century by don Bettega, the priest of Canal San Bovo, and upon that by don Daniele Sperandio, the priest of Caoria from 1922 to 1935.
9. Shortly after Caoria, in 1758 another chapel was consecrated in Prade, and others were built throughout the valley a few years later. According to the priest who resided in Canal San Bovo in the 1890s, this was the outcome of the *cristianesimo di campanile* (i.e. a kind of Christianity used to celebrate community identity and distinctiveness vis-à-vis other communities) that permeates the priests' teachings. In a note he wryly writes, 'Do you want quarrels? Build chapels!' ('Volete delle discordie? Fabbricate delle cappelle!').
10. The records of the priest of Canal San Bovo of the late nineteenth century suggest that relationships between Canal San Bovo itself and the other villages have been characterised by mutual distrust since the eighteenth century.
11. Various quarrels between the priest of Canal San Bovo and the priests of Caoria, Prade and Ronco arose over the fact that the priests and the people of the above villages were required to attend the Corpus Christi procession in Canal San Bovo every year. In 1815 the above priests refused to do so. It is worth noting that in Caoria the Corpus Christi procession was not allowed until 1912.
12. This is a very interesting aspect which deserves a study in its own right. In fact in this work the limited range of archival sources consulted comes from my being an anthropologist and not an historian, and the role of priests in forging local identity still awaits its analysis in Alpine historiography.
13. This was in turn the outcome of Tyrol's position of economic marginality and political irrelevance within the framework of the Austro-Hungarian Empire.
14. It is in this period that a Tyrolean provincial consciousness developed alongside a strong sense of German identity, particularly in the German-speaking part of the region. However, this consciousness did not involve loyalty to the central government in Vienna, but was rather influenced by anti-Enlightenment political forces such as the local nobility and the clergy (Cole 2000).
15. The symbolic incarnation of Tyrolean liberty and religiosity.

16. Various descriptions of the area and its people (especially in English) came from the British mountain climbers who visited the valley of Primiero in that period. Unfortunately, as the Vanoi valley never appealed to climbers, written accounts about this area were not produced.

17. Several barns in the high meadows (or *masi*) were built in that period.

18. This was also the case of the village of Prade in the 1890s. That the relationships between Canal San Bovo and the outlying villages were characterised by acute parochialism (*odio di campanile*) is clearly explained by the priest of Caoria, Giuseppe Fidelangelo, in a letter sent to the Diocese of Trent on 2 January 1904.

1. Map of Italy, highlighting Trentino.

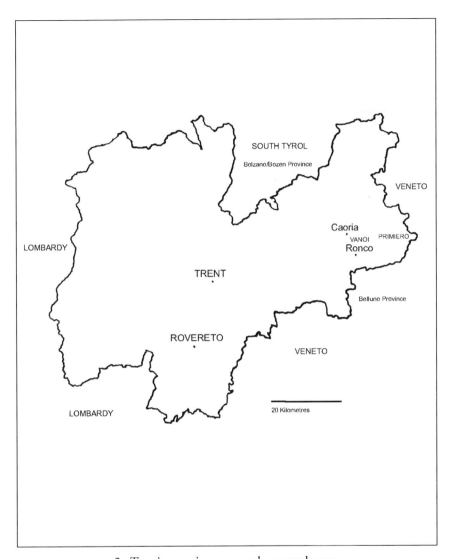

SOUTH TYROL

Bolzano/Bozen Province

VENETO

LOMBARDY

Caoria
VANOI
PRIMIERO
Ronco

TRENT

Belluno Province

ROVERETO

VENETO

20 Kilometres

LOMBARDY

2. Trentino: main towns and case study area.

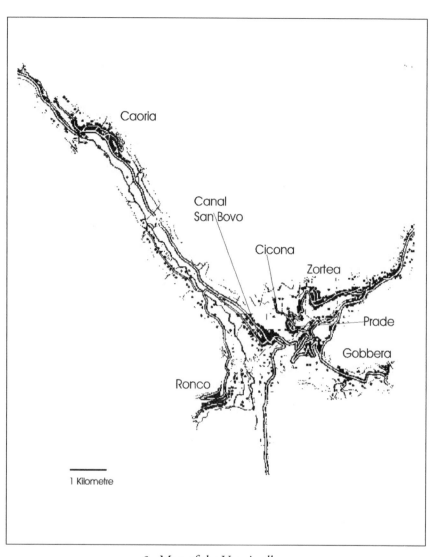

Caoria

Canal
San Bovo

Cicona

Zortea

Prade

Gobbera

Ronco

1 Kilometre

3. Map of the Vanoi valley.

4. Panoramic view of Caoria in the 1940s.

5. Caoria in 1992.

6. Panoramic view of Ronco.

7. Ronco: nowadays only a few retired perform agricultural chores.

3
A PRIVATE SPACE: THE PRESENT-DAY ORGANISATION OF VILLAGE LIFE

Introduction

On entering the villages of Caoria and Ronco the occasional visitor cannot help noticing the huge open spaces, formerly used for grazing, which stretch outside the inhabited area. Images of such landscapes are reminiscent of the portraits of Alpine communities that can be seen in postcards, which convey an idea of the countryside as an intangible resource defined by its appearance, to be consumed visually. In other words, it is a vision of the countryside as part of the leisure experience, something to be 'communally owned' as a source of enjoyment. This is certainly the way the Alpine landscape is perceived by most of those who visit the valley over the weekend, particularly urban dwellers. In fact this association between Alpine landscapes and openness is largely illusory, and the researcher soon realises that what conveys ideas of 'openness' to an outsider may be attached a different meaning by those who live in the area. On walking through an open meadow, for example, tourists are likely to be approached by the owner living nearby, who asks the unaware visitors to keep off, on the grounds that they are treading private property. Encounters like this are not rare. Although private property (*proprietà privata*) signs do not abound in the valley, the oblivious tourists are promptly reminded of the fact that there is a boundary that should not be trespassed. Thus, despite the absence of a material boundary, such a boundary may be present in the minds of the people. However, this attitude does not simply mirror a concern with the protection of a physical space. In the village of Caoria this impression proves founded when the visitor reads, in the locally published brochure or at the entrance of the village museum, that tourists are invited to 'respect the intimacy of the inhabitants'. In a sense, it looks as though emphasis on what is private is not simply expressed by territorial boundaries, but informs social relationships as well, and particularly the way a group of people relates to persons and things that are not part of the group itself. As a matter of fact a notion of 'private' very often emerges in conversations, particularly in relation to the association between people and 'private' spaces: it is an image of the social world in which each individual actor should occupy a specific domain. Villagers' stress upon divisions and upon the necessity to protect property boundaries and keep things and people 'in place' (*a posto*) as they used to be in the 'old days' expresses this idea very well. This emphasis upon the notion of 'in place' and its association with boundaries and divisions raises the question of how far this is reflected in the ways social actors interact with each other.

The starting point of my investigation was the discovery that the aforementioned divisions were often mentioned when alluding to the village of the 'old days', and there was an acute awareness that the village was no longer the same. The view that in the past everything was 'in place', i.e. that such boundaries were not questioned, and that the community was 'self-sufficient' was expressed on several occasions by my informants, both in Caoria and in Ronco. The statement *el mondo de 'ncoi no l'e giusto* ('the world of these days is not right')[1] well describes the opposition between an ordered past and a 'disordered' or 'chaotic' present: there is a shared conviction that men and women used to have their own separate domains in society, that they were 'in place', and that every household had its own landed property whose boundaries were never crossed by strangers. By contrast, there is a commonly held view that at present nothing is 'in place', and that both physical and symbolic boundaries are often blurred. How an ideology about order and the awareness that the world of the 'old days' is vanishing can coexist is the theme I am going to explore.

Kinship and Residence

Perhaps the most appropriate way to start this exploration is by looking at one of the 'natural' divisions of the social world, that is to say kinship and residence. In the Vanoi valley, as elsewhere in the Alpine crescent, the villager's social world consists of two antithetical types: that of the household, whose basis is deemed to be mutual trust and affection, and that of the outside, characterised by mistrust and often by hostility. The positive values of village life are, at least nominally, centred on the family; both in Ronco and in Caoria the solidarity of close relatives remains one of the underlying elements of social organisation. As in other Alpine valleys, the household provides the basis of social actors' perceptions of who they are within the social world to which they belong (Minnich 1998: 51). Kinship creates moral claims and obligations (Fortes 1969: 242), and internal solidarity vis-à-vis the outside world. In theory close relatives represent a category of relationships which divides one's kin from strangers; in practice, however, the distinction between the two worlds is modified by a number of relationships, which include friendship and marriage, that link the different family groups to each other in different ways.

Kinship in the Vanoi valley is cognatic, that is to say that descent is traced equally through both the father and the mother. A man's close relatives as a category of relations include all kinsmen on both his mother's and his father's side to the level of the third ascending generation, and laterally to the degree of second cousin. Villagers seem to be embedded in a kinship network: the statement **noi son parenti** ('we are related') encompasses a wide range of people that also include those who are only distantly related. Third cousins, for example, may be alluded to as 'relatives'; this idea of relatedness shows that the local notion of kinship is very wide, and suggests that, as in many northern Mediterranean villages, even in this area a person is a member of a community through membership of a family.[2] The household represents the foundation for the people's self-understanding, though this does not entail that the 'family' is necessarily a focus of attachment in place of extra-village and state institutions in the same way that it is in the South of Italy (see for example Banfield 1958).

That the idea of relatedness informs much of village thinking is revealed by the endless conversations about who is related to whom, which may be heard in many social settings. The idea of 'real' villager entails membership of 'real' families,[3] that is to say families that have resided in the village since time immemorial. In a sense, kinship does not simply come into play as a biological fact, but also an an idiom: taking a hint from Schneider's well-known study of American kinship (1980: 59), 'the family is a paradigm for what each relation is and how they should behave toward each other'. This applies to a village in which all are related, at least at the level of self-representation. In reaffirming their relatedness through the reconstruction of their kinship connections the inhabitants of the valley also create the boundaries of their world. Both in Caoria and in Ronco there is an ideal congruence between kinship and territorial boundaries, as is shown by the villages' division into small clusters (**colmèi**) named after the families that first settled there.

In both communities most of the inhabitants are able to trace their genealogies back to the third ascending generation (ego's great-grandparents), with greater emphasis on the male line. Ancestors are seen as part of the history of the family and linked with the living generations, especially when the ancestor in question was a distinguished person, or when a set of his descendants is named after him. I use 'family group' here for such a set. The villagers' own term is **ratha** (literally 'race'): this reflects the idea of genealogical depth, which may be missing from the term 'family'.[4] Family group names are referred to as family nicknames (**soranomi**), which both in Caoria and in Ronco are used much more often than surnames, given the many cases of homonymy.[5] These are handed down through the male line, and have force within the community only. Thus, when one is asked **di che ratha si tu?** ('Which "race" are you?'), one is expected to answer by giving the nickname of a father's family group; in the case of illegitimate children, however, one may also reply with that of one's mother, though this may be embarrassing. That such nicknames have force only in the community suggests that they act as markers of differentiation for the 'core' families of the village, and that they maintain the boundary between members and nonmembers of the community. As with a patronimic, a given family nickname vanishes if there are no sons born to a married couple.[6]

As a rule, a villager's 'most important' relatives are members of his/her elementary (or extended) family, which also includes one's uncles and aunts, great-uncles and great-aunts, and one's first and second cousins. At the degree of third cousin people are termed as 'very distant relatives' if ego is on good terms with them, otherwise kinship ties are denied. The idea that kinship may endure beyond the degree of second cousin becomes patent when, for example, a given household needs extra help for work in the vegetable garden or in the meadow: the recruitment of an extra-household labour force is likely to occur between close relatives (siblings, first cousins, etc.), and sometimes even between second or third cousins.

At present the majority of the households consist of single nuclear families; both in Ronco and in Caoria all the people I know live in two-storey houses with adjacent stable (**tabià**) where livestock were kept until some years ago. Although nuclear families are very often separate in the sense that they have a separate kitchen, it is also common for married couples to inhabit part of a building shared with the husband's relatives. At present most of the houses in Ronco and in Caoria are inhabited all the year round,[7] aside from those owned by strangers or by villagers who work in urban centres. This pattern has undergone some changes during the last few decades, especially in Caoria, where new houses have been built. However, before the demise of agro-pastoral economy young married couples used to live virilocally with the husband's parents and siblings, which suggests the existence of a model of household in which a senior man is ideally the main decision-maker.[8] In some cases it was the groom that had to go to live in a house next to the bride's parents: this was not very frequent, and I heard that in the 'old days' it was embarrassing for a man to do so, for this led covillagers to believe that he was not able to support his wife and did not own enough land.[9] This type of marriage was called **in cuc**, i.e. just like the cuckoo.

As already noted, until the demise of agro-pastoral economy most of the families resided in **colmèi** named after them. This division is clearly illustrated by the cadastral maps of the nineteenth century, which portray Caoria as a set of clusters at some distance from each other. Even at the time of my fieldwork the inhabitants of Caoria and Ronco used to refer to each other using the name of their respective households: in other words, such names are metaphors for social relations.[10] Even though nowadays this rule is not always abided by, I found that most of the newly married couples, especially in Caoria, still set up residence next to a house inhabited by close relatives (usually the husband's parents, and often siblings or first cousins), which may be the one formerly owned by paternal grandparents. Despite this tendency, the construction, in the 1990s, of new houses in Caoria in an area previously farmed gave a few newly married couples the opportunity to move to a part of the village where no close relatives live nearby. In Ronco, by contrast, going to live here or there in the village does not seem to matter as much as it used to: there may be married couples that set up home neolocally outside the valley both because of lack of job opportunities, and also in order to keep away from a social environment in which every member has access to knowledge about every other member.

As in many other rural communities, village endogamy was quite common until a few years ago. Marriages with outsiders were not encouraged by the community: a stigma was attached to those, especially women, who married a stranger, on the grounds that they were considered unable to find a spouse in their own village; this suggests that in the 'old days' it was deemed preferable to get married to someone of the same community: as Innocenza (b. 1942) stated, 'Only those who were desperate to find a spouse were willing to marry an outsider'. At the same time marrying within the village entailed the possibility of joining together one's landholding with one's wife's plot. This practice used to be widespread in the Alpine area when people had to rely on agro-pastoral activities as the main means of subsistence (Poppi 1980: 78), and also functioned as a device to maintain a strict control over land use and rights (Viazzo 1989: 25). Villagers are very ambivalent about village endogamy: during my fieldwork all the people I talked with stated unhesitatingly that nowadays it does not make a great difference whether a person decides to get married to an outsider or to another villager. If anything, it is often the case that young women get married to an outsider in order to 'escape' parental control, though it seems reasonable to believe that permanent emigration abroad or to urban centres in northern Italy has also played a significant part in reducing village endogamy. Even the men I came across no longer mind, at least nominally, about marrying *in cuc*, and the expression itself is never used by villagers, apart from occasions when they tell stories about the past. However, even though the Caorians interviewed deny that there is a great difference between virilocal and uxorilocal marriage, I found that there is still nostalgia, on the part of men, for the 'old days' when virilocal residence was much more common than it is now. Apart from the very few married couples that set up home neolocally in the valley, in the majority of the cases women still set up residence next to the husband's parents. So, if the two spouses live in different clusters before marriage (albeit in the same village), it is women who usually leave their place of residence. This is certainly the case in Caoria, where there are just five non-Caorian men who found a partner there, while there are thirty women who came from the outside to marry a Caorian.[11]

Aside from a few cases, women coming from other villages find it difficult to adjust themselves to the social environment of the community where they take residence. They end up being addressed by the collective nickname used for the people of their places of origin, and are never talked about as full members of the community where they settle. Consequently, although it seems assumed that every resident is looked upon as a member of the community, in fact this applies to those who were born and have resided there. Likewise it is still highly desirable for a man to keep residence where he was born and where his parents and forefathers have always lived.[12] A survey of the households of Caoria and Ronco has revealed that this system still works to a certain extent: men keep residence, while women change it. In the 'old days' the relationship between Caoria and Ronco could be described, in Lévi-Straussian terms (1969), as something similar to an 'exchange' of women who 'move' from one community to another.

It seems reasonable to suppose that this pattern of virilocal residence was maintained by inheritance practices. Although the information on this aspect is confined to what informants said in the course of conversations, it is clear that such practices played a decisive role in the reproduction of the social system. Under Italian law a share of the patrimony (the so-called *legittima*) must be divided equally among the heirs entitled to it, irrespective of sex, but the rest can be disposed of as the testator chooses. In the Vanoi valley the house and the *masi* were usually left to sons, along with as much of the better land as possible, whereas daughters used to get the rest. Even now the *masi* are looked upon as male property, as an extension of the owner. Inheritance practices, in other words, entailed the transmission of a patrilineal identity.[13] Although in both villages there is emphasis on the necessity to divide things equally, in fact property used to be divided unevenly, and conflict among the heirs entitled to a share of the patrimony was very likely to arise. In a sense, many ties of close kinship subsume rivalries and latent hostilities, as shown by various cases of siblings (even those living next door) who avoid each other for this reason. Thus, attitudes towards patterns of inheritance are characterised by ambivalence: on the one hand villagers explain the fragmentation of property as a dimension of social harmony;[14] on the other, they complain about the absence of a system of ideal impartible inheritance, such as that formerly practised in the German-speaking South Tyrol, on the grounds that such a system would keep things 'in order'.

It is significant that not only is it preferable for many men to avoid marrying *in cuc*, but also to have sons, rather than daughters, in order to ensure that someone of the same family group remains in the same house and carries the family name.[15] This suggests that the continuity of a family group is conditional on having sons who 'keep' the name and continue to reside in the same place.[16]

Thus, in spite of the fact that male villagers (even young ones) usually deny that a patrilineal ideology permeates marriage customs, in fact actual practice provides evidence that the idea of the continuity (and social reproduction) of the paternal family group is still attached considerable importance. One of the consequences of this is that women, through marrying out of their villages, also 'move' through the communities, and are not committed to 'locality' as much as men are: in other words, locality may have a different meaning for them. So, the issue is not only what ideas the notion of locality conveys, but also *who* talks about it. This point is further explored in the following section.

Men and Women: Public and Private Domains?

The aim of this section is to assess the applicability of the conceptual opposition between 'public man' and 'private woman' (and, implicitly, 'dominance' and 'submission') to the social context under study, and to see how discourse and practices of 'masculinity' and 'femininity' are constructed in sociability. This is also meant as a further exploration of the idea of 'private' in an attempt to assess its potential as an analytical tool to describe the local community in relation to the encompassing nation-state. It must be stressed that, although the term 'private' is often used in this work, it does not follow that the *dramatis personæ* use it. Sometimes they make use of the Italian *privato*, but they also have other words or expressions to describe such a domain, as will be seen later on. I use the term 'private' mainly as an analytical tool to translate the concepts used by informants.

The pervasiveness of such a notion becomes patent in the analysis of the domains occupied by men and women. As in many other Alpine villages, it is surprising how easy it is to get in touch with village men, whereas getting acquainted with village women may take longer, especially for a man. A commonly held view is that men can be seen in the bars, whereas women are likely to be found in their houses or in the back streets, rather than in 'public' places. This ideal separation seems to reflect a distinction that has been found elsewhere in the Alpine region and in the rural world in general. In Ronco, and especially in Caoria, men fraternise with whoever they come across in 'public' places (especially in the wine bar), whereas women seem more enmeshed in their families and their kinship networks. They exchange visits and errands with female relatives but, at least apparently, do not socialise beyond the kinship sphere.

However, we may take a hint from Reiter (1975: 252): 'Although "official" power is vested in the more formal, public arena occupied by men, women consider their own domestic realm as more important and more formative. Men deny the importance of women's activities and see themselves as predominant in village life'. This raises the question of whether the distinction of the two spheres actually entails a power differential between the two, given that women may wield power without directly participating in formal political institutions. The public/private dichotomy in the study of gender has been criticised on various grounds:[17] for example, it has been argued that this distinction is merely ideological, and that subordination in one sphere may be offset by power in another (Hirschon 1984: 19). Another issue is the degree to which the kinship realm has importance for women's lives: the assumption that women are necessarily bound to the domestic domain and to the kinship realm would lead to the conviction that the opposition between 'private woman' and 'public man' is fixed, and would clash with the widely held view that women, by marrying out of their villages, also move from one place to another.

One significant distinction related to the gendered division of space is that between the situation of *'sti ani* (the 'old days') and that of *'ncoi* ('these days'):[18] despite the apparent fixity of such divisions, informants (especially men) agree that the 'old days' (i.e. until the 1960s) were characterised by 'stability', in that 'men's and women's realms were kept separate' (***omini de una banda, femene de l'altra***), and men's predominance in the 'public' spheres was never questioned: while men were free to roam where they wished, women were restricted to the village and home. By contrast, most men complain that nowadays the boundary between the two realms is increasingly blurred. Clearly, until some years ago it was women only who did the cooking, cleaning and washing. Now that several women, especially the young ones, have a paid job outside the domestic domain many men have to be competent at some of those tasks when the spouse is away.

Despite the blurring of the boundaries between such domains, in some cases such realms can be easily distinguished. One of the domains that is looked upon as 'typically male' is the village bar.[19] In Italy the bar or *osteria* is regarded as typical of villages, conjuring notions of rurality and working-class culture, a place of sociability. In anthropological literature it is described as the focal institution of 'public' life as opposed to the 'private', domestic sphere dominated by women.[20] Although the public man/private woman dichotomy has been questioned on various grounds, anthropological case studies still depict the bar as the 'public' domain of men, and the domestic realm as the 'private' domain of women. This idea, as I will try to suggest, is partly unfounded, as the notion of 'public' necessarily conveys ideas of a place (or domain) that is accessible to everybody. Assuming that the bar represents the 'public' side of the community would entail overlooking the multiplicity of meanings that it can take on in the social context under study:[21] as Dubisch suggested in relation to a similar context (1993: 280), concepts such as public and private 'need to be grounded firmly in specific ethnographic contexts'.

Each bar in the valley has its own steady clientele, which normally includes those who live in the neighbourhood or are related to the bartender (usually a woman in her sixties). The bar represents the men's house as opposed to domesticity and loneliness. There is a shared conviction, among my informants, that *'sti ani* the bar was the place for 'true' men where a certain kind of 'male' behaviour was allowed, and there are various stories about social behaviour in the bars of Ronco and Caoria. As Nives (b. 1957) put it, *l'era come el far West* ('It was like far West'), implying that quarrels and brawls were frequent there, and that heavy drinking was not only allowed but, in a sense, mandatory in order to be part of a group of men: it was a culturally coercive activity. Although women and children may be seen in the bar now and again, *'sti ani* it was only adult males who were allowed there, even though in theory everybody could be admitted, irrespective of age and gender. As Tullia (b. 1949) said, her father, an outsider in Caoria, used to be sharply criticised by other Caorians for taking her to the bar to have an ice-cream when she was a child, on the grounds that the head of the family should leave his children at home. In the 'old days' men began to frequent the bar when coming of age, and those who tried to go there before the attainment of adulthood were usually forced to leave by the elderly (*i veci*).[22] Clearly, by frequenting the bar on Sunday morning while the holy mass is said, men join the company of other men and avoid attending the religious service in the village church, a place frequented mainly by women.[23] However, attitudes towards the Catholic Church should not be interpreted simply as the result of the declining power of the Church itself: a report on the parish of Caoria, sent to the Diocese of Trent on 19 August 1864, contains a complaint about the men of Caoria, who frequent the wine bar instead of attending the holy mass.

The bar used to be, until quite recently, the place where villagers gathered to play cards or other games, some of which are now forbidden. Until not long ago men used to go on playing various games such as *morra*[24] until late in the night. At the time of my fieldwork these were not as popular as they used to be,[25] nor did they seem to have the same socialising role that they played until recently. Such games were part of being 'adult male', in that they enabled actors to display male aggressiveness and assertiveness. Even now becoming a 'true' man may be conditional on being a heavy drinker (but not a drunkard). This means that men going to the bar usually ask for a glass of wine or a 'strong' coffee with *grappa* or cognac,[26] but very seldom for a glass of water or juice.

In spite of aggressive behaviour, in the bar a day-to-day interaction among covillagers builds up a local 'community'. This becomes very clear on Sunday morning, when most men gather in the two biggest bars in Caoria, and entertain there to exchange news about the village or comment on local politics. Thus, bar attendance is a highly patterned activity, as revealed by the strict etiquette that regulates social drinking, especially when someone asks for a drink;[27] one usually buys a round for the others who, in turn, reciprocate shortly afterwards. When everybody has paid for a round the bartender usually joins in and offers another one for free. Those who exchange rounds of drinks are normally those who go to the same bar every Sunday (and sometimes in the weekdays as well). As Vale de Almeida (1996: 90) suggested in relation to a similar context, this also expresses the political ideal of the fundamental equality of men. As a rule, these people have a priority to initiate a round of drinks, but strangers are very seldom allowed to buy a round,[28] and in certain cases they are not even allowed to pay for their own. This suggests that this sort of 'balanced reciprocity' builds a community that is restricted to certain people only and that generosity towards strangers serves to maintain the boundary between villagers and strangers themselves.[29] In a sense, a relation of reciprocity is established and reinforced among covillagers, whereas one of asymmetry is established between the villagers themselves and the stranger.

The ethnographic information about the bars in the valley is by no means unusual, and social behaviour of this kind may be noticed in many Italian rural villages. This information brings us back to the widely shared idea that the village bar is necessarily a 'public' domain: it may be so, but in relation to what? That this type of balanced reciprocity is confined to villagers only suggests that in engaging in an exchange of this type not only do these people cement the idea of community and comradeship, but also build up a symbolic boundary between 'us' and 'them', between those of the village and strangers. My contention is that the bar may be considered the 'public' side of the village chiefly in relation (and in opposition) to the 'domestic' domain dominated by women, but it is the 'domestic world' of those who think of themselves as representatives of the community. If anything, as I will try to show in the following notes, its 'local' character also makes it the place of 'cultural intimacy'.[30]

The fact that those who frequent the bar are people who have lived in the village for a long time means that the bar itself functions as a 'venue of communication' in which news about the village and the outside are exchanged, and where only those familiar with a sort of 'coded language' can join. The local dialect, for example, is the only idiom used there.[31] The village bar becomes the arena where one comes to know about community affairs, and hears any kind of gossip. It is also in the bar that stereotypes usually spread.[32] The tender of one of the bars in the valley, for example, is laughingly referred to as *il gazzettino* ('the chronicle') because she is deemed a source of news about her village and its inhabitants. As already said, the idea that the bar is the ideal setting for 'male gossip' is the main reason why some villagers avoid going there: if they started doing so, their private affairs would suddenly become known to everybody in the community.

That an outsider can hardly partake of the exchange of information that takes place in the bar becomes patent when, for instance, s/he steps in while some villagers have a glass of wine or half a pint of beer after work: conversations suddenly come to a halt, and the people who happen to be there turn to look at the unwelcome visitor, and remain silent until the person asks the bartender for a drink or information. Eventually, when the visitor leaves the bar, all villagers engage in a conversation about the person's accent, the way s/he behaved, the clothes s/he wore, how much money s/he had, and so forth.[33] This presence may provide an opportunity for making fun of the stranger him/herself, especially when this person does not show familiarity with the mores of the village. However, when a stranger starts frequenting a given bar on a regular basis, villagers' attitudes may change, though they are likely to keep on asking him/her several questions such as, for instance, where s/he comes from, how long s/he expects to remain in the village, and so forth. This sudden shift of attitude is deceiving, for locals strive to get information about the outsider, but very seldom talk about themselves, and in doing so they succeed in maintaining a boundary between the stranger and themselves. This is a very common attitude among villagers in dealings with strangers, which shows that in local discourse not only is it important to protect one's own boundary, but also to violate others'. This ideal, as will be seen later on, informs interpersonal relationships too.

The bar, as the place of male sociability, is the setting where membership of the community becomes patent, where one can easily assess who is friend of whom, and whether one is taken into high or low consideration. The case of the bars of the valley suggests that men do not necessarily occupy the 'public' spheres of the community. It may be argued, instead, that the bar is the setting where men become the upholders and defenders of the 'private' knowledge about the community. However, such attitudes are also expressed by the way in which some bartenders interact with customers: this varies according to whether the customer is a villager or a stranger; it is worth noting, for instance, that although prices are fixed (i.e. not negotiable), in fact some categories of customers always pay whereas others seldom do so. As a rule, in the valley outsiders have to pay as much as stated by the price list displayed at the entrance. Thus, customers are issued a receipt stating the exact amount paid.[34] By contrast, during my fieldwork receipts were seldom issued to villagers, and in the local restaurants the amount they were asked to pay was normally lower than that paid by strangers. At that time there were prices for 'Italians' (*'taliáni*, i.e. Italians coming from outside Trentino) and prices for locals. This was a socially recognised way of operating, and not necessarily a 'hidden transcript', as Scott would have termed it (Reed-Danahay 1993: 229). So, it was considered improper for a villager to ask the bartender for a receipt. However, when uniformed inland revenue inspectors (the so-called *finanza*) come to the valley bartenders phone each other in order to avoid being caught selling drinks or food without issuing receipts. That villagers very seldom ask the bartender for receipts is another demonstration that they approve of a covillager paying as little as possible to the state.[35] Clearly, some bars represent the context where official rules are challenged, or where the 'intimacy' of village life is kept beyond the reach of state regulation. Contempt for laws is also evidenced by male behaviour in the bar. Foul expressions, for example, are frequently heard,[36] though the bar is not the only place where swearing is common.[37]

From the examples just discussed it may be suggested that the bar is the context where opposition to law-enforcing agents and certain norms of behaviour may be manifested in various ways. So, if concepts such as 'public' and 'private' are relational, then the bar may be termed 'public' in relation to the domestic sphere, but becomes a 'private' space in relation to the outside, and to the state in particular. It is not purely coincidence that in their anti-state propaganda the autonomist parties that garnered so many votes in the valley, especially the Northern League, made use of a language (usually sexist) that is often heard in the bars. Hence, in the 1990s masculinity was portrayed more by means of contempt for rules than by physical strength as it was in the 'old days'.

It goes without saying that the domains inhabited by men are by no means confined to the bar. However, the importance that the bar has in the social context under study is related to the widely shared idea that laws should have no force there, and points to an association between the village bar and a 'private' space. This idea of 'private space' in which the state is absent is used in other contexts, as will be seen, and looms large in political discourse too. So, inferring that men inhabit the 'public' spheres of the village is a gross simplification, as it implies that these are termed 'public' on the grounds that they are 'out of the house'. Especially nowadays, this idea is unfounded, and the dichotomy between 'public' and 'private' is not so rigid. There are various domains, aside from the bar, that are 'typically' male: all the workplaces where considerable physical strength is required are characterised by a predominantly, not to say overall, male presence.

Until the demise of agro-pastoral economy it was only men who performed certain activities out of the village during the warm season, especially in the upper pastures, and even nowadays it is extremely rare to find women among the herders, let alone among the lumberjacks. In a sense, in the 'old days' the workplace was the ideal setting for displaying physical strength and 'maleness'. Heady (1999: 75) has shown in his study on the Carnic Alps that hardness is an integral part of male identity, which does not simply denote strength and ability to sustain hard work, but is also a personal quality which enables a person to make his own way in the world. At the time of my fieldwork strength was predominantly, albeit not exclusively, a quality ascribed to men: in fact various women in the valley, although lacking the physical strength of a lumberjack, have the strength of character which gains them respect in their community and outside.

Despite men's emphasis on strength, it was clear that its significance was declining. Unlike the 'old days', nowadays the men who are employed in the new sawmill are required to have a good knowledge about the machinery that makes the sawmill work, and physical strength, albeit an important factor, is no longer crucial. In a sense, while in the 'old days' man's role was primarily that of 'domestication' of nature through performance of agricultural, pastoral and forestry activities (and manual work in general), nowadays men no longer participate in an 'untamed' nature or, at least, taming it is no longer essential for survival.[38] However, men are still expected to 'protect' women and children (i.e. the 'weak') from the hostile world of the outside, and the community against the intrusive law-enforcing agents by resisting rules and laws. This also applies to the political sphere, as will be seen. Men's role in the protection of the 'private' certainly enables them to perceive themselves as autonomous persons and the homestead as a clearly bounded and viable domestic institution.[39] This sense of autonomy is still seen as an authentic expression of what it means to be a Caorian. Male identity, especially in Caoria, is also the consequence of a rhetoric that defines the 'true' man as a self-reliant figure and as the upholder of regional (and local) virtues, particularly the protection of freedom from outside rule that has been ascribed to Trentine and Alpine peoples (Fedel 1980: 25; see also, for Greece, Herzfeld 1985a: 21).

As a man, I experienced more difficulty in exploring women's domains. The first impression that the researcher receives is obviously that men travel and have social ties outside the domestic sphere, whereas women do not. That the kinship realm, especially in the 'old days', was of paramount importance to women's lives is a truism: kinship still is women's way of life, especially among the old ones, and much of the visiting in the village is between kinswomen. When I visited women at home, I often met close relatives (usually a sister or a first cousin) visiting at the same time for coffee, and most male informants claim that women stay at home and do not go out very often. In spite of this claim, when walking through the main streets of the two villages (especially in Caoria), the researcher is very likely to come across women rather than men. It is women who usually go shopping in the village or run errands for their husband. It is also common to see women walk arm in arm with one another.

While, as I said earlier, places such as the bars or the administrative offices are men's domains, houses and back streets symbolically belong to women: it is where women gather after going shopping, usually in groups of three or four that include close relatives or very good friends, and exchange news about the village and its people.[40] In one of the villages where I conducted my research, for example, there is a *congrega*, a group of three or four women who gather every day, especially in the summertime, at about ten in the morning by the public fountain near their houses (where laundry is sometimes done) to exchange (and spread) news and gossip about other villagers. One of the consequences of this repeated exchange of information is that other women avoid the place at that time for fear that they might be noticed by the group, and that gossip about them might spread. The local store is another place that some women prefer to avoid, as its staff includes the daughter of one of the aforementioned *congrega*, who usually tells her mother about the villagers who go to the store, what they bought, how much they spent, how things are going for them, and so forth. Therefore, although in the 'old days' the domain of women used to be that of the house, in fact they were and still are able to take control of 'public' places (or where domestic activities go on) and spread news and gossip (and, implicitly, affect 'public' opinion) in a way that men cannot. Female gossip may put one's reputation at stake, and while men are away the villages are in female hands.[41]

Another domain that is largely in female hands is that of the church, and church attendance shows this very clearly. Although the holy mass is said on a daily basis in both villages, it is on Sunday morning that church attendance is easier to observe, for most of the villagers remain in the valley over the weekend. Church attendance, however, is no longer as impressive as it was until the 1960s, and it seems reasonable to believe that this has been affected by depopulation and by the declining power of the Catholic Church. Nowadays, both in Caoria and in Ronco, roughly one villager out of four attends the holy mass on Sunday morning on a regular basis. The gendered division of churchgoers is one of the underlying features of church attendance: by and large, in Caoria women sit on the rows on the left, while married men accompanied by their spouses sit on the other side (or stand at the back of that side); in Ronco men occupy the front rows, whereas women stay at the back,[42] and the holy mass is always attended by the same people who occupy the same seats every Sunday. In Caoria only fifteen to twenty churchgoers out of roughly one hundred are men, whereas in Ronco churchgoing men are fifteen out of about fifty. Most of the men, especially in Caoria, prefer to sit in the bar next to the church while the mass is said. In the weekdays it is women only who go to church, especially those in their sixties and older. Such a division between churchgoing women and bargoing men is not unusual, as in most Italian rural communities women are allocated the task of dealing with the spiritual life of the household. Morever, churchgoing is part of an ethic of submission that is conceptually opposed to that manifested in the bar,[43] in which a 'male' behaviour is socially approved. It is not purely coincidence that the Caorian men that I came across (particularly those between the ages of thirty and fifty) see themselves as partaking of a 'wild', 'unruly' environment as opposed, for instance, to the 'churchgoers' of Ronco.[44] A statement, which summarises this idea, goes that ***chei de Ronc no l'e cathadori, ma δ̀ent de cesa*** ('the people of Ronco are not hunters, but churchgoers').

Contrary to what might be expected, the collected data partly challenge the widely held assumption that women do not see themselves as social and economic agents. That women are not necessarily village-bound has been suggested by other factors: recent studies about emigration from the valley to central and northern Europe in the twentieth century have shown that such waves also included women, and that their labour was not unskilled (Grosselli 1989: 113). This was the case of those who temporarily emigrated to Vorarlberg, in western Austria, at the turn of the century, to work in textile factories. Furthermore, cases of women of the valley who engaged in emigration abroad in the 1950s and 1960s (particularly to Britain, France, Germany and Switzerland) are not rare. Interestingly, going abroad was not perceived as a constraint, but as an occasion to go out of the village and 'see the world' ('vedere il mondo'), even though this was not encouraged by the clergy.[45] This will to see the world, expressed in the course of interviews, seems to contradict the conventional image, usually static, of local communities. If I were to take on board Gupta's and Ferguson's viewpoint (1997), I would be led to infer that what happened was a sort of displacement of communities, and that the idea of community itself hides the significance of movement and change, which have always had an important part in the lives of the people born in the valley. In spite of this, there is no evidence that because of movement the people in question feel displaced. Movement in itself does not displace anything (though displacement entails movement). In the end, most of these people came back, and movement did not become part of their self-identity. In Trentino, in particular, this was the case of people living in the valleys, that is to say those owning landed property of a small size.[46]

Most of the women interviewed explained that they were contemplating the possibility of remaining abroad, but had decided to do otherwise because of their husband's insistence that they come back to the village.[47] Thus, commitment to 'locality' (and particularly land) seems to be expressed by men, and not so much by women.[48] As an outcome, it seems arguable that in the valley the idea of 'female domesticity' is largely the product of a male ideology legitimated by the Catholic Church. Both sexes occupied and occupy, to a greater or lesser extent, public and private spheres. Yet the above dichotomisation is ideological, for the two spheres are integrally connected:[49] they simultaneously define and sustain each other. Women may have important roles in the public realm (and all the more so at present), and men may have significant associations with the private one.

Nowadays, as I noted, it cannot be inferred that women occupy 'private' domains only: rather, the blurring of the boundary between 'public' and 'private' domains was the situation I was confronted with during fieldwork. The few university students of the valley who are taking degrees in Trent, Padua or Bologna are for the most part young women, and in 2001 the only person resident in Ronco, holding a university degree, was a 26-year-old woman. This does not imply that women give up the role of mothers or carers, but rather that getting married around the age of twenty is no longer felt to be a moral obligation. Another significant aspect of this blurring is that physical strength is no longer as important as it used to be. The spread of clerical jobs in Trentino has had significant consequences for women. At present most of the young women in the two villages have a long-term or permanent employment in the public sector, especially as clerks, whereas the able-bodied men with no special skills have to apply for seasonal jobs. However, it should be noted that while most of the able-bodied men of Caoria have a job in their own village, the young women who hold a driving licence spend the day, and often the entire working week, out of the valley.

Women's option for work outside the home was dictated both by the need for income and by the desire for freedom from parental control. Although it seems certain that women are, practically and symbolically, the core of a home/family, now domestic work and childcare complement work for a wage, and are no longer so central in women's lives. At the same time a permanent job in an office may be better valued than a seasonal one spent looking after livestock or felling trees. Although generalisations may be a bit reductive, I think it is safe to suggest that the ways in which men and women view work in the 1990s are strikingly different: for men, work establishes a continuity between past and present, as most of them still perform the activities formerly done by their fathers and forefathers. So, the idea that the community is a social system that reproduces itself over time is affected by men's views. Women, by contrast, seem to view work as a device to break from 'tradition': they derive pride from their work as long as this gains them a certain degree of autonomy from the household. Thus, what I was witnessing during fieldwork was not a 'shift to modernity', but a situation of transition, in which some of the values of rural society (among which is that of male dominance), albeit questioned, still figured prominently in local discourse.

In sum, it seems reasonable to suggest that it is men who are committed to 'locality' and to its social reproduction, whereas women move (or are more willing than men to move) through 'localities'.[50] Ideas about 'locality' and its social reproduction permeate male, rather than female, discourse. Women continue to be seen as mobile elements in a world of male stability.[51] Yet their mobility does not entail subordination: rather, women seem increasingly detached from 'locality', and tend to look 'beyond' the village instead. They equate moving out with moving up. Men, on the other hand, protect 'locality' and the 'private' against intrusive outside agencies.

Of Land and Landowners: Honour and Fame

As I noted at the beginning of this chapter, the 'private' represents one of the main subjects of conversation in virtually any social setting. It looks as if both in Caoria and in Ronco there is an obsession with its protection, and this is expressed by ideas about landed property. In particular, the fear that a stranger might set foot on someone else's property seems to suggest that a 'private property idiom' looms large in village thinking. This section seeks to provide a partial interpretation of this 'obsession' and shed light on the relationship between landed property and ideas about 'locality'.

The occurrence of a 'private property idiom' may seem paradoxical in an area in which for centuries the collective inalienable property of forests and high-altitude pastures has been the basis of the economy of these communities. Yet we can make sense of this idiom if we allow for the fact that direct control over privately owned land is predominant in the valley under study, in Trentino (Zaninelli 1978: 34–42), and throughout the Alpine region as well. One of its characteristics is fragmentation and dispersion, as shown by the fact that most of the holdings in and around the villages are just a few square metres in size.[52] Apparently no form of sharecropping system occurred in the area under study, and cadastral registers provide documentary evidence that the inhabitants of the valley have maintained direct control over land since as early as the late seventeenth century.[53] The fact that agriculture has never been a profitable economic activity in the valley, but just a subsistence-oriented one, in all likelihood hindered the development of a system of large landownership and the settlement of a landowning nobility there. After all, it was the scarcity of cultivable land around the dwellings that, until the 1960s, compelled households to spend about eight months in the high meadows (the *masi*) every year to pursue agricultural activities in combination with grazing and haying. That several landholdings around Caoria and Ronco have been owned by the same family groups for generations is suggested by the custom of naming the land after the **ratha** that owns it, although such names do not necessarily appear in cadastral maps. One of the elements that characterises the local landholding system is in fact the ideology of continuity of ownership, as suggested by the widely shared idea that a landholding should retain its name and should not be alienated to nonrelatives or strangers.[54] However, it seems arguable that this strong sense of individual and ideally inalienable property also derives from the fact that land communally owned (i.e. forests and high-altitude pastures) cannot be alienated, and so it is embedded in an idiom in which land and places are associated with persons.

The significance that landed property assumes in the valley is shown not only by attachment to land and by the owner's identification with it, but also by the commonly held view that one of the greatest achievements in the life of a man is the acquisition of a sizeable amount of land. The term that defines the capacity of a person to acquire it is that of *grandezza* ('greatness'). However, the term *grande* ('great') is also used to refer to whoever succeeds in achieving a certain degree of economic independence, so as to be able to solve one's own problems without asking other villagers or relatives for help.[55] *Grande*, however, may have negative connotations too, as it may refer to those, once poor, people, who suddenly have made a fortune and started putting on airs and looking down upon covillagers.

It is common in both villages for those who have acquired a considerable amount of land during the last few years to ostentatiously boast of this, even though, unlike the 'old days', at present owning land has little or nothing to do with economic activities. During my fieldwork a man of the valley used to pride himself on the fact that he could reach the top of the mountain overlooking his village without trespassing beyond the boundaries of his own property, which he refers to as *el me* ('mine'). Another man expressed the same sense of pride, as he acquired several landholdings from those who left the valley in the last few years. He spoke of himself as a sort of large landowner, even though the landholdings he has taken over have little economic value, in that they are located on steep hillsides or by the river, where houses can scarcely be built.[56]

Achievement of independence and autonomy and becoming *grande* are conditional on another important factor: hard work. Both in Caoria and in Ronco villagers think and talk a great deal about it, and contrast their capacity to work hard with the unwillingness to do so of the inhabitants of other villages or urban dwellers in general. Aside from ideas about hard work, villagers' capacity for sustained hard work is impressive: especially in Caoria it is rare to see people sitting on a bench and doing nothing, and it is equally embarrassing for a man to be seen inactive. As Gustavo (b. 1928) once stated, 'We [Caorians] are always working, but we do it for ourselves, not for other people'. Although his statement expresses the ideal of homestead (and individual) autonomy that looms so large in local discourse, in the valley it also serves to contrast this ideal with the (widely shared) view that across the regional border with Veneto (particularly in the lowlands) farmers used to work land belonging to large landowners rather than their own holdings.[57] That Caorians identify themselves as 'peasants' (*contadini*), rather than herders, is a case in point: it is a reference to their direct control over land, which gains them a sense of ideal independence, as they do not have to surrender their labour to others. This is antithetical to the activities of the herders, who work for the municipality and look after livestock belonging to someone else. Yet this also expresses the ideal of self-reliance, as epitomised by the dictum 'Aiutati che Dio t'aiuta' ('Rely on your own means, and God will help you'). On the one hand, this attitude is reminiscent of a conceptualisation of work in terms of family production and moral community;[58] on the other hand, this ideal does not clash with a conception associated with the wage economy, but is a combination of the two. 'Real' work is work alienated from production for large landowners or factory managers, and is associated with the private domain.

My focus so far on individual assertiveness should not blind us to the fact that actors also engage in cooperation with each other: any household aims at economic independence while at the same time maintaining links with other households. However, while cooperation between families was essential when agro-pastoral chores were the main economic activities, now the people who earn a wage or a pension are more reluctant to ask others for help, given that this would clash with the ideal of self-reliance, especially for men. However, villagers stress this ideal of independence and autonomy to defend their sense of worth when and where the prestige of farming is on the wane.[59] That hard work is highly valued as a means to build and acquire property and to engender a sense of self-reliance would be reminiscent of what might be termed as a 'Protestant ethic' (see for a comparison Abrahams 1991: 17–18), if it were not for the fact that the area is Catholic, at least nominally. In fact, the Catholic Church played an important role in casting hard work as a means to acquire private property, especially in the 1950s and 1960s, to oppose the idea of collective property championed by Italian Communists (Guizzardi 1976: 207; Antonelli 1981: 48–49). So, it seems arguable that the Catholic Church championed values that already informed local discourse. That casting hard work as a value may also be a political statement is revealed by the widely shared belief, especially in Caoria, that its inhabitants are of an 'Austrian race'. This enables them to associate themselves with the hard-working and putative efficient German-speaking people of South Tyrol and central Europe.[60] At the time of my fieldwork this association partly echoed the Northern League's political propaganda, which used to cast northern Italy's wealth and efficiency as part of a Germanic, central European legacy. Yet as will be seen later in this book, the Northern League's emphasis upon hard work as a quality that distinguishes northern Italy from the South is an appropriation of an old rhetoric: while the Catholic Church made use of it to forge a Catholic identity, the Northern League instead deployed it to create a territorial one.

One of the intriguing aspects of the landholding system of the valley is that despite the fragmentation of property and the significance that this assumes for its owners, it is rare to find boundary markers. Property is jealously guarded against outsiders, and landowners seem to assume that all covillagers know where their property boundaries lie: formal boundaries are drawn up on cadastral maps, but can hardly be seen in actuality. When owners of adjacent landholdings are close relatives, the absence of such markers is not a problem; by contrast, when these people are neither related nor on good terms, the boundary may become an object of contention. This is very likely to happen when, for example, two fields are not clearly singled out by a 'natural' boundary such as a brook or a footpath. In the two villages there is often disagreement over who may have access to a given tract of land, or simply over rights of passage. Both in Caoria and in Ronco people often quarrel with their neighbours over the entitlement to walk through a meadow or use the parking area in front of a house. Even nowadays arguments often ensue when someone crosses the boundaries of someone else's landholding and chops timber or makes hay there without permission. Venetians, for example, are often alluded to as trespassers. Stories about people who accidentally trespassed across the boundary of a meadow, and were verbally attacked by its owner or even threatened, are frequently heard. Even these days there are landowners in Caoria, for example, who spend a lot of time watching their own landholdings lest an outsider might set a foot in them. Both in Caoria and in Ronco this has led to several quarrels, sometimes even between brothers. There was the case of a man in Ronco in his late sixties who, when I was doing my fieldwork in that village, came to blows with his elder brother because the latter was driving through the former's landholding.

That one's boundaries are guarded against outsiders does not entail respect for someone else's boundaries. There are various stories about a Caorian (now deceased) who was known as a person who often 'moved' the boundaries of his own property in order to 'enlarge' it. The act of 'enlarging' one's own property should not be merely seen as an attempt to appropriate natural resources such as meadowland, but also as one of the ways in which formal boundaries are contested and, to some extent, violated too. Although cadastral maps state exactly what belongs to whom, in fact it is difficult to ascertain who is making use of what. The fact that a person owns a piece of land does not imply that the person actually controls it. Similarly, some of my informants refer to communal land as 'their own' land as though they were its actual owners. This local-level idea of private property has little to do with property formally owned by the people involved. If anything, it may be suggested that property is associated with a kind of expertise and knowledge of the territory that one acquires through frequentation or when going hunting, as will be seen in more detail later on. Although concepts of public and private are creations of an established authority such as the state or the municipality, in fact private property may take on a local meaning. For example, the act of trespassing across communal land to chop timber without permission may be a way of expressing contempt for laws, just as protecting one's own private property boundaries (the ones drawn on official maps) is a necessary condition to achieve respectability in the village. I heard a story about a Caorian who, a few years ago, placed a gas container on communal land, not far from his *maso*, and fenced that patch in spite of the fact that this was illegal. When this became known in the municipal offices, two officials were sent to levy a fine on that man, and to get him to remove the gas container. When the officials reached the place, they came across the man waiting for them, wielding an axe. So, the two men decided to go back to Canal San Bovo, and the case was not pursued.

This emphasis on protection of boundaries forms part of an ideology, but is not always expressed by actual practice. As a matter of fact, after the demise of agro-pastoral economy (and particularly these days) several landholdings and houses were sold to outsiders very cheaply. There are also cases of local people who acquired property from covillagers for very low prices, and eventually made a fortune by selling such property to tourists or to the public administration. Moreover, the development of summer tourism (albeit limited) in the valley, especially from the nearby Veneto region, posed some unexpected problems, for those who acquired land and buildings in the valley started fencing their newly acquired landholdings, a practice that is still deemed at odds with local customs. When asked about the meanings of property, informants are ambivalent: in Ronco, for example, both men and women share the view that attachment to landed property was very strong in the 'old days', but not now. If anything, they state that quarrels over land arise in Caoria, but not in their own village. That they endeavour to distinguish themselves from Caorians became patent on various occasions: one day, for example, when I was walking along a footpath in Ronco, I asked the landowner who happened to be there whether I could cross his holding; the man answered affirmatively, and advised me not to worry about property boundaries on the grounds that I was not in Caoria. In a sense, by ascribing this kind of attitude to people of another village this man and his co-villagers were getting rid of a mentality they consider obsolete, and they were projecting it on to other people, that is to say people who, by expressing attachment to landed property, live in 'another' time. This apparent lack of interest in property boundaries was contradicted by actual practice. A few days after that encounter, I engaged in a conversation with another man in the same village, who expressed a very similar view about property. When the conversation was drawing to an end, we happened to come across the director of the provincial land registry office of Fiera di Primiero, who was in Ronco for a cadastral survey. As he was going to do his job on a landholding not far from my companion's house, the official approached him asking where he could find the iron plaque used for cadastral surveys.[61] My companion replied calmly that he had destroyed it, because it trespassed the boundary of his property by a few inches, and asked defiantly: 'Do you mean that I am no longer the landowner?'

Stories like this are not rare: in a sense, in trespassing across someone else's property boundaries one does harm to the owner. This is a significant factor that has been overlooked by most anthropologists working in the Alpine region. Landed property does not represent an economic asset, especially these days, but is involved with the owner's personality and with the particular nature of his identity in society.[62] Heady (1999: 103-5) found that in the Carnic Alps, too, rights to ownership are closely linked to a sense of identity: any action against any part of one's property is not merely resented for the economic loss that might be involved, but because such action represents an action against the owner. In a sense, it seems arguable that possession of territory is a mechanism whereby identity is fostered and reinforced.

Nowadays landed property, especially that in the *masi*, is attached a symbolic value: it may be regarded as an 'extension of the self'. Some stories about the 'old days' in Ronco well illustrate this point: when agro-pastoral chores were the main economic activities in the valley, most of the villagers did not have enough cash to buy goods and foodstuffs at the village store. At that time the rich families of the village controlled the local bank and the cooperative store, and these were willing to let covillagers purchase such products and invoice them at the end of the year. However, various villagers, owing to a crop failure or to a cattle epidemic, were not able to pay for the bill of the store.[63] Thus, those who had to settle their debt were compelled to sell patches of land to the manager of the store who, in doing so, could acquire landholdings very cheaply. Consequently, cases of people who had to sell their land and leave the village were frequent. More importantly, these people did not come back, as it was assumed that a person without land in the village had no reason for returning there: in other words, without landed property one was no longer considered a 'villager', and landed property used to play and still plays an important part in the definition of a villager.

Although joint ownership of land and buildings is very common, disagreement often arises among co-heirs as to the share one is entitled to, so that decisions are seldom taken and a meadow, not being cleared on a regular basis, soon becomes densely overgrown. For this reason, nowadays attempts at consolidation are rare. In all likelihood the absence of a system of impartible inheritance in the valley led to the fragmentation and dispersion of the holdings and fostered the occurrence of quarrels among the heirs entitled to a share of the patrimony. Nowadays several houses in the villages and most of the huts in the *masi* are co-owned, with the result that, given the difficulty in reaching an agreement over the renovation of the buildings, many of these are abandoned and fall into disrepair.

During the last thirty years, however, massive waves of emigration from the valley compelled many people to leave or sell their land, especially to tourists from the nearby Veneto region or to the better-off of their village. Thus, many buildings in the *masi* were acquired by outsiders and turned into weekend dwellings. By contrast, for the villagers who, in spite of economic hardships, succeeded in keeping their property, the *masi* have become a source of pride, a commodity with which the owner is most strongly identified. The *maso*, with its own meadow surrounded by woodland, evokes both ideas of domestication of nature, and of ideal inaccessibility, given that it is usually located far away from the village. However, as soon as the *masi* shifted their function from places of work to houses for the weekend, they also became yearned-after commodities for the potential heirs. The transfer of *masi* by inheritance often created tension among close relatives as a consequence of uneven division of landed property, and the cases of *masi* destroyed by sudden fires are usually interpreted as a form of vengeance by those who did not inherit the share of the patrimony they wanted.[64] Clearly, owning a *maso* forms part of a mechanism through which villageness is maintained and further asserted, especially these days. However, the emphasis attached to the *maso* in Trentino is also a recent development, as it has to do with tourism and with the significance that the *masi* have acquired in the nearby South Tyrol, both as weekend houses, and as economic assets.[65] This increased significance could also be interpreted as an attempt to establish a relationship of cultural continuity with South Tyrol, and so it was affected by the cultural policies of the provincial government of Trentino, as will be seen later in this work.

Between the 1960s and the 1970s the alienation of land occurred under favourable circumstances for the outsiders who acquired it: the tourists who first settled in the valley could purchase land and houses cheaply, as tourism in the valley had not yet developed, and locals were not used to bargaining prices with outsiders. A term that is often used, particularly in Ronco, to describe most of the strangers owning land and houses in the valley is *invadenti* ('intrusive'), which alludes both to the way in which they appropriate land, and to the way they interact with locals. Both in Caoria and in Ronco there were complaints that with the alienation of land the village was losing its specificity and identity, and this was seen as the result of the progressive erosion of an idealised village autonomy. Thus, although the concern with property I was confronted with was an outcome of the demise of the agro-pastoral economy, it also mirrored an acute awareness that the idea of the bounded community inaccessible to outsiders was progressively declining.

While being considered a villager is still conditional at least on owning land and buildings in the community, gaining respect in the village entails keeping and acquiring landed property, and residing in the house inherited through the paternal line. The high value placed on this is partly reminiscent of one of the classical themes of Mediterranean anthropology, that of 'honour and shame'. I do not imply that men necessarily have a notion of 'honour' or that they make use of this term; as I said earlier, the term deployed in Caoria is the Italian *grandezza*. However, unlike 'honour', *grandezza* is neither achieved through control over women (given their mobility in the past and at present) nor by simply getting married and building up a household. Being married is preferable to remaining single, but may not be essential for the achievement of respectability in the village. Control over women, as has been seen, was possible only to a limited extent, as shown by the fact that temporary emigration of women was common as early as the turn of the twentieth century. Given that women are more 'mobile' as they move through 'localities' and are therefore difficult to 'control', one way in which respectability can be attained is the acquisition of a large amount of land through hard work and by exercising the authority to keep strangers out of it, that is to say through the ability to create boundaries difficult to trespass.

Although inherited private property is not necessarily the only determinant of family members' activities, it acts as an idiom whereby several men express the achievement of respectability on the one hand, and a sense of self-reliance on the other, i.e. it embodies the capacity to solve one's problems without asking other people for help. This is a constituent part of being a Caorian and a Trentine. Especially now that the cooperation between homesteads is declining, the autonomy of each household has become a central tenet of social life. This sense of autonomy seems in tune with the view that things and people should remain in their 'own place', which entails both protection of one's own boundaries (both physical and symbolic) and respect of others', at least ideally. However, this is partly contradicted by actual practice, as shown by the fact that invading someone else's domain (both at the level of appropriation of land and at the level of social interaction) is deemed as important as protecting one's own private sphere, especially among men.

Even though it is tempting to look upon the transformation of rural families as a shift from 'co-ownership' to a partnership between workers, in the Vanoi valley co-ownership and partnership between workers are not the two ends of a continuum, unlike what has been observed in relation to other parts of southern Europe:[66] rather, hard work remains the means whereby private property is acquired and maintained, but hardly entails partnership between workers. Landed property, being associated with manhood, has come to represent an 'extension of the self', something that the 'true' villager has to protect from the outside.[67]

Conclusion: Locality of Gender

The material presented in this chapter made the point that a notion of 'private' informs the way people interact with each other, and the ways they relate to the outside. However, the identification of the person with one's land seems to show that ownership itself is also an idiom which defines who a person is in the social landscape. Implicit in what has been said is that at the turn of the millennium this idea of 'locality' still reflects largely men's views: especially these days the idea that masculinity is asserted through the protection of one's own boundaries (and private property) and through opposition to and appropriation of the nation-state informs the distinction between the community and the outside that looms large in village thinking. This idea is embedded in an idiom of strength which, as has been seen, forms an integral part of becoming and being a man. An intriguing aspect of this concern with protection is that it was occurring at a time when countless privatisation initiatives were taking place all over the national territory, and the nation-state was no longer the dominant framework controlling the national economy.

The above considerations of men's role in the valley are reminiscent of what Blok (1981: 434) wrote about the notion of 'honour', particularly the idea that this notion may develop in the absence of state control, where people have to rely on various forms of self-help to guarantee the immunity of life and property. His view, however, rests on the assumption that with the expansion of scale this notion has no *raison d'être*, so that it remains confined to groups of people whose sense of identity and 'honour' is dependent on membership in local communities (1981: 436). I think I have shown that with modernisation a sort of 'honour' does not vanish, but may be redefined and reformulated in response to changes: it may become an idiom through which commitment to the community and opposition to some aspects of nationhood such as domination are expressed, all the more so in response to changing political and economic circumstances. This does not entail that women do not have a sense of locality. Rather, it means that to remain in the village and spend one's life there is no longer their first option. The ideal role of men remains associated with protection of locality and with resistance to the state, especially at a time when the national government was imposing high taxes on property: in other words, when it was no longer perceived as a funding body, but as a law-enforcing agent. In the 1990s this ideal of independence, particularly economic independence from the nation-state which stems from hard work, was central to the rhetoric of the autonomist parties (notably the Northern League), whose electoral success was conditional on their ability to mobilise themes already existing in local culture.

In a sense, men's and women's different ideas about independence (and, implicitly, of locality) seem to mirror differing ways to come to terms with modernity. For men, a sense of independence is achieved by reliance on one's own means and on ability to protect one's own domain. So, taking a hint from Strathern (1988: 65), it may be argued that 'idealised masculinity is not necessarily just about men; it is not necessarily just about relationships between the sexes either', but may be a constituent part of a system for the reproduction of a bounded community. By contrast, for women this sense is achieved by moving outside locality, by breaking with what they call 'tradition': so, while men long for independence from the state, women long for independence from men. The practices through which independence from the state is achieved will be explored in the following chapter.

Notes

1. This theme is explored in chapter 5.
2. See, for a comparison, du Boulay (1974: 75), Loizos (1975: 63) and Silverman (1975: 179).
3. See Strathern (1981) for a comparison.
4. Family nicknames may be patronimics in the strict sense of the word. Thus, for instance, the 'Tonoi' form a group of the Cecco family who descended from a founding ancestor called Antonio. Similarly, the 'Vincenth' form a group of the Loss family descended from a man named Vincenzo. As a rule, the family group is named after a founder ancestor. The founder ancestor may have been a large landowner, someone who became a person of means, or the oldest of a family group which settled in Caoria. Interestingly, the Caorians asked to trace their genealogy were not able to go further back than the ancestor that named the family group, whose portrait or picture may be seen pinned to the dining-room's walls of most houses.
5. It is not coincidental that the churchyards' tombstones contain family nicknames alongside the names of the deceased.
6. Poppi (1980: 73) found the same situation in the Ladin-speaking Val di Fassa, not far from the Vanoi valley.
7. It must be noted that until the 1960s the houses in the village were inhabited chiefly during the winter.
8. This ideal is often contradicted by actual practice, for in some households, in both villages, it is women who 'rule'. I heard of two men in Caoria who went mad because their wives were very authoritarian, and eventually committed suicide.
9. As will be seen later in this chapter, respectability in Caoria is closely entwined with property and property relations.
10. Waldren (1996: 78) found the same phenomenon in Mallorca.
11. In 2001 there were 369 inhabitants in Caoria, 54 of whom came from outside the village. Among the outsiders who came from other villages of the valley there are two men (one from Canal San Bovo and one from Ronco) and ten women (two from Canal San Bovo, four from Ronco, and four from the remaining villages).
12. This was the case of one of my informants, who decided to take residence in the house of his late paternal grandfather rather than move to a newly built one in the centre of Caoria.
13. Bourdieu (1976: 122) and Abrahams (1991: 113) have made the same considerations for southern France and eastern Finland respectively.
14. See Herzfeld (1985b: 170) for a comparison.
15. I heard of various married couples, both in Caoria and in Ronco, who begot many daughters until they eventually had a son.
16. This is consistent with the ideal of a social system that ideally reproduces itself over time, which informs so much of village thinking.
17. See, for example, Strathern (1980), Collier and Yanagisako (1987) and Moore (1988).
18. A more detailed analysis of the distinction between these two concepts can be found in chapter 6.
19. The woman working behind the counter is the only one that can be seen there.
20. See, for example, Driessen (1983: 125). In a sense, village women find the bar an 'unruly' setting that contrasts somewhat with domestic order. That in the past most of the men going there used to get drunk (*ciochi*) is a sufficient reason, for women, to limit their visits to the bar to a few occasions.

21. The considerations on the social role of the bar in the two villages under study rely on ethnographic data collected for the most part in Caoria, where the presence of four bars made this investigation feasible. Such considerations apply to Ronco only to a limited extent, as depopulation and other factors reduced meeting opportunities considerably.

22. It was only after conscription that young men were allowed to go to the bar and court village girls.

23. Interestingly, the few men attending the holy mass in Caoria usually stand at the back of the church.

24. A game similar to that of the English children's 'scissors, paper, stone' that involves two competitors making gestures with their arm and shouting at the same time. Now it is illegal because of its tendency to lead to fights.

25. This is certainly the case of those that are now forbidden.

26. In Italy this is known as *caffè corretto*. In Caoria some men claim that coffee without *grappa* (that is to say *espresso*) is not 'true' coffee.

27. Usually this is a glass of white wine, the cheapest thing one can buy.

28. Obvious exceptions are those who are unknown in the community.

29. Stewart (1991: 48) made the same point in relation to the Greek island where he conducted fieldwork.

30. By 'cultural intimacy' I mean 'those aspects of a cultural identity that are considered a source of external embarrassment but that nevertheless provide insiders with their assurance of common sociality … It consists in those alleged national traits …that offer citizens a sense of defiant pride in the face of a more formal or official morality …' (Herzfeld 1997: 3).

31. Those who speak Italian or another dialect in the bar are often frowned upon, and are sometimes advised to speak the local dialect if they are familiar with it.

32. It is not coincidental, I think, that electoral campaigns in the valley are usually held in the village bars. That politics is debated there suggests that, even now, this remains a realm dominated by men.

33. Heady (1999: 112–13) reported a very similar experience in the Carnic Alps.

34. This is compulsory all over the national territory in order to prevent tax evasion. At the end of every year bartenders (and traders in general) are required to state to the inland revenue how much they gained, and are consequently obliged to issue receipts to all customers. This law was introduced in the early 1980s, when it emerged that most of the Italian traders used to state a lesser income than actually earned.

35. This was a recognised way of operating when I conducted the bulk of my fieldwork between 1995 and 1996, but was much less common when I visited my fieldsite in 2001.

36. This is why women seldom or never go to the bar, except after the holy mass on Sunday morning or in early afternoon when the bar itself is empty. That women do not come to the bar frequently became clear one day when I was sipping coffee in a bar in Caoria; a woman in her forties from Canal San Bovo stepped in, asked the bartender for a cognac, and eventually lit a cigarette. When she left the bar, one Caorian who was sitting there wryly commented that in the 'old days' things like that were very unlikely to happen.

37. Ecclesiastical reports about the valley of 1864 state that swearing was quite common at that time, especially in Caoria.

38. An exception to this is hunting, which is practised almost exclusively by men, and is still conceived of as a way of 'domesticating' nature and of asserting control over territory and resisting rules and laws: it represents, in Scott's terms (1985), an 'everyday form of resistance'.

39. See for a comparison Minnich's case study of the Julian Alps of northeastern Italy (1998: 125).

40. This does not mean that men use a different space in different ways: men may congregate in the streets too, but at different times, when women are busy cooking and invisible to public view.

41. As I was told at the initial stages of my fieldwork, one has to be very careful as to what to say and to whom, because 'gossip is faster than light'.

42. Apparently this division is not as clear-cut as it was until some years ago.

43. Le Bras (1976) made a similar point.

44. This point is further developed in the next chapter.

45. This is patent in some articles, published in the local church magazine '*Voci di Primiero*', aimed at discouraging young women from taking temporary employment in urban centres.

46. Renzo Grosselli, personal communication.

47. This was usually the case of those who owned land and a dwelling in the valley.

48. These considerations rely on the recorded material collected in the valley by Renzo Grosselli in 1993, available at the Emigration Office of the Autonomous Province of Trent. Such material provides evidence that it is usually men who are more willing to come back to the valley after a long period spent away.

49. See for a comparison Cole (1991: 88).

50. Young women's attitudes toward education and work seem to contrast with young men's, and this aspect emerged during a conversation with an informant from Ronco, currently an undergraduate student in Sociology at the University of Trent. She recounted some cases of young men of her area who were attending the final years of high school, and suddenly decided to quit school and undertake instead manual jobs in their village or thereabouts. She described this behaviour as a sort of 'crisis' that many young men of the area experience between the ages of seventeen and eighteen. According to her, this 'crisis' stems from their realisation that while a high school degree has yet to be obtained, there are people of the same age group who already have a job, earn a wage, and own a car, and therefore many young men come to the conclusion that it does not make much sense for a person to remain a student until the age of eighteen or nineteen if one can undertake a job at an earlier age without moving from one's own village. I have not conducted research on this phenomenon, but it certainly deserves in-depth investigation. However, if the above information proved correct, it would strengthen the argument that commitment to locality permeates men's discourse.

51. See Loizos and Papataxiarchis (1991: 15) for a comparison with modern Greece.

52. Ortolani (1932: 85) recorded this phenomenon in the 1930s.

53. This is one of the main features of Alpine ecosystems: communal tenure is usually associated with higher-altitude zones where grazing is done, whereas fields and meadows in lower-altitude zones and higher meadows are subject to individual tenure (Viazzo 1989: 20–24). See the previous chapter for a definition of 'higher meadow' or *maso*.

54. This is evidenced by the fact that in each village it is deemed preferable to sell land to close relatives or neighbours. That this system worked until very recently is revealed by the fact that many families have occupied the same house for generations, and suggests that the transmission of landed property was not simply an economic issue, but also a moral one.

55. In fact this seems a constituent part of Trentine identity, and not just of the local one. I found the same attitude in the city of Trent: some friends, who live there, explained that for a non-Trentine being respected by Trentini is conditional on one's capacity to be self-reliant, otherwise one is very likely to be looked down upon.

56. In spite of the airs he puts on, he is known as a very stingy person, and in the past he often tried to negotiate the price of a glass of wine while visiting the bar of his village.

57. Caorians seem uniform in this view, although it is very hard to generalise as far as the Veneto region is concerned.
58. See, for a comparison, Lampland's considerations on rural Hungary (1995: 274).
59. Roberts (1989: 24) made this consideration in relation to rural Finland.
60. This attitude became very widespread in northern Italy after the rise of the Northern League. Heady (1999: 219) found very similar views in the Carnic Alps.
61. This is fixed to the ground in specific spots such as, for example, the top of a mountain or any place from where one can have a panoramic view.
62. The idea that landed property may be conceived as an extension of its owner has been recorded throughout Greece as well (e.g. du Boulay 1974: 17 and Hirschon and Gold 1982: 65).
63. Some people still pay the bill on a monthly basis.
64. In the valley this happened twice during my fieldwork.
65. It must be noted that, unlike Trentino, in the German-speaking South Tyrol the *masi* are inhabited all year long. See Cole and Wolf (1974) for a detailed exploration of the cultural significance of the *maso* in the other province.
66. See particularly Collier's Spanish case study (1997: 114).
67. As Pine observed for highland Poland (1996: 445), the house (and, implicitly, private property) may exist in opposition to extra-village and state institutions.

8. Men's domains: the village bar.

9. Women's domains: the back streets.

10. A *maso* high on the mountainside.

4
KNOWING ONE'S LAND:
HUNTERS AND POACHERS

Communities of Hunters

The exploration of the idea of 'private space' has shown how far a 'private property idiom' informs village thinking and, particularly, social relationships. Although this idiom should be seen in historical perspective, it seems clear that throughout the centuries the protection of the boundaries of the communities and of one's domain has been an important concern for the inhabitants of the valley. In the 1990s, as has been shown, this concern was mainly engendered by the alienation of landed property to outsiders, and by the progressive erosion of the villages' ideal autonomy. In this chapter I will extend this exploration a step further, and will look at the ways in which social actors create and protect a 'private space'. I will try to pursue the idea that the creation of a 'private space' has also a political dimension, as it involves asserting distinctiveness vis-à-vis the encompassing society and the nation-state in particular. The creation of such a space may be expressed by what social actors do in everyday life, by practices that apparently have nothing to do with politics. Among such practices hunting is one of the most important.[1]

An exhaustive understanding of hunting entails the analysis of several themes, particularly that of humans' ambivalent attitude to nature and culture. In Western society hunting has been seen as a 'ritual replay of a number of central themes in our lives... especially our problematic relationship with nature' (Kayser Nielsen 2000: 63), and has also been treated as a discourse about human relations through which participants make declarations about themselves and the way they perceive their world (Marks 1991: 268; Hell 1996:

216). My analysis of hunting is confined to the aspects that relate to the main issues discussed in this work, to the idea of a practice that serves both to stress distinctiveness in relation to the homogenising forces of 'modernity', and to come to terms with 'modernity' itself. I seek to illustrate how hunting may also express a thematisation of social actors' views of politics, and that it may function as a device to stress the valley's distinctiveness vis-à-vis the nation-state. So far, anthropologists have dealt with hunting and politics (notably political ideologies) separately; the ethnography of hunting in the study of agricultural societies has been regarded chiefly as the investigation of the ways humans seize control of nature. The study of politics and political ideologies, in turn, especially in the West, has so far largely overlooked the political dimension of the appropriation of 'nature', though the existence of such a dimension has been acknowledged by recent studies on environmental issues. Overall, the political and the appropriation of nature have been kept separate. This analysis of hunting seeks instead to show that 'nature' may turn into a 'political' issue in the same way that politics may be understood and interpreted through the prism of 'nature'.

My interest in hunting arose from the fact that, as I will show, it forms an important part of local identity. Anthropology's focus on this theme, especially as regards Western society, is associated with an interest in transgression of law and rebellion.[2] However, recent anthropological literature has also shown that, far from being an exploitative activity, hunting also establishes a relationship with the natural environment. Ingold (1994: 11), in particular, argued that hunters keep a dialogue with it, and that for them there is no contradiction between the conservation of the environment and the practice of hunting. The idea of conservation, as has been observed, is central to locals' claims to its control; but how far is this idea of conservation compatible with that of resistance to outside agents, and how far does it apply to the valley studied?

The casual visitor coming to the valley for the first time cannot help noticing how much importance is attached to hunting, in spite of the fact that the hunting season lasts only from mid September until early November. As some villagers put it, hunting 'is in the blood' (*l'e nel sangue*), or 'it is a disease' (*l'e una malatia*): this implies that once a person starts he is unlikely to stop. If I were to take villagers' statements at face value, I would be led to think that going hunting is essential to make a living, and that it is an activity in which every man engages. Despite this emphasis, nowadays hunting is not a subsistence activity, but a social one, often accompanied by eating together afterwards. Venison is no longer a good reason for going hunting, for its availability at the local butcher at an affordable price makes hunting itself an unprofitable activity. Also, the annual fee for the game licence amounts to about £500, and the price of a gun (excluding ammunition) may be well over £2,000.

Especially in the bars *la catha* (hunting) is one of the main topics of conversation, and in Caoria there is a long-standing tradition of telling stories about the hunters' exploits. Most of the men of Caoria that I know went hunting at least once in their life, and each of them has or had a father or grandfather who used to be a hunter. It looks as if hunting represents a stage in the life of a man through which it is mandatory to go: even now most Caorians take pride in the fact that they have been able to shoot a big deer or catch a mountain cock, and stories abound as to the ways in which local hunters succeeded in shooting prey in remote and inaccessible places. The importance attached to hunting is also revealed by the collections of trophies that all hunters keep, usually the heads of the animals, which project from the walls of their living room, or the antlers of roebucks or deer. Hunters also keep several pictures of hunting forays, especially those portraying the hunter himself holding the antlers of a freshly shot animal. Moreover, despite the high costs, in the mid-1980s some Caorians travelled as far as Hungary to pursue those animals (e.g. the wild boar) that cannot be found in the Alpine area.

As will be seen in more detail later in this work, the oldest story about the village is that of the hunting foray for the last bear in the valley. This recounts how, in the winter of 1840, three hunters of Caoria succeeded in killing a big bear that was wandering around their village. The story, of which nearly all villagers know a version, was published in a local magazine in 1935 (Fontana 1935). Those from whom I heard it did not seem to care so much about when this happened, as about the event per se. Somebody, for example, stated that the bear was shot in the early nineteenth century, somebody else that it was in the 1930s, and so on, and everyone knows a different version of the same story. Apparently it is not so much the written story that is known, as its many variants; this suggests that there is no 'true' story of the kill of the last bear, probably because it was told so many times that eventually it became a sort of myth.

Most of the Caorians (both men and women) I have been talking with do not know about the origins of their community; however, while chatting with some of them I received the impression that the only thing they know about the distant past (*'sti ani*) is that there were plenty of bears until someone of the village shot the last one. The event is talked about as a shift in the history of the area: when the last bear was killed, humans (symbolised by the three hunters) 'appropriated' nature. In a sense, there are grounds for suggesting that the event is attached importance as it symbolised the end of a state of 'wildness'. That some Caorians invented the tradition of the burning of a straw bear to celebrate the new year is a case in point. Nowadays hunting provides an idiom through which the men of the valley can discuss and debate their local identity and the valley's relations to the outside; it is clearly connected to the villagers' orientation towards the forest, and particularly to humans' relation with nature and its appropriation. However, during my stay in the valley I realised that its significance could also be related to the social, economic and political changes that the valley was undergoing.

In the mid-1990s there were fifty-eight hunters authorised to hunt in the municipality of Canal San Bovo. However, almost all the men of the valley participated in a hunting foray at least once in their life. Most of these are permanent residents, whereas those who do not reside in the area either have relatives there, or hold a special permit. Given the huge forested area that surrounds the village of Caoria, most of the hunters of the valley are from Caoria itself.[3] The animals that may be hunted in the valley include most of the Alpine species, particularly the deer, the roebuck, the chamois, the fox, the hare and the mountain cock. Those most often targeted are the deer and the chamois; as I said earlier, the importance attached to them is revealed by the trophies and by the collections of pictures. Nowadays, on the black market, deer antlers may cost up to £400, and the price of a mountain cock tail may be as much as £120.

Central to an understanding of hunting in the valley is its relationship with law: national and regional laws circumscribe the boundaries within which game is taken. In Trentino a strict game law is enforced by uniformed gamekeepers and officials appointed by the provincial Forestry Department, and prosecutions for infringements are not uncommon; these officials are stationed in Caoria and Canal San Bovo, and patrol the forested areas surrounding the villages. Unlike the other Italian regions, where it is the national Forestry Department that deals with hunting, in Trentino it is the provincial authority and the military police that enforce game law. Since Caoria does not have a mayor, the official appointed by the provincial Forestry Department (who often acts as gamekeeper too) is the only person exercising some authority there.[4] In Caoria there has been one since the mid-nineteenth century. On the one hand, he is a permanent resident who interacts with the local people on a daily basis, who in turn may relate to him to as a fellow villager; on the other, he is an outsider who has to adjust himself, to some extent, to the customs of the community of which he has become a member. So, because of their membership of the community both the official of the Forestry Department and the gamekeeper encountered some difficulty in exercising authority there.[5] The other aspect worth noting is that although the relationship between the local authorities and hunters seems vertical, evidence shows that it is not always the case. While the officials have the authority (and the duty) to enforce laws, they are also subject to the hunters who hold key appointments in the local government: for example, at the time of my fieldwork the secretary of the local hunt club was the municipal *assessore* (councillor) of agriculture and forestry, and the former secretary acted as the director of the local bank for many years.

The local hunt club (*Gruppo Cacciatori*) controls de facto hunting practice in the valley, and mediates between the local hunters and the provincial authority in Trent that issues the licences. The club is headed by a president elected on a regular basis,[6] and an appointed secretary collects the fees. As obtaining a hunting permit has become difficult and expensive, membership of the club clearly confers a strong sense of identity for those involved and a corresponding sense of exclusion for the 'uninitiated', i.e. those not familiar with the mores of hunting or those who did not succeed in getting the licence. In other words it creates solidarity, especially vis-à-vis the outside.[7]

Despite restrictions, Trentine and local hunters enjoy some benefits that those of the rest of Italy have not, as it is only the members of the local hunt club that have access to the hunting preserves in the municipal territory.[8] As prescribed by the old Austro-Hungarian game law (still in force in the region), local hunters may not hunt in the other municipalities of the region Trentino-South Tyrol but may, in turn, do so in most of the other regions throughout the national territory. Permit holders include those who have resided for a minimum of five years, former residents who have relatives in the valley, and 'guests' who are not residents and do not have kinship ties in the area, but may hold a special permission issued at the discretion of the hunt club.[9] In a sense, the hunt club 'protects' the municipal territory from strangers through restricting the number of people allowed to hunt in the valley. Hunters in the valley include men in their late teens and older. Until a few years ago the first hunt usually took place around the age of fifteen, when a youth began to participate in forays alongside his father. Although hunting is not permitted until the attainment of adulthood, many villagers started earlier, on account of the fact that the patrolling of hunting areas was not strict until the 1980s, and the law was seldom enforced. Moreover, it is only since the late 1960s that would-be hunters have been required to pass a test to get a hunting permit.

The hunters who were asked whether the first hunt was considered a way of attaining adulthood for the young man (or a sort of *rite de passage*) denied that it has ever been attached such a meaning. Despite this, there is evidence that until the 1960s it was mandatory for the young boys of the valley who were coming of age to shoot a mountain cock (*lyrurus tetrix*, **gal forthèl**), a black bird known for its elaborate love ritual. It is no accident that this used to happen shortly before undergoing the medical examination that selects those fit for military service in the national army, that is to say in the Alpine infantry.[10] The youths were expected to reach on foot the top of a mountain between late April and early May, and shoot the cock. On the day of the medical inspection the conscripts used to wear a hat adorned with the tail of the cock either shot by the youth himself, or handed down from father to son, but often purchased from a local hunter.[11] In a sense, the hunt of the mountain cock used to function as a sort of ordeal intended to instil fortitude in the youths.[12] In fact, as Giuseppe (b. 1930) once said, in Caoria the youth's ability to shoot the cock was highly valued: those who were not able to catch one were likely to be mocked by the men of the village, particularly by the elders, on the grounds that they were deemed unable to become 'true men' (**veri omini**). It is not purely coincidence that the feathers which adorn the conscripts' hats are the same that often adorn those of the hunters on special occasions: this suggests that the hunt of the mountain cock serves to make a symbolic claim to manhood and, implicitly, that to engage in hunting is a proper way of becoming and being a man. In this regard, the association that local hunters make between a large deer and virility suggests that they '…implicitly identify themselves with at least some of the animals they pursue, and by killing them, they symbolically transfer some of their qualities to themselves' (Howe 1981: 293).[13] So, hunters seek after deer antlers as trophies, carefully distinguishing the worth of a trophy according to the number of tines on it on the grounds that the more tines, the more 'balls' (***coioni***) a deer has.

A factor which determines what and where to hunt is the degree of difficulty that catching a prey entails. In this regard, the statement 'Shooting game from one's own dwelling would be too easy' (Walter, b. 1955) is very telling, as it implies that endurance and strength are essential attributes of the 'true' hunter (***vero cathadòr***). It means that the prey per se is deemed worthless unless considerable effort is necessary to catch it, and that 'true' hunting should be practised far away from the village. Emphasis on the hunt of the mountain cock stems from its difficulty, which may also be related to distance. This is why it sometimes happens that a hunter spreads the news that he succeeded in shooting a deer in an inaccessible place even though he might have done so within walking distance from the village.[14] It is not so much the prey that matters, as the endeavour that has to be made to catch it. This is consistent with the ideal of 'strong' people already mentioned, and with that of 'hard work' that pervades so much of village thinking.

Until a few years ago it was customary to load on a van the freshly shot animal as though it were a trophy, and show it to the fellow villagers who congregated in the local bars. Nowadays this seldom happens given that the ascendancy of environmentalist movements in the national political arena and the establishment of the natural park have made hunting a sort of 'semi-illegal' activity. As an outcome, local hunters prefer to put their prey in a plastic bag without displaying it in public places, and taking a freshly shot animal to the local bars to evoke admiration is now looked upon as a way of making a fool of oneself, what Caorians call a ***blagada***. That the display of freshly shot animals has become uncommon is also related to the ecological changes brought about by the demise of the agro-pastoral economy: while until a few years ago it was necessary to walk a long way to pursue any prey because of the extensive cultivated area surrounding the villages, now the forest encroaches on the villages themselves; consequently, coming across roebucks or foxes around or in the inhabited areas has become frequent, and catching them has become easier and is no longer a source of pride. Therefore, animals such as the chamois or the deer are preferred because they are more difficult to shoot, even though their flesh (especially that of the former) is of a worse quality than that of the roebuck. This is why the roebuck itself is no longer deemed an important prey. Thus, nowadays the village elders complain about the fact that present-day hunting is no longer 'true' hunting, for shooting animals from a long distance has become much easier both because of the availability of good guns, and because stray animals can often be found at the edge of the inhabited area, especially after dusk.

As hunting no longer functions as a subsistence activity, now it serves to assert man's appropriation of nature and, to a certain extent, to draw a boundary between insiders and outsiders, and between women's worlds and men's worlds. This is especially true these days since, as has been noted earlier in this work, men live in a world in which the lines of demarcation between the sexes are blurred, and where the presumptions of male 'superiority' are being challenged. Interestingly, although the hunters I have been talking with never said explicitly that hunting makes a symbolic claim to manhood, they implied this when they said that he who is not a hunter is a churchgoer. In the valley this is especially the case of the inhabitants of Ronco, irrespective of age and gender, who are alluded to as devout churchgoers, but are not known as hunters. Since it is mostly women who attend the holy mass, it could be offensive, for a hunter, to be referred to as a churchgoer: it would entail a denial of manhood. For example, the hunters of Caoria are scornful of those of nearby Castello Tesino on the grounds that their neighbours' hunt club includes some women among its members. The conceptual opposition between hunters and churchgoers becomes patent in the course of public events; it manifests itself, for example, in the church during the Sunday morning mass, which hunters seldom or never attend. In a sense, in local discourse being a churchgoer means subscribing to that ethic of submission and respect for rules and authorities that hunters, as 'men', find unacceptable, as will be seen in another section. So, for example, during my fieldwork hunters very seldom participated in religious events, such as processions (even on the patron saint day), or in state-sponsored commemorative ceremonies.

The conviction that hunting is exclusively a male domain was challenged in the late 1960s, when an 18-year-old woman of Caoria obtained a hunting licence, and became part of a group of men. In doing so she attempted to prove that a woman is able to engage in the same activities in which men engage; she was partly successful, given that her ability to pursue game was proved on various occasions. Eventually it was her skill that made her fellow hunters envious of her; she gradually became an outcast, and consequently decided to give up her hunting licence after a couple of years. No other woman of the valley went hunting until 1992, when one from Zortea, in her early thirties, passed the test and obtained the permit. As she told me, she did so on purpose in order to challenge widely shared ideas of male superiority. Now she is looked upon as a very skilful hunter; she accomplished this as she was able to pass the test to get the licence, while other men of her village failed it. When I visited her at home she proudly showed me a huge number of trophies (mostly roebuck and deer antlers) that she and her husband have caught. Her collection includes mountain cocks too, whose tail, as already mentioned, is considered a symbol of attained manhood. Her case is reminiscent of the issues explored in the previous chapter, and suggests that it is when the boundaries between men's and women's domains are blurred that making symbolic claims to manhood becomes problematic.

Hunting and Poaching

Now, as just noted, the rules governing hunting have shifted from local, customary norms to formal laws enforced by uniformed strangers. This led me to assume that national and regional laws are effective, and that all hunters take them for granted. I realised that this is not always the case when I asked one of the hunters of Caoria when hunting is permitted, and he answered 'Year round', or when I asked a villager whether he was a hunter, and he defiantly replied 'No, I am a poacher'. Although such statements sounded like jokes, in fact they also suggest that rules are not always abided by. This became clear when another informant proudly told me the detailed story of how he managed to catch a couple of roebucks without licence during the winter, and take them through the village, passing in front of the Forestry Department Office without being noticed. Although it is difficult to state whether this actually happened, there is no doubt that the person in question used to be a poacher, as he was brought to trial twice for hunting without a permit or outside the hunting season. More importantly, this person was not the only poacher in the area: cases of poaching in the valley are not rare, and some of those who called themselves 'poachers' actually went poaching. Yet their priding themselves on being poachers was surprising on account of the fact that whoever infringes hunting laws may be put in jail.

If I were to take such statements at face value, I would be led to argue that not only does poaching evoke admiration, but that it also acts as a form of resistance vis-à-vis the established authority (Cartmill 1995: 777–8), and that it may be associated with freedom and rebellion. That road signs in the valley are often used as targets clearly expresses hunters' attitudes towards law-enforcing agents. Poaching may take on the dimension of a struggle in which property rights are contested, and is a permanent feature of agrarian life whenever the established authority and its agents are unable to control it (Scott 1985: 265). Nowadays this relates to the widely shared idea that there was a time (the 'old days' or *'sti ani*) when all the people of the valley could hunt without permission and without restrictions, because the law was not enforced and there were no environmentalists contesting the locals' moral entitlement to hunt.[15]

The occurrence of poaching in the valley is accounted for in various ways: one Caorian, who never went hunting (although this person defiantly declares himself a 'poacher'), once said that it was poverty that, after the Great War, pushed villagers to go poaching, thereby implying that poaching was a subsistence option.[16] Although it seems clear that poaching was widespread long before 1914, he was arguing that it was a result of the Great War itself. According to him, its spread in Caoria and in the valley was due to external factors, such as the arrival of the Italian troops and Trentino's subsequent annexation to Italy. In saying so, he made it clear that it is not his fellow villagers' fault if there are poachers in the valley. In his view, the origin of poaching was not 'local': rather, it was the outcome of an 'intrusion' from the outside. Although his views suggest that it is national and regional laws that define what is hunting and what is poaching, the ethnographic information shows instead that this distinction is not so clear-cut. If anything, as will be seen, the notion of territory seems central to an understanding of this tension. So, for instance, when the hunters of Caoria talk about poaching, they do not so much allude to covillagers as to the outsiders coming from other valleys or municipalities. In a sense, it looks as though it is their being outsiders that makes them poachers. This is true not only of Castello Tesino and Imer (the nearby municipalities) but also, to some extent, of Prade, which is in the same *comune*. This implies that the local definition of a 'hunter' entails in turn the definition of a moral contrary, that is to say that of a 'poacher': the hunters of the valley declare themselves 'hunters' in the same way that they refer to those of Castello Tesino as 'poachers'.

As a matter of fact, quarrels often ensue, especially between Canal San Bovo and Castello Tesino, when the law is not obeyed. This is why Caorian hunters are keen to stress that they hunt in 'their' place (*sul nos*), and refer to outsiders (usually those of Castello Tesino) as poachers on the grounds that they are always shooting animals outside their municipal boundaries. Disputes abound as to whether an animal has been shot within the municipality of Canal San Bovo or within that of Castello Tesino.[17] When hunting was a subsistence activity, both the inhabitants of Castello Tesino and those of Canal San Bovo used to go hunting outside their municipal boundaries, and Caorians had often been caught by hunters of the other *comune*, and in many cases had to give up the prey just shot. There is a dictum in Caoria, ascribed to the inhabitants of Castello Tesino, which runs 'What is ours is ours, and what is not ours will become ours' (*chel che l'e nos l'e nos, e chel che no l'e nos lo ciapòn*) that stresses the latter's 'intrusive' character.

Stigmatising the people of Castello Tesino has become a sort of joke. As a Caorian once stated, 'They [the people of Castello Tesino] are of another "race…", as the elders used to say, it is an imported "race", a "race" of Turks, Slavs, and Sardinians. …they speak a different dialect, nobody here speaks like that'. In saying so he was implying that not only are they strangers, but also that they are a mixture of 'imported races'; they are not a 'pure race', but 'matter out of place', in Douglas's terms (1966). In depicting outsiders as incomprehensible to insiders he was also defining them as culturally marginal (see for a comparison Herzfeld 1987: 162–3). In this regard, history is often invoked as an explanatory key to the differences between the people of the two adjacent municipalities; as a man of Caoria, now in his fifties, stated: 'They are more uncouth than we are. It is a matter of origin. ...don't you know the story? They came from a penal settlement of the Republic of Venice'.

The conviction that a poacher is tantamount to 'matter out of place' is consistent with the idea that hunters should shoot animals without trespassing the boundaries of their municipality: it is a statement about legitimacy, and particularly about the ideal of remaining in one's own place and avoiding being 'intrusive' that looms large in political discourse too. In fact this is an ideal that does not always reflect actual practice. Being able to hunt outside the municipal boundaries may be at odds with the idea that people and things should stay 'in place', but does not clash with the ideal of male assertiveness and aggressiveness that is both a constituent part of being a hunter, and is consistent with the ideal of *grandezza*. This is why several men of the valley take pride in declaring themselves 'poachers'. This suggests that even nowadays assertive masculinity is mainly expressed by means of contempt for rules and particularly national laws.

If I were to take social actors' statements at face value, hunting and poaching would be very easy to define: they would mean that those who present themselves as 'poachers' implicitly acknowledge the fact that hunting without a licence or outside the municipal boundaries is illegal. As it is the regional and national laws that prescribe who can hunt and who cannot, and what can be hunted and what cannot, then it would be safe to describe the relationship between hunting and poaching as a tension between 'permitted' and 'prohibited'. Although this seems to be the case, such a view hides the complex discourse that most hunters use in defining hunting and poaching. To this issue I turn next.

'Bounded Fields': Hunting and Property

The widely shared view that hunting identifies who is 'in place', and poaching who is 'out of place' suggests that the legitimacy of hunting centres on the notion of property. That in Trentino each hunt club controls a specific area encompassing a municipal territory has various implications, and accounts for the social actors' stress on the idea of control over some stretches of land. This is epitomised by the statement, 'We are the lords here' (**qua comandón noi**), which also implies that locals can make their own rules regardless of the disapproval of the established authority. Yet the idea that the land is 'ours' may have different meanings, for normally hunters do not 'own' the territory where they go pursuing game.[18] Rather, that the members of a given household have a very detailed knowledge of some stretches of land, usually at high altitudes, far away from the villages, and within walking distance of the landholdings where these people own a *maso*. This is the area that each family group 'controls' in that it is where its members normally go making hay, picking berries and mushrooms or hunting, even though this expertise does not entail the existence of property rights. This also means that they know the material boundaries within which they can do so without going 'out of place', which may be marked by a brook, a row of trees, the edge of a meadow, and so on.

As I observed, 'owning' the land has little to do with property rights, but denotes a certain degree of familiarity, and even identification, with the territory. In fact most of the rules that govern hunting in the valley are not written. This became patent when I heard the president of the hunt club (a Caorian) say that the hunters of Canal San Bovo are 'foreigners' (*stranieri*) while in Caoria. His statement was at odds with the fact that any inhabitant of the *comune* holding a permit is allowed to hunt throughout the municipal territory, irrespective of the village of residence. In spite of legal rights, there is evidence that the hunters of Caoria hunt around their own community, those of Canal San Bovo do so around their village, and those of Prade around Prade itself. Although there are few formal restrictions as to the area where hunting is permitted within the municipality, there is nevertheless a strong bond between the hunters and the stretches of land where they shoot game. That hunting is inseparable from territory is suggested by the fact that this land was normally 'inherited' through the male line. This is consistent with the statement that hunting should be 'in the blood', and even nowadays any hunter pursues game in the area that was frequented by his father, paternal grandfather, and sometimes even his ancestors. Hunters explain this division of the land as a means to avoid quarrels with other hunters, which accords both with emphasis upon protection of one's own boundaries, and with the widely shared view that people and things should remain 'in place' (*a posto*).

Thus, territory could be 'handed down' from father to son, the young hunter could become familiar with a stretch of land when going hunting alongside his father, and written agreements were not necessary. As a result, a hunting territory could be named after the family group that pursues game there, although there is no evidence of this on official maps. In a sense, naming the land becomes part of that process of appropriation of nature and territory that in local discourse is still attached considerable significance, and hunting land becomes an 'extension of the self'. Federico's (b. 1963) family group, for example, has been hunting in the same place for generations, and Marcello (b. 1932) pursues game in the area where he used to go making hay when he was very young. A consequence of this unofficial mapping of territory is that the 'formal' boundaries that define what is hunting and what is poaching and the 'informal' ones do not necessarily overlap.

As suggested in the previous chapter, landed property is not simply an economic asset, but is involved with the owner's personality; a hunter is identified with the land he 'possesses', and the mapping of hunter-gatherer terrain, as

Appadurai notes (1995: 205), becomes part of the process by which locality is materially (and symbolically) 'produced'. The conversations I had with some hunters centred to a significant extent on the issue of the legitimacy of hunting, i.e. who can pursue game and where. However, often implicit in the distinction between hunting and poaching in local discourse is the idea that those who 'protect nature' (i.e. those who hunt 'in place' and 'know' the territory) should not be required to hold a licence. Permanent residents who 'control' and 'own' a stretch of land but do not hold a licence are not alluded to as poachers. As Federico (b. 1963) said, 'You may make a distinction between killing as a sport and hunting as a passion to protect [*sic*] the mountains… When you catch a prey you… [should] take it home, and eat all you can without wasting anything. One of the things I cannot stand is hunting in pursuit of the trophy or just for the sake of shooting'. If hunting is a 'passion', he added, it is not thought of as 'poaching'. So, while hunting without a licence or outside one's municipal boundaries is considered illegal, hunting without a licence in one's own territory may be legitimate.

When discussing the legitimacy of hunting, all those who practice it rejected the assumption that the main object of hunting is killing animals, and for a simple reason: if there were no game hunters would not go hunting. If anything, central to the definition of a hunter is that he is a 'cultivator': 'Many people say that the hunter destroys. This is not true. The hunter protects too'. (Nando, b. 1918). 'The hunter is like a cultivator of animals, as it were, whereas the peasant grows plants, since he knows well his territory. …If hunting is done properly, he may be able to increase the number of animals even though he kills them …but if you shoot anything you see …that is poaching'. (Raffaele, b. 1962). 'If you want to grow something, you have to cultivate it …so you watch if a roebuck remains in the same area or moves in search of females …and from time to time you give him a piece of salt …You have to know your territory'. (Federico, b. 1963). Thus, hunting 'produces' locality as it creates the boundaries within which the hunter 'cultivates' his animals. It involves mastery of nature in the same way that it establishes a relationship of sharing. Like the 'cultivator', who looks after his fields and crops, the hunter pursues his prey when the time is ripe, that is to say when the animals he intends to pursue have already reproduced themselves, for the life cycle to go on uninterrupted. Wildlife, from the above persons' standpoint, has to be 'cultivated' just like fields.[19] However, this idea does not apply to all animals: deer, for example, need to be shot for the 'damage' they cause to the natural environment.

It is not entirely clear to what extent such ideas reflected what my informants have read in books or magazines; be that as it may, the striking aspect is the conviction that the hunter is not a killer, but is tantamount to a cultivator. This accords with Hell's view (1996: 207) that in southern European countries hunting is associated with the idea of free right of gathering, whereas in central and northern Europe hunters share a conception of hunting as 'harvest'. The ethnographic information discussed suggests that hunting in the Vanoi valley is thought of as 'harvest' too, even though the boundaries within which hunters may 'harvest' are not drawn on official maps. The association between hunting and cultivation explains why social actors never blamed their fellow villagers for hunting without a licence. This is reminiscent of the distinction between 'territoriality' and 'tenure'. Although both terms denote the appropriation of space by humans (Ingold 1986: 130), the term 'territoriality' is usually applied to hunter-gatherers, whereas 'tenure' is used to refer to agriculturalists. While 'territoriality' serves to convey information about the location of individuals dispersed in space, 'tenure' is a mode of appropriation, by which persons exert claims over resources dispersed in space (Ingold 1986: 133). Even though the concept of 'tenure' has been considered inapplicable to societies of hunters and gatherers, at least in non-Western societies, it is central to an understanding of the relationship between hunting and politics. The ethnographic data just discussed suggest instead the existence of a conceptualisation of hunting land which seems to convey ideas of 'tenure'. As I have just pointed out, although local hunters do not 'own' that land, they treat it as private possession. While from an outsider's viewpoint hunting may seem an expression of 'territoriality', in local discourse it is 'tenure'. As David Anderson notes in relation to a different context (1998: 82), in order to understand the entitlement of persons to land one must consider how persons attend to the landscape, and in this case entitlement implies a proper way of 'knowing' the landscape. The relation between hunting/poaching and property provides an alternative understanding of hunting: in local discourse hunting without licence is tolerated as long as it is practised within one's own boundaries. Law should be enforced against strangers but, from the hunters' viewpoint, not against 'owners'. Hunting turns into poaching when it is practised by strangers: they do not 'cultivate' the land, because it is assumed that, as 'strangers', they have no interest in doing so.

Hunters' control over 'property' became an object of debate between 1985 and 1990 as the outgoing Christian Democrat mayor (a Caorian) strongly opposed hunting and endeavoured to inhibit it by forbidding vehicles' access to the roads that go to the hunting preserves. The main issue was not just that by inhibiting hunting the mayor was suppressing a tradition, but also that he was questioning the hunters' claims to 'private property' through the actual enforcement of laws, which in turn would have made control over territory much more difficult. At the time of my fieldwork he was referred to as an 'intrusive' bureaucrat, the kind of behaviour that runs counter to the ideal of local politician who does not interfere in local affairs. In the 1990 municipal elections the local hunters joined forces to present a coalition (symbolised by the head of a roebuck) whose main aim was to throw the mayor out of office. Eventually the coalition (whose candidates included for the most part hunters and their close relatives) succeeded in capturing just a small number of votes (7.6 percent) in the municipality, mostly from Caoria itself, but the mayor was not reelected.

The idea of 'cultivator' not only projects positive traits on who 'cultivates' the land, but also legitimates his action. Implicit in this is the view that who 'knows' territory also 'owns' it: through its symbolic 'cultivation' territory is turned into 'private' or 'individual' property. Who 'cultivates' the land has an implicit right to 'harvest': the notion defines who can harvest and who cannot, and consequently defines a 'moral order'. That each hunter controls a given tract of land prevents competition at the same time that it legitimates hunting without licence.[20] Thus, it may be suggested that the local notion of poacher differs from the 'legal' one in that it is not so much a permission that entitles a person to hunt in a given area, as his 'owning' the land. The notion of poacher is projected onto strangers, on the grounds that they are potential destroyers, for the land they hunt in is not theirs.

The establishment of the regional park in the early 1990s and the rise of environmentalist movements clearly inhibited hunting throughout the region by means of restrictive laws and through a strict patrolling of the area. Although the villagers' property rights were not questioned, the idea that their right to 'control' territory was challenged by the park caused much uproar. This contributed to a partial delegitimisation of hunting, and probably for the first time the people of the valley were confronted with a way of relating to landscape and nature that reflects urban views, as will be seen later on in this work: on the one hand the establishment of the park involved the imposition of a notion of the countryside as 'landscape', i.e. as an intangible resource defined by its appearance, to be consumed visually. In other words, it was a vision of the countryside as part of the leisure experience, something to be 'communally owned' as a source of enjoyment (Macnaghten and Urry 1998: 201). On the other hand, this idea of a 'public space' had to coexist with an increasing importance attached to 'private property' which, at that time, was also the result of the privatisation initiatives taking place all over Italy.

In fact the debate over landscape was mainly caught in the symbolism of power relations: it was not so much environmentalism that was looked upon as a problem, for social actors used to speak of themselves as paragons of ecological virtue. The main issue was not environmentalism per se, but who should talk about it. What was contested was the idea that conformity to an environmentalist directive entails the acceptance of rules imposed from the outside. As I hinted in an earlier chapter, the creation of the park also brought about the transfer of a sizeable amount of land from the provincial administration to the park itself, and the enforcement of conservation laws. However, the extent to which the park took action to prevent the forested area from advancing and encroaching on the villages still remains unclear. Be that as it may, most of the villagers were led to believe that the forest's advancement was due to the park itself, and that the protection of nature that it advocated would result in a landscape gone wild or, worst of all, a landscape left to nonlocal agents, which would be at odds with the local-level idea of the 'clean' environment discussed so far.

Nowadays the local notion of hunter, coupled with that of cultivator, acts as a rhetorical weapon to challenge the environmentalists' campaigns against hunting on the grounds that such environmentalists are outsiders, and therefore do not 'know' the place. This consideration brings us back to the idea of cultivation of territory, and particularly to the view that since nature is encroaching on the village, it has to be reappropriated. Such a view, as already noted, legitimates the local hunters' actions on the grounds that they keep the landscape 'clean'. However, in doing so social actors also cast the nation-state as the 'outsider' or the 'intruder': they accomplish this through the appropriation of an environmentalist language to champion the idea of a 'clean' landscape managed by locals as opposed to a 'wild' one appropriated by nonlocal (or national) agencies by means of restrictive laws.

If the ability to 'master' nature is a sign of high 'civilisation', then the local hunters question state authority on the grounds that the latter's rules and laws have brought about the territory's degradation. This highlights the tension between a 'private' property that is kept clean and tidy by locals, and a 'public', 'disordered' one administered by nonlocals or by the nation-state. This attitude accords with both a Christian Democrat and a Leaguist idea of an administrative unit in which the main decisions are made by locals, and in which outside agents play very little or no part. In a sense, the image of the hunter who evokes admiration is akin to that of the politician who remains 'in place', acts on behalf of the community, and prevents nonlocal (or national) agencies from interfering in local affairs.

In sum, the distinction between hunters and poachers in legal terms fails to take into account the social actors' views, and the discrepancies between rules and strategies. Hunting serves to reinforce material and symbolic boundaries vis-à-vis the outside and, consequently, to legitimate them: what hunting entails is a 'social' appropriation of the territory as opposed to a political/administrative one. Conservation of the landscape appears as a way of protecting locality: hunting, in turn, becomes functional to the 'production of locality', the process through which landscape is symbolically turned into an extension of its 'owners'. This idea accords with the widely shared belief that prosperity is conditional on the territory being managed (and controlled) by locals, and not by impersonal, nonlocal agencies (Filippucci et al. 1997).

The Appropriation of Tradition: Hunting and 'Ethnic' Identity

From the ethnographic information discussed so far, hunting emerges as a way of constructing landscape and, paradoxically, also as a way of making territory an object of aesthetic contemplation. In this respect, what unites some of the theorists on landscape (Bender 1993; Hirsch 1995; Ingold 1995) is the view that landscapes themselves are constructed by people interacting with spatial areas. Ingold (1995), in particular, in developing his 'dwelling' perspective, has argued that landscape has to be understood as the world as *known* to those who have dwelt there, who do dwell there, who will dwell there. Landscape is a place of memory and temporality. As the same author suggests (1993: 161), the inter-penetration of past, present and future centres on practices which produce the social character of any such landscape: these persist 'as long as people are actu-ally engaged in the activities of dwelling' within that particular landscape. I intend to focus on landscape from a slightly different perspective, and pursue instead the idea that interacting with a physical space is also involved with the ways political identities are inscribed onto landscape itself.

As I noted earlier in this chapter, all hunters keep collections of pictures of hunting forays, and they pride themselves on showing them even to the casual visitor. Most of these photographs portray the hunter when the foray is over, namely when the prey has already been shot. Such pictures show that hunting forays follow a rather fixed pattern, and suggest that they are like rituals for the people involved; I found further evidence of this when two informants made this point very explicitly, and said that 'hunting is a ritual' (*la catha l'e un rito*). So, for example, the custom of putting a bough of fir tree in the mouth of the freshly-shot animal can be seen in every picture, even though it does not seem to have a practical function but only a symbolic one. When I asked a hunter for an explanation of this, he simply answered that he had always done so, and that it was a very old custom. Despite this conviction, other interviews revealed that the custom is not exactly a local tradition, as it was 'imported' from South Tyrol a few years ago. Although it was alluded to as 'local' and 'very old', in fact the custom represents a very recent 'appropriation'.

The curious aspect of this adoption or appropriation was that such a custom is among many others that local hunters took from the adjacent German-speak-ing province. In all likelihood the availability of publications (mostly picture books) about hunting customs in South Tyrol explains why these are known in the valley. What seems most significant of hunting 'the Tyrolean way' is that it is described as an elaborate ritual. Those who were asked about the occurrence of such customs in the valley answered that the local hunters have them because the valley was under Austrian sovereignty for six centuries. However, they also stressed that it is good to have the same hunting customs, because 'in Austria, unlike in "Italy" they know how to hunt': what distinguishes local hunting is its being 'Tyrolean' or 'Austrian'. The way of carrying the gun on the shoulder and the mountain cock tail that adorns the hunter's hat on certain occasions are examples of how this appropriation is given practical expression. This 'appro-priation' seems a contradiction in an area in which hunting symbolises 'auton-omy' and resistance to outside authority. In fact, stress on autonomy and resistance are not at odds with the appropriation of a Tyrolean tradition, given the significance of the Austrian/Tyrolean legacy in the valley under study and in Trentino as a whole. If anything, inventions and appropriations serve to legitimate distinctiveness and claims to 'private property'.

The view that 'local' (that is to say 'Austrian') and 'Italian' hunting (*la catha de l'Italia*) are different is predicated upon contrasting ways of attending to landscape and conceptualising wildlife. According to some Caorians, the difference is that local hunters aim at the pursuit of big game, whereas 'Italians' target birds. Since in the valley birds are not highly valued, they are usually left to those who occasionally come there to hunt with a special daily permit, whereas local hunters keep big game for themselves. This difference also rests on the idea that Italian hunting is not 'true' hunting, for in 'Italy' (that is to say in the lowlands across the regional boundary) it is not necessary to walk a long way through the gorges to pursue a prey, and therefore it is much easier. In other words, the notion of 'true' hunting conveys ideas of strength and endurance, and is appealed to in local discourse to imply that 'Italians' are neither 'true hunters' nor hard workers. The hunters of Castello Tesino are derogatorily labelled 'Italians', for they pursue birds, which in the Vanoi valley are not even targeted by locals; however, in portraying them as 'Italians' they implicitly ascribe to them the 'intrusive' character that is deemed typical of the nation-state.

The hunt of the mountain cock, mentioned earlier in this chapter, is an example of a 'local' tradition which has been lost because of the restrictive laws imposed by state administration. As Raffaele (b. 1962) said, 'The mountain cock used to be pursued in spring. Now it has been hunted in autumn for ten–fifteen years, but not by villagers, because this is a custom that comes from "Italy" …which these people [i.e. Caorians] do not look upon as a local tradition…' Now, as the above man argued, this tradition has lost its 'local character' because the mountain cock cannot be shot when it performs its love ritual, and so is left to a few 'Italians' (i.e. daily permit holders coming from the Veneto region). This is an interesting shift in meaning: what used to function as a sort of 'ritual of initiation' or *rite de passage* is now described as an Austrian tradition; it no longer matters what it means, but where it comes from. In other words, it is only nowadays that this custom becomes imbued with such a meaning. Until a few years ago this was looked upon as local, and nobody was aware that Austrian hunters have the same custom. Its 'Austrian' origin has come to the fore now that this tradition is left to 'Italians'. Mountain cocks participate in the Italy–Austria/Tyrol debate in a prominent way, as for many hunters of the valley they were inherently local or Austrian until they became Italian with the enforcement of the Italian game law.

The dichotomy between Italian and Austrian hunting has other implications, for it is not simply customs in common that define the valley's partaking of a 'Tyrolean culture': rather, it is the similar way Austrian and local hunters relate to landscape that defines what is 'local'. Local hunters argue that they 'protect' nature through the 'cultivation' of their animals and prevent competition and conflict with other hunters by means of an informal agreement, as each hunter pursues game in a tract of land that he 'owns'. Interestingly, their ability to keep their territory 'clean' is interpreted as a result of the fact that they had been under the sovereignty of the Dual Monarchy for a very long time. According to some Caorians, in 'Italy' nobody 'owns' the territory, several hunters end up shooting the same bird, and quarrels ensue. This idea highlights two distinct notions of hunting: the local (or Austrian) one, aimed at the protection of the natural environment, and the 'Italian' one, which takes the form of a competition. The distinction between Austrian or local 'harvest' and 'Italian' gathering does not simply reflect different ways of looking at landscape. As Dalla Bernardina (1993: 41) observed, the administrative boundary between the provinces of Trent and Belluno represents a dividing line between two contrasting ways of hunting: the 'northern' one that is practised in one's own 'property'; and the 'Mediterranean' one that is practised in areas that nobody 'owns'. In the Austrian Tyrol hunting is restricted to the people who own a hunting preserve, and so evoking a Tyrolean hunting tradition conveys ideas of exclusive rights over hunting land.

There is an interesting parallel between ideas about hunting and local views about inheritance practices. As I have noted in an earlier chapter, one of the salient features of the landholding system in the valley is the fragmentation of the landed property that is the outcome of a system of strict partible inheritance. When I discussed the matter with some informants, they wryly pointed to the fact that when there are too many people entitled to inherit a share of a landholding or a building it is very difficult to reach an agreement as to the use that should be made of it. So, these people end up quarrelling, no agreement is reached, a meadow becomes covered with trees and weed-infested, and a house falls into disrepair and eventually crumbles. Interestingly, they stressed that a system of impartible inheritance, such as that formerly practised in South Tyrol,[21] would prevent this from happening, as one heir is enough to manage property. In saying so, they seem to imply that when too many people have access to a house or a landholding this can hardly be managed. In a sense, this seems the same logic that informs 'local' or 'Tyrolean' hunting. In stressing this, hunters were pointing to the necessity of drawing clear-cut boundaries in order to define what is owned by one individual and what is owned by another.

In ascribing the custom of the 'cultivation' of territory to an Austrian or Tyrolean cultural tradition local hunters assert their partaking of that tradition, and blend landscape with ethnicity. However, they do so through drawing on an idealised image of Austria as portrayed by the media as a 'clean', and 'ordered' country which may contrast with a putative 'disordered' Italy in light of the bribes scandal that led to the demise of the governing political party, the Christian Democratic Party (DC). It seems reasonable to believe that appealing to a 'Tyrolean' tradition is a device to stress that the valley has little in common with the 'intrusive' nation-state, which is represented, in the municipality, by the military police (*Carabinieri*) and its officials from the South. This also becomes a statement about a distant past or 'structural nostalgia',[22] in Herzfeld's terms (1997: 109), which rests on the conviction that before the arrival of the 'Italians' the valley was 'independent' and 'self-sufficient'.

In the 1990s the dichotomy between Austrian and Italian hunting emerged as a social problem, as a result of the symbolic confrontation between the local and the national, the periphery and the centre. This also took the form of a confrontation between the North and the South, central Europe and the Mediterranean, as long as hunting reflects two contrasting ways of relating to landscape: what seems to be a local issue eventually takes on a 'transnational' dimension. While the distinction between the two highlights the tension between a vision of the countryside as part of the leisure experience and land conceived as private property, it also reflects the dichotomy between the domestic and the public domain and the moral evaluations attached to them. Clearly, giving hunting an ethnic flavour also reflected the political developments of the mid-1990s, when the regional administration was championing the establishment of an Autonomous European Region of Tyrol (Euregio) and was attaching emphasis on common cultural traits between Trentino and South Tyrol. In appealing to a Tyrolean tradition, local hunters also appropriated the principle that keeping a place 'clean' is a sign of moral superiority, and that those who show 'disrespect' by littering it are judged to be inferior or the 'other'.[23] The difference between the two types of hunting eventually replicates that between an 'ordered' private property administered by locals, and an 'open' one controlled by the nation-state to which everybody has access, and which nobody has any interest in 'cultivating' or keeping 'in order' simply because it is open to everybody. Implicit in this is also a moral evaluation of the nation-state and public administration in general, and hunting becomes part of the process through which the nation-state itself is cast as the 'other'.

While it is tempting to believe that hunters express attachment to the Tyrolean legacy simply as a reflection of the ideas propagated by party leaders, in fact it is not so much political ideologies per se that are at stake, as the way these relate to local knowledge, to a bodily knowledge and cognition by doing. Social actors draw selectively on such political messages, and translate them into familiar terms to legitimate their claims. Traditions have to be appropriated because the valley is considered 'without traditions', or does not have traditions that clearly distinguish it from the adjacent valleys or from the surrounding Italian-speaking provinces.

The analysis of hunting suggests that political parties do not simply superimpose ideological messages on local society: rather, local society acts as a motive force by making use of local-level ideas about private property. Hunting, which is associated with boundaries, traditions, property and autonomy, expresses such values very well. While it is tempting to infer that the political messages, such as those of the Trentine-Tyrolean Autonomist Party, are taken for granted, in fact they are appropriated to meet local needs: they may have specific meanings for the élites that advocate them, but this may not hold true in a social context in which the main issue seems to be local boundaries rather than politics as a set of abstract ideas.

Conclusion

The ethnographic material discussed suggests that there are multiple interpretations of hunting. Clearly, it is a ritual reenactment of the fear of uncontrolled natural forces; it represents a statement about the past, a distant past when man's control over territory, accomplished through the 'cultivation' of wildlife, was not questioned. In this regard, the identification of the hunter with the cultivator is also a transposition of the ideology of private property that permeates so much of village thinking, which is now ascribed to the valley's partaking of a 'Tyrolean' or 'central European' culture. It is practices such as turning landscape into private property, both materially and symbolically, that carry a sense of historical connectedness for the social actors. This local practice helped to naturalise the connection between the Austrian past and the idea of autonomy which is appealed to by both the inhabitants of the valley and the regionalist political formations.

Hunting involves cultural heritage in practice in that, as a way in which humans interact with landscape, it conceals memories and myths. It shows that cultural heritage is also something that happens: in other words, it may be an activity. However, while it may be argued that hunting primarily consists 'of a culturally inherited thematization of our view of nature' (Kayser Nielsen 2000: 64), the material discussed suggests that hunting may also thematise social actors' views of politics. It is functional to making landscape the context for contesting aspects of nationhood such as domination and encompassment. Landscape, in turn, becomes a powerful symbol: it is imagined as the embodiment not just of the community, but of the region as a whole. It provides a metaphorical setting to validate the view that the protection of nature is an integral part of defending the community and, by extension, the region: in other words, it becomes a political myth. Although politics and the appropriation of nature have been seen as antithetical, it may be suggested that the two are not necessarily opposed: rather, it is also the appropriation of nature that may form the background against which politics is debated and understood.

NOTES

1. I collected most of the data on hunting in the village of Caoria, and little information came from Ronco. As hunting is almost exclusively a male domain, most of the considerations in this chapter are one-sided, for they mainly reflect men's views.
2. See for example Peres (1998).
3. Of about 11,000 hectares in which hunting is permitted within the municipal territory, over 8,000 fall within the forested area surrounding Caoria.
4. He is one of the very few in the village, aside from the hunters, allowed to carry a firearm.
5. There is, for example, a long-standing enmity between the local hunters and the official of the military police, a southerner based in Canal San Bovo.
6. At present the president is a Caorian.
7. Hunting in the valley cannot be thought of as a diversion for the upper classes. If anything, it is the conviction that local hunting is different from that practised in other Alpine valleys that confers a sense of identity for those involved, as will be seen in another section.
8. Quarrels with the nearby municipalities over the control of the hunting areas are not uncommon. In the summer of 1996, for example, the *comune* of Pieve Tesino, which embraces a sizeable amount of land in the upper Vanoi valley, claimed rights on a hunting preserve that falls within the *comune* of Canal San Bovo, alleging that the latter had sold it to Pieve Tesino in 1906.
9. This was the case of the president of the Autonomous Province of Trent or of some freemasons, and usually people in high places.
10. This custom disappeared in the 1980s, owing to depopulation and to the fact that shooting the mountain cock in spring is no longer allowed.
11. Poppi (1980: 67) has written about the same custom in the Val di Fassa, not far from my fieldsite.
12. The hunters I interviewed denied this, even though I received the impression that they said so in order to stress that they have nothing to do with what they call 'primitive' peoples.
13. This also applies to the mountain cock, which used to be targeted when performing its love ritual.
14. There are several anecdotes on this subject. One was about a hunter known as a liar. One of his stories runs that he shot two roebucks in a very steep and inaccessible place; being unable to take them to the village because they were too heavy a load, he managed to capture another roebuck that dragged the other two to Caoria. Likewise it is still customary to spread the news that three or four roebucks have been shot instead of one or two in order to gain a good reputation in the village.
15. Although there has been a gamekeeper in Caoria since the mid-nineteenth century, it is not entirely clear how far laws have been enforced since then.
16. His statement is reminiscent of the Greek case study analysed by Herzfeld (1987: 45), notably of the view that Greek bureaucrats' corruption is what remains of the Ottoman legacy, something that came from the outside.
17. There are several anecdotes on this subject. One, for example, has it that a few years ago a hunter of Canal San Bovo shot a big deer not far from the administrative boundary between Canal San Bovo and Castello Tesino, and news quickly spread throughout the valley. Some days later police came to levy a fine on him on the grounds that the deer had been shot within the *comune* of Castello Tesino. The man refused to pay the fine, and two or three cadastral surveys were necessary to ascertain that the animal had been caught in the municipality of Canal San Bovo, just a few metres from the boundary.
18. Normally this belongs to the municipality, especially that high in altitude.

19. It is not purely coincidence that in the summer of 1997 the president of the hunt club was busy organising a conference on hunting, held in Caoria in late 1998, designed to show that hunting is aimed at the 'protection' of the mountains.

20. This applies to several informants, on account of the fact that they admitted that they had been hunting without a licence prior to the attainment of adulthood, even though they do not look upon themselves as poachers.

21. See the work by Cole and Wolf, '*The Hidden Frontier*' (1974), for details about inheritance practices in Trentino-South Tyrol.

22. By 'structural nostalgia' I mean a 'collective representation of an Edenic order... in which the balanced perfection of human relations has not yet suffered the decay that affects everything human' (Herzfeld 1997: 109).

23. See, for a comparison, Argyrou (1997: 159).

11. Caorian hunter with a freshly-shot fox in the 1930s.

12. The prey is caught: Caorian hunter holding a deer's antlers.

5
THE VIEW FROM BELOW: CONSTRUCTIONS OF OTHERNESS

Introduction

Binary schemes such as modernity/tradition and centre/periphery have often been deployed in anthropology in the analysis of the relationship between the national and the local. Like 'identity', they have long been seen as relational concepts. However, while the relationship between centre and periphery usually functions as a relationship of power, there is ambivalence about the notion of tradition, both as it is used by intellectuals, and as it is understood in local discourse. Traditions are aspects of identity within a historical context. On the one hand, the notion of tradition can be used by both intellectuals and ordinary people to define a national or local identity; on the other hand, labelling a human group 'traditional' may be tantamount to 'orientalising' it, as the notion of tradition may convey ideas of 'otherness'.

The Vanoi valley has been depicted both as a repository of regional traditions that have been lost elsewhere in Trentino, and as backward. Ideas of backwardness, by their very nature, are largely the product of power relations: they imply the existence of a 'centre', such as a nation-state, seen as the embodiment of social agency and the basis of legitimate social and political power. However, at a time when the idea of modernity erected on the foundations of national society is questioned, concepts of identity and otherness need to be analysed by taking into account different viewpoints. Identity is constructed through interplay with the 'other' (Gefou-Madianou 1999: 414), and otherness may be an ongoing process in the same manner that identity construction is. Nowadays the relationship between 'tradition' and 'modernity' is posed as one of the most significant issues facing the valley, and social actors have to cope either with a loss of identity that 'modernity' is likely to bring about, or with the alternative of veering too close to 'tradition'. But how far do these dichotomies inform individual actors' definitions of local identity in the valley? Clearly, the rise of regionalism in northern Italy in the 1990s posed the question of how people construct identity and difference in a changing political situation, and particularly of the applicability of this binary modernity/tradition distinction. While until recently the nation-state acted as an agent of 'modernity', with the advent of regionalist political formations 'tradition' suddenly became a banner for contesting the state as the embodiment of legitimate political power.

The changes in the political landscape had repercussions in the valley studied too (as in most of Trentino), even though in that area the Italian state has never had the same significance that it has in other Italian regions: in the valley, for example, it is only the post office and the *Carabinieri*[1] that represent it. The city of Trent, where most of the national offices in the province are based, is about 100 kilometres from the valley. Especially in Trentino, it is the municipality[2] (*comune*) and the province (*provincia*), rather than the state, that loom largest in the lives of most of its inhabitants. The researcher visiting the province soon realises that the overwhelming majority of the public offices are owned by the *provincia* itself, whose logo (an eagle) can be noticed in almost every corner of Trentino. The limited presence of the state apparatus at the local level has certainly influenced the people's 'sense of place', but local particularism in the field of law has also played an important part.[3] Although in Trentino the state has hardly been looked upon as the embodiment of social agency, the political and economic changes of the 1990s had the effect of further questioning its legitimacy, at least at the level of discourse. Thus, in this chapter I look at the notion of otherness as a counterdiscourse whereby individual social actors invest this idea with moral meanings and achieve a sense of agency.

Perceptions of Campanilismo

'Qui di campanilismo si nasce e si muore'
'Here you are immersed in *campanilismo* from your birth to your dying day'
(Carlo, b. 1981)

In the anthropological literature on Italy of the 1970s and 1980s the term used to define a set of village-centric attitudes vis-à-vis strangers is the Italian word *campanilismo*, or local chauvinism. This is translated into English as 'parochialism', *campanile* being the church belltower, symbol of independence (Pitt-Rivers 1954: 30; Silverman 1975: 16). On the one hand, the concept expresses pride in the qualities of the place of birth, and stresses the difference between it and other places; on the other hand, it connotes a narrowness of outlook

(Cohen 1977: 107; Pratt 1986: 140).[4] *Campanilismo* implies that those who live in the same place share something, and it occurs when there is a certain degree of isolation of a local population, but nevertheless some contact exists (Pratt 1986: 41).[5] It is not purely coincidence that the anthropological literature often refers to Mediterranean villages as 'little republics'.[6] The term highlights the 'particularist' character that is deemed typical of peasant villages, expressed by a strong sense of 'our place' as opposed to the outside world (MacFarlane 1978: 32).

Campanilismo necessarily entails the expression of positive sentiments towards one's own community, and the definition of village boundaries is crucial: although boundaries between nations or regions are more manifest than those between small communities, for the members of such communities 'local' boundaries are instead more significant, in that they are related to intimate areas of their lives (Cohen 1985: 13). In the Vanoi valley, too, ideas of distinctiveness figure centrally in local discourse: it is reasonable to believe that the world outside the two communities studied is imagined as a set of concentric circles, the village community being at the very centre, surrounded by the neighbouring villages that are in turn surrounded by the adjacent valleys.

This focus on attachment to place and village boundaries may look a bit naïve at a time of increasing mobility, and may be reminiscent of the typologising approaches of classical anthropology of some years ago, now a subject of criticism. As a matter of fact Gupta and Ferguson (1997: 37) argued that people have always been more mobile, and identities less fixed than has been postulated. Malkki (1997: 52–53) too made the point that the rooting of peoples and the territorialisation of identity is part of a taken-for-granted way of thinking. As we have seen in chapter 2, villagers have been mobile too, and emigration abroad has long been part of their lives. However, this mobility does not necessarily affect the representations of identities: although identities are far from fixed, they are represented as fixed, both by the people and in political discourse. While for the researcher identities may appear fluid, from the viewpoint of those who reside in a certain place there is very little or no room for fluidity in the definition of localness. So, the problem that local identity raises is not so much one of authenticity, as one of representation.

At the simplest level *campanilismo* centres on a conviction about the special qualities of the place and its people. The researcher meets this very early on: the inhabitants of Caoria and Ronco, named collectively after the place (**Caorióti**/Caorians and **Roncaroni**), often claim to have the best air, the best climate, the most wonderful landscapes, to be the most honest and hospitable people, and so on. As Aida (b. 1931) once said, 'It is like Paradise here in Caoria. You can trust everybody, and you can even leave your door unlocked'. Behind this is also the idea that the village community is 'ruled by laws and standards of morality and ranged against a non-moral world outside' (Bailey 1971: 14). However, when the researcher reaches the valley s/he soon realises that there are some discrepancies between what actors say and actuality: the valley is badly connected with the outside, the climate is quite harsh, especially during the winter, and visitors coming to the valley for the first time may not find residents particularly welcoming. The researcher visiting Caoria or Ronco cannot help noticing that every villager expresses a very strong sense of attachment to his or her place, often epitomised by the statement 'I am a "true" Caorian/***Roncarone*** and I am proud of it'. The significance of place is also expressed by the high number of chapel shelters, symbols of universal devotion transformed into vehicles of local sentiments.[7] These often mark the boundary of a village or hamlet, and act as lines of demarcation between what is 'in' and what is 'out'.

In the valley there are two main forms of *campanilismo*: one, which has already been mentioned, is the attachment to one's own *campanile*, the church belltower that symbolises the village community; the other, with its pejorative overtones, manifests itself in the sense of hostility vis-à-vis the outside world, and is the attitude towards the neighbouring valleys or the state.[8] The system in which villages are rivals within the valley, and different valleys are rivals within the district, and different districts are rivals within the province of Trent may be termed as a system of segmentary identities: so, in spite of rivalry among villages, Caorians declare themselves as inhabitants of the Vanoi valley as opposed to those of Primiero but, at the same time, they present themselves as inhabitants of Primiero when they want to distinguish themselves from the urban dwellers of Trent, and they proudly identify themselves as Trentine as opposed to the ***belumàti***[9] living a few kilometres away across the regional border. The village bar, as has been seen in chapter 3, is the ideal setting for observing the 'community' and its attitudes towards strangers, particularly when a nonvillager steps in, and the bar suddenly turns into a 'private' space. This also illustrates an aspect that urban dwellers call peasant mentality: the suspicion that surrounds all dealings with strangers arising from a fear of being cheated.

In the valley *campanilismo* is also expressed by the idea that ecological and administrative boundaries should overlap: although the physical boundaries of the valley and those of the municipality roughly coincide, there are tracts of land within the valley that belong to the neighbouring municipalities. Some people ironically said that one can hardly move in the valley without setting a foot in another municipality. However, while there is a shared feeling that the territory of the municipality should encompass the valley in its entirety, there is also a conviction that the local government is unable to enlarge the municipality's size because the other *comuni* have more powerful and skilful representatives in the provincial government. This sense of powerlessness deriving from an awareness that the municipality is unlikely to grow in size is antithetical to the importance attached to the ability to enlarge one's boundaries, as has been seen in an earlier chapter, particularly as a condition to gain respectability in one's community. At the time of my fieldwork quarrels between the *comune* of Canal

San Bovo and those nearby often ensued: territorial boundaries became objects of contention, and the main issue was not so much how to enlarge the *comune*, as how to defend its boundaries from others attempts to incorporate land. As a matter of fact the conversations among villagers that I happened to hear often centred on the legitimacy of administrative and individual property boundaries. A brook that marks the boundary between the *comune* of Canal San Bovo and that of Castello Tesino, a few kilometres north of Caoria, is a case in point: it is called the 'brook of the quarrels' (***boál de le beghe***) because of the quarrels that arise between the two *comuni* when hunters are caught shooting game outside the territory within which they are authorised to do so.[10] Another disputed boundary is a forested hill that lies next to the village of Ronco which, in spite of its proximity to the village, falls within the territory of the adjacent *comune*, Cinte Tesino. The ***Roncaroni*** I came across claim that the hill was illicitly appropriated by the other municipality, and according to them the hill was owned by an old woman of Ronco, until she was persuaded to bequeath it to the nearby *comune*.

A similar story, which everybody in the valley knows, is about Cainari, a hamlet that lies within Castello Tesino, although it forms part of Ronco. The story goes that 'once upon a time' the *comuni* of Canal San Bovo and Castello Tesino were quarrelling over where to fix the boundary markers (in the form of milestones) between them. As no agreement could be reached, eventually it was decided that the representatives of each *comune* would set out from their villages at an agreed time and that the boundary markers would be placed where they met. When the representatives of Canal San Bovo reached Ronco, and found that nobody was approaching from the other side, they decided to stop at the local inn, have some wine, and play cards. Soon after they stopped playing they realised that the men of Castello Tesino had already passed the hamlet of Cainari which, as the story runs, has belonged to the other municipality ever since.[11] In 1951 its inhabitants petitioned the municipality of Castello Tesino in order to have their hamlet separated from that *comune* and incorporated into that of Canal San Bovo, but their request was rejected. The struggle over boundaries and the 'illicit appropriation' of the hamlet of Cainari became the subjects of a play staged at the theatre of Ronco in the summer of 1994, which was well received by the villagers who attended it. What such stories have in common is that they question the legitimacy of administrative boundaries on the grounds that part of the territory that used to belong to the community was 'stolen' by nearby *comune*.

Campanilismo now manifests itself mainly in the form of contentious relationships between the municipality and the neighbouring ones, particularly Castello Tesino and Pieve Tesino (not to mention the Primiero valley) over the control of natural resources (water, woodland, game, etc.), and at the level of discourse. *Campanilismo* as a form of physical violence no longer occurs. The stories I heard date back to the 1960s or earlier, and are mostly about skirmishes between groups of youngsters of neighbouring villages. It is a topic about which informants do not like to talk. Some of these stories are about people of the nearby villages who came to Caoria and Ronco to court a village girl and were met by a barrage of stones. This used to be a very common device until the 1960s to preserve village endogamy, and to prevent local girls from getting married to outsiders,[12] or simply from establishing liaisons with them.[13] Such attitudes often led to bad relationships with the inhabitants of other communities, which could develop into acute antagonism.[14] This often manifested itself in the form of open brawls in which groups, mainly of youngsters, took part. There were different locations where fights could take place, the usual ones being the boundary between two neighbouring villages, as was the case of the communities of Canal San Bovo and Prade.

Village endogamy as a device to defend community boundaries against strangers used to be an integral part of *campanilismo*. As noted in chapter 3, 'in the old days' it was deemed preferable to get married to someone of the same village. Parish records provide documentary evidence that until the demise of agro-pastoral economy both in Caoria and in Ronco marriages between first and second cousins were not uncommon. However, in spite of this marriages with strangers used to take place from time to time both in Caoria and in Ronco. In Caoria, for instance, when a local girl was about to get married to a stranger, the bride's unmarried age mates used to go to the very edge of the village after the religious ceremony to await the newly married couple. The groom was then handed an old axe, and was asked to cut a log;[15] then, according to the local custom, he had to pay for as many rounds of drinks as his wife's age mates could swallow while he was cutting the log. This was meant as a sort of symbolic compensation for the stranger's 'stealing' a village girl. This custom disappeared not long ago, and it was widespread in other areas of the Alpine crescent like the Carnic Alps (Heady 1999). This form of control of village boundaries points to the role of youths in limiting and outlining community membership recorded elsewhere (Bendix 1985: 67–68), and both in Caoria and in Ronco it represented a form of control by the adults of the community acting through their unmarried sons. Taking a hint from Peters (1972: 112), it can be suggested that 'by deflecting responsibility onto an irresponsible group of youths the adult community is able to maintain its own integrity'.

In spite of the ideology of boundedness just mentioned, there is also a long-standing tradition of intermarriage between Caoria and Ronco. In the 'old days' marriages between Caorians and **Roncaroni** were not encouraged, but they were not disapproved of either. Various people living in Caoria were born in Ronco (usually women who married out), or have ancestors who came from there. Conversely, some residents of Ronco descend from Caorians or identify themselves as Caorians. Marriages between members of the two communities were not frowned upon, on the grounds that these people consider each other of the same 'kind', that is to say 'poor' people and 'hard workers': as a Caorian said, 'we are all 'poor' people here' (***Noi qua son tuti pora δènt***). This idea of 'poverty' is further explored in the sections that follow.

Contesting 'Modernity'

The hypothesis that people's ideas of locality may be taken as descriptions of social units, as the idea of 'poverty' suggests, becomes patent when it comes to the analysis of 'modernity'.[16] The term 'modernity' is hardly used in the valley. Rather, the dialectal term ***moderno*** means 'strange', 'odd'. A 'modern' person is usually alluded to as *educato, distinto, evoluto* or ***studià***, as is the case of those holding a university degree. Both in Caoria and in Ronco ideas about 'modernity' usually come to the fore when villagers talk about the village of Canal San Bovo (the municipal seat) and its inhabitants, and project negative traits on those people. If I were to take my informants' statements at face value, there would be grounds for inferring that the relationships with that village have never been particularly friendly. In the two villages there is a collective nickname attached to the inhabitants of Canal San Bovo: ***strasinasachi***, namely, 'those who drag the sack'. The term does not make any sense unless it is borne in mind that in local discourse 'to drag the sack' means avoiding carrying a burden on one's shoulders, and conveys images of laziness. Unlike Caoria and Ronco, whose inhabitants describe themselves as hard workers, the inhabitants of Canal San Bovo are not known for their ability to sustain hard work. A woman of Caoria now in her seventies made this view very explicit: 'I do not like to go to Canale [San Bovo], because the people there think of themselves as ***siori***.[17] They behave like city dwellers …we do not hate them, we like them, but they are different from us. Do you know what we call them? We call them ***strasinasachi***'.

The idea that work 'inside' is opposed to nonwork 'outside' should be subjected to the same kind of scrutiny that has attended the analysis of the sense of distinctiveness. The significance of this opposition lies in the meanings attached to certain economic pursuits as markers of local identity, and is highlighted by the fact that, as has been seen in an earlier chapter, the overwhelming majority of the able-bodied of Caoria and Ronco are manual workers. By contrast, nowadays clerical jobs are the main economic activities in Canal San Bovo, given that the municipal offices are based there. Various people of Caoria and Ronco left their village for Canal San Bovo to undertake a clerical job in the public sector, the bank, or the provincial Forestry Department. The idea that those who work in administrative offices do not do real work is fairly recent, and is chiefly the outcome of the demise of agro-pastoral economy.[18] Behind this is the idea that 'true' work is manual work, toil. This brought about the differentiation, in local discourse, between 'hard work' and 'nonwork', especially in a valley where agro-pastoral pursuits were the main economic activities until the 1960s, and where those who work in public offices belong to families who could afford to send them to school to obtain educational qualifications.[19]

The Caorians and ***Roncaroni*** who undertook clerical jobs and came back to the village after retirement had some difficulty in reintegrating themselves in their place of origin, and some ended up being treated like 'strangers'. This was also the case of those who emigrated to large urban centres such as Padua, Milan or Turin to work in factories. However, those who had clerical jobs in the public administration became 'outsiders' to a greater extent for, while they remained village residents, they were believed to have taken on 'urban' habits. The Caorians who went 'urban', for example, are often alluded to by their covillagers as 'shit put on a stool' (***merda montada sul scagno***), on the grounds that they do not work at all and look down upon manual workers. I think it is reasonable to postulate that in local discourse clerical workers typify those who are employed by the state (referred to as *statali*), as epitomised by the statement that these people 'do not do anything at all' (*i statali no i fa un catho*). There is a widespread conviction that these people adopted the 'aristocratic' and 'urban' customs of Canal San Bovo by frequenting the bars there or the cafés in Fiera di Primiero instead of joining their fellow villagers in their village bar. One takes this attitude by wearing one's best clothes when going to the 'urban' centres of the nearby valley of Primiero in order to be treated like an 'urban' dweller, and not like a *cafone*.[20] These are alluded to as villagers just by reason of residence, but not by character, for presenting oneself in an 'urban' manner is deemed tantamount to putting on airs or raising oneself above others.

The idea that the city may be the centre of 'modernity' is contested in various ways, and collective nicknames are cases in point.[21] These usually are derogatory, and are also ascribed: in this case the term ***strasinasachi*** implies that *all* the people of Canal San Bovo are morally inferior on the grounds that they behave like urban dwellers and are not hard workers. 'You see, they sit on a bench in a square, watching who is coming and who is going, and doing nothing' (Andrea, b. 1922). This is antithetical to the high value Caorians place on the capacity to work hard discussed in the chapter 3. That the inhabitants of Canal San Bovo are called ***strasinasachi*** reveals the existence of community nickname systems which are common features of rural life in Europe and the Middle East (Gilmore 1982: 686). In the specific context of the valley under study collective nicknames have a boundary-maintaining function too, and contribute to the community sociocentrism or *campanilismo* of rural life. This nicknaming is more than drollery, for it summarises different sorts of prejudices, masks, insults and aggression, and forms part of local identity.

Much of the anthropological debate on nicknames, and especially the literature of the last twenty years (e.g. Gilmore 1982, 1987), focuses on the affective content and on the psychological motivations of name substitutions and distortions. This analysis, however, is confined to an exploration of collective nicknames as a device to categorise strangers. The importance of family nicknames, in the valley, is shown by their high number in the municipal records of the last century (Romagna 1992: 151–5). However, unlike family nicknames, those referring to outsiders have a different character, in that they are used, sometimes jokingly, as boundary-markers between those who are 'in' and those who are 'out', and often with negative connotations. They are personal in that they often describe the character of the person to whom they are referring, and they are collective because they are shared by all those who come from the same place. In other words, nicknames distinguish those who are members of the community from those who are not. A man from Ronco who moved to Caoria in the 1980s to marry a local girl is called *pendol* as a native of Ronco. Paolo (1903–74), a man from another Trentine community, used to be called 'the bull' (*toro*) because of his aggressive character, and his wife Margherita (b. 1922) is referred to as *la francese* (the Frenchwoman), because she was born in the French side of Switzerland, or simply *la tora*, because she was married to the late *toro*. Likewise in Ronco Adriana (b. 1937) is called *la perugina* because she is native of the Perugia province, and there are other examples like these. What unites such nicknames is their fixity. Once they are attached to a person they are not changed. Residence only does not entitle one to be referred to as a villager: although Adriana has resided in Ronco for many years, she will always be called *la perugina* because of her origins. So, nicknames suggest that villageness is hardly negotiable: one is either an insider or an outsider.

Nicknames may project negative traits on those to whom they are attached, but may be neutral too. Similarly, personal nicknames sometimes stress the marginality of the person in question through labelling him/her as 'wild' or antisocial. In this respect, the idea that the people of another place speak an incomprehensible language is often deployed to project negative traits on them. This is the case of the inhabitants of Castello Tesino, whom a retired school-teacher of the valley defined as 'a bunch of immigrants who speak an incomprehensible mixture of dialects that nobody understands'. In labelling them as 'immigrants', many Caorians also cast the people of Castello Tesino as 'matter out of place', in Douglas's terms (1966). That they speak an 'incomprehensible mixture' of dialects is taken as evidence that the language they speak is not 'pure'. In this regard, even the stories about the struggle for boundaries may serve to stigmatise the people of the nearby municipalities: the conviction that the ancestors of some people used to be deceitful or thieves is considered a 'proof' that their descendants are the same. This is the case, already analysed, of the inhabitants of Castello Tesino, who are attached the labels of poachers and thieves, and in both Caoria and Ronco different stories are quoted as evidence of this.[22]

That the origins of people may explain behavioural idiosyncrasies became patent when Liliane (b. 1946), a Swiss woman who came to live in Ronco in the late 1970s, told me about the character of the people of Castello Tesino, whose municipal boundary lies a few hundred metres from her home. According to the story she heard in Ronco, those who first settled in the Tesino plateau were bandits. For the above person this could account for the fact that such people look like bandits. 'Not only do they [the people of Castello Tesino] descend from bandits, but they also look like bandits'. This is not a matter of negative traits only, but is rather a way of establishing (and accounting for) relationships between people living in a territory. When I was talking with a woman of Caoria about a man of Castello Tesino she knows well, she made similar considerations: she remarked that such a person is a hunter like his father, who was in turn the son of another hunter, that is to say a 'typical' man of Castello Tesino. He is 'typical' both as a member of a family group and of a territorial unit. In other words, behavioural traits, just like collective nicknames, are thought of as ascribed and inherited; in village thinking being a native of a given place necessarily involves being attached a set of labels (including nicknames) which identify those who live there. As I noted, the inhabitants of a given place are ascribed fixed characteristics, and underlying this ascription is the idea of reproduction: strangers reproduce strangers, and strangers replicate strangers ad infinitum. On the one hand, this is consistent with the view that self-definition entails the construction of moral contraries (McDonald 1993: 227); on the other hand, such an idea accords with the imagery of a village as a system that ideally reproduces itself over time: villagers reproduce villagers in the same manner that strangers reproduce strangers. In spite of the awareness that there are exceptions to the rule of reproduction, such a rule is invoked to account for similarity.

Another significant aspect is that the construction of distinctiveness between the villages of the valley means stressing the difference between the city and the countryside. The overwhelming majority of the Caorians and **Roncaroni** I came across represent themselves as country people, rustic, *cafoni* as opposed to the urban dwellers or those who think of themselves as such. They pride themselves on the fact that they preserved their traditions vigorously. However, this pride is also tantamount to a claim to 'purity' against outside corruption that often takes on the form of an extreme localism (see, for a comparison with Greece, Sutton 1994: 245). This attitude is reflected in the tendency to dismiss many artefacts coming from urban centres on the grounds that they are **moderni**. Interestingly, as I noted earlier in this chapter, the dialectal term **moderno** is not the equivalent of 'modern' as in Italian, but means 'odd'.[23]

The idea that the 'purity' of the country life may be opposed to the 'corrupt' life of the city is hardly new, and has already been discussed in various works (see, for details, Ching and Creed 1997). Suffice it, for now, to focus on the relationships between the villages of the valley. The idea that the people of Canal San Bovo behave like 'aristocrats' (*aristocratici*) on the grounds that they look upon themselves as 'urban' dwellers is at odds with the idea of a group in which all should be equal, and in which hierarchies should not exist. Therefore, while someone in Caoria and Ronco may feel the need to behave in an 'urban' way as a marker of prestige, most of them resist outside influence, and decide instead to behave like a *cafone* as a marker of distinctiveness vis-à-vis the *aristocratici*.[24] Likewise the different views that most of the people of Caoria and Ronco, irrespective of age and gender, hold about each other seem to question the assumption that the notion of 'modernity' is shared by everybody.

An analysis of the uses of collective nicknames illustrates how 'modernity' may be manipulated. The collective nickname attached to Caorians is *orsi* ('bears'), which carries a heavy symbolic load. In the valley, especially in Canal San Bovo and Ronco, calling Caorians 'bears' is quite common (see also dei Chechi 1930: 32). The term has a number of meanings both in the local dialect and in Italian. In local discourse, an *orso* denotes an antisocial person who lives isolated and has no kind of social interaction, a reference to the behavioural idiosyncrasy of the animal that lives alone and not in packs. The term also connotes rough and uncouth people, who are spatially and socially 'marginal', and conveys ideas of wildness. This idea permeates much of local discourse but, as will be seen, it may be used in different ways. In Ronco there is a shared conviction that Caorians, albeit good people, are 'uncouth' (*grezzi*), on the grounds that some of them still pursue agro-pastoral activities. This view is at odds with actuality, since there are more people in Ronco who perform such tasks than in Caoria itself, even though the former are not attached the stigma of 'wild' people. Ideas about strangers in Ronco have an oppositional character too, for they emphasise difference. There is a conviction, which all my informants in Ronco seem to share, that **Roncaroni** are more 'civilised' (*più evoluti*) than Caorians, who are in turn spoken of as backward people: as a young woman of Ronco told me, 'We [**Roncaroni**] call them [Caorians] *orsi*'. The Caorians I talked with, by contrast, seem to share a different view of the 'other': they proudly describe themselves as different from and in opposition to somebody else, notably those of Canal San Bovo, who adopt urban habits.

What unites ideas about the inhabitants of Ronco is the fact that they are identified with positive values, and in Caoria they are usually described as 'people of the same kind' (*δènt de la stesa sort*). However, three negative traits are projected on them: the first one is that, albeit good people, they are deceitful; the second one is that they are churchgoers. This is rather striking: while in Ronco going to church on a regular basis is deemed a sign of education, Caorians, particularly men, denigrate them for this very reason. Conversely, what unites **Roncaroni**'s descriptions of Caorians is the view that they are 'wild' (*selvatici*), whereas for Caorians wildness and strength are constitutive of their identity. The third negative trait projected on the people of Ronco is that they are bad-looking. As a Caorian man remarked, 'Have you ever noticed that all **Roncaroni** are bad-looking?' That **Roncaroni** are derogatorily spoken of as churchgoers does not mean that Caorians do not go to church: Ronco and Caoria have roughly the same church attendance, that is to say one inhabitant out of four. If anything, the Caorians I talked with never prided themselves on this, probably because going to church involves loyalty to the Catholic Church and expresses an act of submission to its authority.[25] Furthermore, since it is women who for the most part attend the holy mass, for Caorian men going to church is tantamount to a negation of manhood.[26] In Ronco, by contrast, being a churchgoer does not represent a problem: rather, it is a marker of 'civilisation' conceptually opposed to being a hunter or a 'wild' person. By contrast, in Caoria being close to nature and resisting urban (and church) influence is deemed a virtue. This, as will be seen in the next chapter, also reflects different ways of relating to the larger society and of perceiving history. So, different notions of 'civilisation' emerge: in Ronco the term *orso* connotes backwardness; in Caoria this is ultimately a symbol of strength and domination over (and appropriation of) nature, and validates the view that people may prefer to retain their original identity in spite of the stigma attached to it (Hurwitz Nadel 1984: 112). Implicit in all this is a point already made in this chapter: as stereotypes do not discriminate between individuals, all the people are deemed the same and every village is described as a system which ideally reproduces itself over time.

Another aspect expressed by such stereotypes is the belief that the natural environment may affect and determine the behaviour of those who live in it: that is to say, people's behavioural traits are deemed to be shaped by the natural environment that created them; a harsh environment produces harsh people.[27] In Ronco the behavioural idiosyncrasy characterising whoever lives in Caoria is accounted for by the natural environment: as Caoria lies at the very end of a narrow valley, those who live there cannot but be narrow-minded. The Caorians I talked with, by contrast, form a virtuous counter-image of themselves, a denial (or manipulation) of stigma: it is the natural environment that makes them strong. This, as can be seen, may be termed as a form of belief in environmental determinism with very different meanings in the two communities.[28]

Apparently, the idea of marginality carries with it the assumption that 'modernity' spreads from the centre to the periphery, and in every village there is a notion of 'centre' and 'periphery'. The 'centre' may be the village itself in relation to the other communities, but it may also be the centre of the village symbolised by the civic belltower as opposed to its margins. So, *orso* does not simply convey ideas of wildness, but also of marginality. Marginality, in this case, is also described as tantamount to unwillingness to interact with other people. In Caoria there is a shared conviction that the upper fringes of the village are inhabited by 'wild' people who live isolated, and still pursue agro-pastoral tasks. These are referred to as 'wild' (*selvatici*) also on the grounds that they seldom (or never) interact with their covillagers. The story that 'once upon a time' the upper fringes of Caoria were inhabited by witches is reminiscent of the belief that the boundary between the hamlets of Cainari and Chiesa in Ronco was also a venue for witches.[29] However, there is also a conviction that in order to know about what the 'true' valley is like, one has to go to its 'margins', where there are still people living in the 'old way' (***a la vecia***), that is to say working the soil and milking cows. This is another ambivalence that informs village thinking, in that these people are viewed as old-fashioned at the same time that they are presented as the repositories of 'traditional' (i.e. authentic and local) knowledge.

In the *campanilismo* complex, as can be seen, village boundaries are crucial. They differentiate between what is in and what is out, between what belongs to the village community and what does not. They are very ambiguous too because what (and who) is at the margins is neither in nor out, and therefore has a half-identity (Douglas 1966: 160). This is the case, for example, of those who live at the edge of the villages or close to nature, and various stigmas are attached to them. During my fieldwork, for example, one of the gamekeepers who used to work in the valley was courting the woman working at one of the local post offices; her father discouraged her from establishing a liaison with him on the grounds that he was an **om del bosc**, i.e. a 'man of the forest', a putative uncouth and wild person. The very fact that people like this man are described as wild because still attached to their own land and farmstead or because they work in the forest poses some questions: for example, why such people are considered 'marginal' or *selvatici*, given that most of the inhabitants of the valley used to engage in agro-pastoral activities until the 1970s. 'The thing is', Federico (b. 1963) said, 'people are no longer used to the smell of dung. Look at (…): she is a handsome girl, and she is not yet married. But who wants to get married to a **bacána**?'[30] In a sense, this also represents a response to the negative traits attached from the outside: by attaching a stigma to another village, social actors are simply 'orientalising' it, in Said's terms (1978), and in doing so they get rid of the stigma of backwardness which is projected on the whole valley from the outside.

All this seems consistent with Ardener's ideas (1989b) about the perception of differences according to which each society (or dominant group) employs a specific system of categorisation. Noncommunication and perceived wildness, for instance, are all characteristics that place a person or group at the margin of society. In rural society, as Ardener notes (1989b: 131), 'the anomaly is experienced as a feature of the "wild", for the "wild" is a metaphor of the non-social…' However, in Caoria the anomaly is Janus-faced, for a stigmatised identity may be identified as a source both of power and rejection. In this case it may be seen as a fleeing from the bureaucratic control of the state, an escape to the wild margins, where communities and societies may be formed anew (Kapferer 1995: 83). What has been said so far poses a number of questions. Although stereotypes portray characters as fixed, simple and unambiguous, they may be manipulated, and the same applies to labels attached from outside. For the people of Canal San Bovo, behaving like an urban dweller may be a symbol of prestige, but for the Caorian who works the soil this may be a marker of moral corruption. The same applies to the notion of 'bear', a stigma attached to Caorians which may instead convey ideas of moral integrity. In Caoria, being 'wild' may mean being a 'true' Caorian: it is not purely coincidence that every year on new year's eve Caorians burn a straw bear in the centre of the village, a celebration of local identity. So, the meanings that 'wild' takes on are the result of an ongoing process of negotiation between a dominant discourse and a local counterdiscourse.

Thus, there are different notions of 'modernity' in each village of the valley, each being highly village-centric. The imposition of 'modernity' from above, in the case of the Vanoi valley, has the counter-effect of creating other views of 'modernity', which may be alternative and opposed to the 'official' one. However, this notion is historically contingent, and there are in turn various levels of 'modernity' in each village community, as has been seen. Such is the example of the conceptual opposition between those living in the village and the 'wild' ones residing at its very edge.

The world outside the valley is viewed and represented in different and complex ways, and is usually associated with the city. The oppositional relationship between the community and the city became strong during the last thirty years as a consequence of depopulation, when several farmsteads in the valley were sold to urban dwellers of other regions, and turned into weekend dwellings. One of the consequences of this transformation is a shared conviction that the strangers who visit the village do so to acquire land and houses and to deprive the community of its own land. The representation of city dwellers and the relationship between the valley and the outside became the subject of the plays which were performed at the theatre in Ronco between 1975 and 1994.[31] These mirror widely shared views about strangers, and city dwellers in particular. No plays were performed after 1994. The negative traits that such plays projected on urban dwellers served to ridicule them and make fun of the 'spoiled' urban way of life in an attempt to question official views of 'modernity'. The play entitled ***En malghèr***[32] makes this point very clearly. It is about tourists from different parts of Italy and abroad, who decide to spend part of their holidays in the Trentine Alps in the summer pastures. It must be noted that the buildings in the high pastures which house herders during the grazing season are often available to trekkers, who can have accommodation for free or for a very affordable price. However, such buildings are not exactly like hotels, and anyone who stops by has to adjust him/herself to a place which is not always clean and comfortable.

The play was in the local dialect, and was performed in the theatre in Ronco just once in 1975, during Carnival. It was put on by the village priest and the youths of Ronco, and attracted a local audience of about 100 people, as many as the theatre could contain. The actors represented two distinct categories of people: the local herdsmen who look after livestock, and the educated urban dwellers of southern Italy. Among them there were also some tourists from Trentino and Germany, who did not play an important role. Most of the play focuses on the contrast between the two main categories, the 'simple' herder and the two 'civilised' urban dwellers from Naples. These, in particular, wear expensive clothes, silk neckties, and carry a big suitcase. When these people get to the *malga*,[33] they complain to the herder, with a thick southern accent, about the lack of a liftchair to take them there. What is even more significant is that these people hold a small red horn, which in Naples and most of southern Italy is believed to keep bad luck at bay. In the play this serves to represent the urban people as more superstitious than the rural ones. The man running the *malga*, by contrast, is portrayed as very humble, but very honest and helpful: he embodies all the good qualities of the countryside, among which is that of 'hard worker'.

Unlike the herder, the southern tourists (who, in the valley, are referred to as the people of 'lower' Italy) often have arguments, and do not seem to adjust themselves to the place. Implicit is also the contrast between different perceptions of the landscape, that is to say between the romantic view of the mountains that the two men hold and that of the **malghèr** who works there three months a year, and has to endure the hardships of pastoral life. Eventually, although these two people do not manage to adjust themselves, it is the humble **malghèr** who solves all the problems and settles the quarrels. It is evident that the play was also meant as the representation of the contrast between the rustic way of life of the local people and that of the city dwellers (but also between workers and nonworkers), who endeavour to look more 'civilised', but turn out to be otherwise.

The performance as an event asserts common identity, at the same time as it emphasises difference between 'insiders' and 'outsiders'. Other plays stressed this contrast more overtly. One of these, 'The Judge', is about an outsider brought to trial, accused of having stolen mushrooms from the communal land and of having trespassed across private property boundaries without permission to do so. This play well expresses widely shared views about outsiders[34] who show no respect for private property and, worst of all, 'steal' the natural resources that 'rightfully' belong to the village community, and when it was staged it was enthusiastically received by those who attended. While it seems certain that some outsiders actually picked mushrooms without permission, it is also reasonable to believe that the stranger brought to trial was a sort of scapegoat, for he was depicted as the cause of the fate of the valley. This image is hardly new. A man of Ronco, now in his fifties, said that before the arrival of strangers, Ronco was a united and harmonious community: although quarrels among its inhabitants occasionally occurred, there was not the selfishness that is so widespread these days. The unity of the village, he added, was symbolised by the absence of demarcation lines between the landholdings; according to him, this is no longer the case, for when strangers came the first thing they did was to fence their newly acquired landholdings. In his view, the presence of fences symbolises the internal divisions and the moral decline of the village, thereby implying that such divisions have been brought from the outside.

There obviously are discrepancies between what informants said and actuality, for divisions in the village were old stories long before the arrival of tourists, as already noted earlier in the present work. Clearly, the ideas of the above man reflected the imagery of a 'united' community opposed to a 'divided' world outside, which is largely idealised. However commonsensical this may seem, this mirrors one of the main concerns of the local people, that of property, and the idea that social divisions are the outcome of intrusions. As already noted, fragmentation of landholdings is the result of a system of partible inheritance, and has little to do with outsiders. Nowadays this excessive fragmentation is perceived and spoken of as a sign of the community's moral decline, particularly as a sign of growing individualism.

Different and sometimes contrasting ways of thinking and talking about 'modernity' seem to coexist. The waves of emigration that brought about depopulation in the valley suggest that urban ways of life were yearned-after models for those who decided to leave the valley for an urban centre in the post-war period and after. However, for those who chose to remain there 'modernity' may not have the same meaning, it may be resisted and, as has been seen, even manipulated. What unites attitudes towards 'modernity' is the production of a counterdiscourse or, rather, the appropriation of the concept. So, for example, by attaching the stigma of 'backward' or 'uncouth' to the inhabitants of Caoria or Ronco the inhabitants of Canal San Bovo get rid of a stereotype that is projected on the valley from the outside. In doing so, they subscribe to 'modernity' as an ideology about town life, and so do the stigmatised who project the stigma on someone else. In the end, subscribing to it involves pushing the stigma to the margins. It is the manipulation of the stigma to the advantage of the stigmatised which enables instead social actors to develop a counterdiscourse, and to reformulate meanings. Rusticity may convey ideas of strength in the same manner that being strong is functional to the protection of one's domain, as we have seen. However, claims to strength do not always derive from being 'local', but may involve blending locality with ethnicity. I turn to this issue in the next section.

'We' and the 'Italians'

In '*The Hidden Frontier*' (1974), now a 'classic' in Alpine anthropology, Cole and Wolf analysed cultural differences between two Alpine villages in the Val di Non, a valley crossing the administrative boundary between Trentino and South Tyrol. These villages lie in two different provinces (Trentino and South Tyrol) and speak two different languages (Italian and German), in spite of the fact that they are scarcely two kilometres from each other. The investigation of cultural differences led the authors to the conclusion that ethnicity is a political tool. Yet the cultural contrast that they found in their fieldsites was seen as the outcome of the villages' interaction with different wider economic, political and ideological fields. So, for example, the authors stressed that, unlike the German-speaking village, a rhetoric of urbanness features centrally in local discourse among the inhabitants of the Italian-speaking community. This was shown by the fact that for the Italian speakers the ideal life is not on the land, but in the city (1974: 281).[35] In other words, the Trentine village was ascribed the characteristics that were deemed typical of the Mediterranean, where the countryside had been culturally and politically subordinated to the city, and where it was expected that country people would abandon rural life if only they could (Cole 1985: 14–15).

Even their analysis posits the existence of 'modernity' spreading from urban centres throughout the country, and setting up behavioural patterns to be emulated by everybody. Although it cannot be inferred that the inhabitants of the valley, in Caoria at least, reject 'modernity' altogether, it may be suggested that, unlike the case study mentioned above, being (or declaring oneself as) a peasant is a constituent part of being Caorian that is not necessarily abhorred. If I were to make a comparison between the villages analysed by the above scholars, I would be tempted to suggest that Caoria seems more similar to the German-speaking village investigated by Cole and Wolf than to the Italian one, as for those who decided to remain in (or to come back to) the valley the ideal life seems to be in the countryside, and not in the city. So, the contrast found between Trentino and the outside, not being built on linguistic differences, poses the question of how far the nation-state actually encompasses the periphery in terms of values. The electoral success of the Northern League and of the Trentine-Tyrolean Autonomist Party (PATT) in the elections in the valley (especially in Caoria) in the 1990s, and the subsequent attempt to establish an Autonomous European Region Tyrol (Euregio) crosscutting national boundaries, seem to show that the nation-state is not always perceived as a repository of 'modernity'. Moreover, sociological research conducted in the mid-1990s in various municipalities in Trentino showed that over 40 percent of the inhabitants of Trentino look upon themselves as closer to the German-speaking people of South Tyrol in terms of 'culture' and values than to the inhabitants of the nearby Italian-speaking regions (Gubert 1997: 475–6). This turned out to be more obvious in rural areas than in urban settings.

As I said in the introductory chapter, the proposed establishment of a Tyrolean European Region raised the issue of regional (or ethnic) identity in an area that had long been identified as Italian in opposition to its German-speaking neighbours. It is outside the scope of this work to discuss in detail the economic implications of the establishment of the above region; suffice it to say, for now, that the project was aimed at the creation of a coherent transit area linking two powerful economic zones, Lombardy in northern Italy, and the Danubian basin of southern Germany. For Trentino this would have meant avoiding being swallowed up, economically speaking, by a large Veneto region (Alcock

1996: 83). However, in order to legitimate the establishment of a large Tyrolean region it was also necessary to create a regional consciousness. Clearly, the huge gathering of Trentine autonomists organised by the PATT on 29 October 1995 affected to a significant extent people's sense of belonging, through a celebration of common cultural traits between Trentino, South Tyrol and the Austrian Tyrol.[36] This emphasis was related to an important change that occurred in South Tyrol in 1992, when it was admitted that the Italians residing there could call themselves South Tyroleans (Luverà 1996: 33), even those unable to speak German. While until the early 1990s the ability to speak German and the local German dialects was central to the definition of who is a South Tyrolean, in 1992 such a notion involved the acknowledgement of the coexistence of two ethnic groups: anybody who lives in South Tyrol is South Tyrolean, irrespective of the ethnic group he or she belongs to. Paradoxically, in 1995 celebrating a regional culture also meant stressing distinctiveness vis-à-vis the Italian regions south of the regional border. This had some repercussions in the Vanoi valley, too.

In fact the fieldworker coming to the valley for the first time soon becomes aware of the distinction villagers make between themselves and those coming from far away, from the rest of Italy in particular, even though the language spoken is the same. This sense of distinctiveness can be noticed in most rural communities; however, in the area studied it may take on an 'ethnic' flavour too, for the term used to address those of the urban world outside Trentino is *'taliáni* ('Italians'). The statement **andòn in Italia** ('let us go to Italy') is still heard when villagers go to Feltre for shopping. When I went to the valley for exploratory fieldwork, in the summer of 1992, most of the villagers I came across addressed me as the 'Italian'. This was all the more striking, as Caorians speak Italian (and the local Italian dialect) as mother tongue, and I could not understand the difference between them and myself in terms of Italianness. It was only later that I realised that the meaning of the term extends far beyond mere philology, into culture and morality, and is used to address strangers derogatorily. An analysis of the ways the term is used reveals that it has various connotations. As a matter of fact, behavioural traits or artefacts that are not normative are dismissed on the grounds that they are *'taliáni*. The distinction between 'we' and the 'Italians' may replicate that between the countryside and the city (and also between rustic/wild and urban), but with some differences. In local discourse, Italy corresponds to the national territory south of the regional border, that is to say the pre-1918 Italian Kingdom. This is central to an understanding of local identity: pre-1918 national boundaries, North and South, Europe and the Mediterranean become lines of demarcation between 'we' and the 'Italians', between who is 'inside' and who is 'outside', and serve to construct difference. In this case, however, the outsider does not belong to a minority group, but to the larger society.

One of the favourite topics of conversation of the local people, men and women alike, is that of the 'Italians' who visit the valley in the summertime. Those who fish around the village without permission, for instance, are always alluded to as 'Italians'. This also applies to the people who go picking mushrooms and berries that 'rightfully' belong to the community. One of the stories I heard was about a man from Venice, typified as the 'Italian', who used to go fishing in the valley. If I were to take all Caorians' assertions at face value, I would be led to believe that there are no more fish in the valley because of that man. In a sense, 'Italians' are ascribed the same 'intrusive' behavioural character that in local discourse is considered typical of the state. Villagers seem uniform in their judgement that 'Italians' cannot be trusted, and in doing so they questioned the image of 'Italy' as a repository of 'modernity'. One day, for example, Giovanni (1919–98) said that 'Italians are good, but are also thieves' (*'talián l'e bon, ma ladro*). The 'Italians' are, in this case, those who come to the valley to purchase land and stables cheaply.

Even the notion of 'Italian', however, has its own contradictions: it may be tantamount to 'nonvillager' as well as a reference to whoever brings in money and buys land. The plays performed in Ronco were clearly targeted at 'Italians', and calling another villager 'You, Italian' is a common joke in the valley. However, while avoiding becoming an 'Italian' and adopting 'Italian' customs is necessary to keep membership of the community, merging into a wider population is perceived as a condition for economic success. This is the case of the son of the late mayor of the municipality, who is one of the largest landowners of Caoria (and also one of the few university graduates of the village). Most Caorians argue that his being half (or the 'typical') 'Italian' has been a decisive factor in his economic success, as his mother came from outside Trentino. Villagers' ideas about him, in this case, seem to associate both Italianness and villageness with 'class' and power: that person became wealthy because he is an 'Italian'. As already noted, the association of Italianness with 'wealth' and of villageness with 'poverty' seems to evoke, once again, the image of a village as a 'social class' that ideally reproduces itself over time. This implies that if the village is 'poor', then one has to go out of the community and turn 'Italian' (or 'urban') in order to enrich oneself. In other words, 'moving out' physically is considered tantamount to 'moving up' socially. Yet it must also be stressed that the person's being alluded to as 'Italian' is associated with his enterprising character and with his ability to appropriate a huge amount of land in and around Caoria at the expense of some covillagers; his being labelled 'Italian' may also be accounted for by his having behaved like an 'intrusive stranger', a characteristic that in local discourse is often ascribed to a putative impersonal and exploitative state. Thus, on the one hand, being addressed as an 'Italian' may be interpreted as an offence; on the other, it is an identity that certain people in the valley (especially young women) endeavour to achieve to escape a stigmatised identity. However, 'Italy' conveys ideas of moral corruption owing to the political crisis that the country was experiencing at the time of my fieldwork. As a woman of a nearby valley once told me, 'We are very Italian here, but now Italy is no good'.

Italianness is tantamount to 'modernity' as long as it is a condition for economic success: becoming rich is conditional on becoming an 'Italian' first, as the above example has shown. By contrast, wildness may be alternative to 'modernity', especially in opposition to the covillagers who try to behave like urban dwellers. Yet ideas about an alternative 'modernity' also rest on the fact that when the valley was subjected to Austro-Hungarian sovereignty education was mandatory, whereas in Italy illiteracy was very widespread. The Caorians who fought in the Italian army during the last World War pride themselves on the fact that *they* taught Italians to read and write; such claims to distinctiveness from the Italian state also draw on the conviction that the inhabitants of the valley have cultivated their own fields since time immemorial, whereas in the nearby Italian-speaking regions working the land owned by large landowners was widespread until the aftermath of the Second World War. Villagers' claims to moral superiority, in this case, are considered legitimated by history, and according to them rest on education and ownership of land. The education they pride themselves on is, as I said above, that of pre-1918 Austria-Hungary. Nowadays the level of educational achievement is one of the lowest in the province and, from an 'objectivist' point of view, ownership of land does not represent a symbol of 'civilisation' owing to its fragmentation. If anything, it may be suggested that it is a symbol of emancipation, of independence from large landowners, rather than one of wealth.[37] It also represents a claim that before the arrival of the 'Italians' the valley had a moral integrity, an idea that permeates much of village thinking and particularly representations of history, as will be seen in the next chapter.

All my informants, irrespective of age and gender, are well aware that they are not Austrians, for they never spoke German, nor has German ever become the official language in the valley. Some of those who temporarily emigrated to Germany or Switzerland in the 1960s to pursue manual and ancillary jobs know some German, but this does not mean that they can speak the language correctly. Nowadays German is taught in national secondary and high schools throughout the regional territory. School children between eleven and fourteen years of age know some basic German, not because they have a chance to learn it from their parents, but because it is a compulsory subject at school. If anything, recent experiences of the local people with German are cited as evidence that this is an altogether foreign language. So, for example, some of the Caorians I met vividly remember what happened during a day trip spent in Innsbruck, an Austrian town not far from the Italian border, in the 1970s. The story goes that a man needed to buy Austrian currency, but he did not know how to do it, because he could not speak a word of German. One of his covillagers volunteered to help him, on the grounds that he considered himself able to communicate in the language. Eventually it turned out that even this person could not speak German: the women at the counter of the bank where they went could not understand a word of what this man was trying to say, and advised him to express himself in Italian instead, which is widely spoken in that town. This story is sometimes cited as evidence that in the village there is little or no familiarity with that language. It is not just coincidence that in Caoria the statement 'You speak German' (*ti parli todésc*) usually means 'You speak an incomprehensible language', something nobody is able to understand.

In spite of their lack of familiarity with the language, they present themselves as an 'Austrian' breed' (*ratha austriaca*). Some Caorians, for example, take pride in appealing to their Austro-Hungarian ancestry in the presence of a *'talián*, especially in the local bars on Sunday morning. Categories such as 'Italian' and 'Austrian' do not necessarily convey ideas of ethnolinguistic identity, at least at the local level. Taking a hint from McDonald's Breton case study (1986: 341), it may be suggested that descent from a *ratha austriaca* does not involve a commitment to language learning, but a biological model of kinship, and particularly a notion of ancestry. So, it is not negotiable. One intriguing aspect, already hinted at in chapter 3, is that while ideas of distinctiveness are shared by virtually all the informants I interviewed, insistence on the village's partaking of a 'Tyrolean' culture seems to be heralded by the men of the valley who are (or were) employed as manual workers, or by the members of the hunt club.[38] By contrast, the women I talked with showed very little or no interest in this issue. This would validate one of the points made in the same chapter, particularly the observation that 'locality' is a notion that figures centrally in 'male' discourse, for the assertion of local identity implies confrontation with the outside.

At the time of my fieldwork the active supporters of the Trentine-Tyrolean Autonomist Party in Caoria used to wear the South Tyrolean green jacket, a marker of Tyrolean identity which has the same function that the kilt has in Scottish culture. The blue apron worn when doing agricultural chores is another such symbol. Yet commitment to the Tyrolean (and Austro-Hungarian) legacy was expressed in various ways. One day, for example, I happened to meet a hunter of Caoria, and I greeted him by saying 'Good morning' in Italian (*buongiorno*); the other jokingly replied with the remark 'Here we say *"morgen"*', that is, 'Good morning' in German (even though this never happens). Also, in Caoria one cannot help noticing the postcards portraying the Austro-Hungarian emperor Franz Josef that are displayed in some of the bars, or the stickers carrying the emblem of the Dual Monarchy. The fact that various informants proudly showed me photographs of their ancestors wearing the uniform during military service in the Austro-Hungarian army is also a case in point. A few years ago some members of the local hunt club attempted to establish a group of Schützen[39] in Caoria, in spite of the fact that in the past such groups were the cornerstone of interethnic Tyrolean autonomy (Poppi 1991: 582), and there is no evidence that they existed in the province of Trent. Eventually the group was created notwithstanding its strict rules based on hierarchy which would clash with the ideals of equality and resistance to authority. It seems reasonable to believe that it was not so much commitment to the values championed by the group that was the reason for its proposed establishment, as the necessity to appropriate some symbols of distinctiveness from South Tyrol and, as a Caorian said, 'to remember the ancestors'.

Although terms such as 'modernity' and 'tradition' (just like West and non-West) have been deployed to describe the relationship between the 'national' and the 'local', this simple dichotomy hides the complex (and, in a sense, subtle) discourses that social actors use in the construction of group identity. Rather, the data just discussed suggest that a distinction between 'North' and 'South', 'Europe' and the 'Mediterranean' is drawn in discussing the traits that define local 'identity' and in contesting the legitimacy of the nation-state. Delanty (1996: 100–3) argued that this notion of Europe (or Mitteleuropa) is equivalent to 'antipolitics', as it affirms the autonomy of society against the state. This distinction seems in tune with the idea that northern Italy (and Trentino in particular) partakes of a 'European culture' as opposed to a 'Mediterranean' or 'southern' one, which was central to the rhetoric of the Northern League and, to a certain extent, of the Trentine-Tyrolean Autonomist Party as well.[40] This rhetoric was in turn expressed by the former's emphasis on the idea of a 'hard-working' northern Italy[41] and by the latter's insistence on unbroken history with the German-speaking South Tyrol. Their appeal to hard work as a marker of distinctiveness was well received in a social setting in which this idea, alongside that of self-sufficiency, permeates local discourse to a large extent. Caorian men look to pre-1918 Tyrol for the values of rural society that are no longer taken for granted, such as the hard work ethic and especially the 'independence' of the village.

While the idea of a 'European' Tyrolean region crosscutting national boundaries took on a specific meaning for the politicians, intellectuals and entrepreneurs who championed it, the same did not hold true for those who experienced 'Europe' in a different way, that is to say in familiar terms: it was not so much political, abstract ideologies that were at stake, as very simple concepts, among which 'hard work', as opposed to 'modernity' as an ideology about town life, is probably the most powerful. In this case the idea of 'Europe' was filtered and mediated by that of a 'region' or 'locality' which embodies the values of a putative hard-working North. This one, in turn, was perceived as the moral opposite of the South symbolised by the 'intrusive' nation-state, and claims to Europeanness were made to stress the valley's (and region's) morality that the nation-state was seen as lacking. So, the uses which were made of the idea of 'Europe' show how questions of local identity itself (or of *campanilismo*) may take on an ethnic flavour when distinctiveness is at stake. This situation is reminiscent of what Heady (1999: 210) found in the Carnic Alps, where distinctiveness is built upon a hierarchy of segmentation extending from the family to the regions of Italy which are seen as embodying certain values, particularly self-sufficiency and ability to sustain hard work. However, identifying with a region can hardly enable social actors to sustain the symbolic confrontation with the rest of Italy. Appealing to Europe and to a Germanic world does instead provide moral coordinates to sustain such a confrontation, because the association with Europe evokes images of efficiency and economic success. In a sense, such an idea enables people to reconcile their appeal to tradition and their claims to autonomy, and particularly to legitimate the claim that autonomous hard work, a necessary condition for economic success in the age of late modernity, has long been a constituent part of local 'culture'.

Conclusion

The ethnographic material discussed in this chapter raised the question of how far the social order propagated by élites and the Italian state is actually accepted. Clearly, the categorical system of local communities reflects typifications of 'otherness' emanating from above (Herzfeld 1997: 157), which cast 'modernity' as a model to be yearned after. Yet taking this model for granted does not do justice to the ways in which alternative notions of 'modernity' are developed 'from below' as a response to state encroachment, on the one hand, and to come to terms with 'Europeanisation', on the other. Casting the Italian state as the 'other' and appealing to wildness represent two responses. Wildness, in particular, turns into a 'civilisation turned upside down' that serves to question the legitimacy of formal hierarchies and the élite's image of a just social order through the manipulation of meanings at the 'lower' levels of society. So, 'modernity' is not given once and for all. In local discourse it does not necessarily represent an ideology about town life, and does not always require the appreciation of the national 'culture'. Rather, it seems to function as a legitimising discourse (not to say a tool) that can be used by different people in different situations for different ends.[42] It was appropriated and manipulated to tie to a particular identity and question aspects of nationhood such as encompassment and domination.

The 'modernity' of which the Italian state was seen as the embodiment emerged as a matter of contestation. However, this contestation was not mere nostalgia, and did not entail replacing the dominant discourse with a 'local' one. Rather, it called into play the hegemonic as well as the 'local': while it is a local discourse that stresses wildness in opposition to 'modernity', it is the dominant, environmentalist discourse, central to the official image of Trentino, that places considerable emphasis on this 'state of nature'. Likewise, the idea of hard work was central to the representations of Trentine people in the rhetoric of autonomist parties. So, the local discourse is not autonomous to the hegemonic one. In a sense, turning 'modernity' upside down represents a form of making do, a way of creating cultural meanings and situations: social actors did not contest 'modernity' as a notion, but mainly reformulated its meanings in response to a changing political and economic situation, and blended it with ethnicity.[43]

Both 'wildness' and appeal to a 'European' or 'Tyrolean' culture were resorted to in an attempt to question 'modernity' as an ideology about town life, and to cast the local community as 'autonomous'. On the one hand, appealing to an (idealised) autonomy is a political act, as it is functional to the retreat from social into group identity that seems to characterise the era of late modernity (Hobsbawm 1992: 5); on the other hand, autonomy points to the emergence of the image of the self-reliant individual recorded elsewhere in the Alps, which is the result of the weakening of the social bonds that tie communities together (Bendix 1985: 77). Yet this image does not obliterate the past, but engenders instead a worldview caught between the values of the community and individualism. Representations of history illustrate this aspect very well, as will be seen in the next chapter.

NOTES

1. The military police.
2. The municipality or *comune* (commune) is the smallest administrative unit in Italy.
3. The region Trentino-South Tyrol has retained some laws which date from Austro-Hungarian times, especially those which regulate the use of land and natural resources.
4. In Italy the term is taken in its pejorative sense. As a rule one does not call oneself *campanilista.*
5. The same author (1980: 43) argues that the ideology of nationalism shares many of the characteristics of *campanilismo*, as the former may be a 'transposition of the ideology of local sub-national identities'.
6. See, for a discussion of this idea, Tak (1990: 90) and Heady (1999).
7. See for a comparison Christian (1972: 101).
8. In 1969 the magazine of the local clergy, '*Voci di Primiero*', published a short article entitled 'Campanilismo' about the *comune* of Canal San Bovo. The article was meant as an attempt to provide an interpretation of the phenomenon in the valley. It is not very clear whether it expressed the people's or the writer's views. In this case *campanilismo* is taken in the pejorative meaning, and not simply as attachment to one's own place. According to the author, there are eight factors that bring about *campanilismo* in the valley: the people's inability 'to get out of their own field' and the frequent quarrels over property boundaries; the high number of villages in a highly diversified environment; widespread mistrust amongst people; refusal to exchange ideas; the leading role of certain families in some villages; uneven allocation of natural resources; the valley's division into various parishes; the power of the elderly who inculcate certain ideas into the young people.
9. The inhabitants of the Belluno province.
10. This phenomenon is analysed in more detail in the previous chapter.
11. Apparently there are similar other stories in the ethnographic literature on the Alps.
12. This was also interpreted as a device to resist changes and innovations from outside. The limited availability of land in mountain ecosystems has probably been another important factor (Burns 1963: 145–8; Viazzo 1989: 276).
13. There were also opposing groups of youngsters within the communities themselves.
14. Dobrowolski (1971: 294) provides ethnographic evidence of this for rural Poland, and so does Peters (1972: 120) for Wales.
15. As a rule the axe was old and worn out, so as to make the task more difficult.
16. '*Three Bells of Civilization. The Life of an Italian Hill Town*' (1975), by Silverman, is a detailed exploration of the uses of this concept in a central Italian village. As the first case study that built a theory on this, it has exercised much influence on anthropological studies on Italy since its publication. However, instead of the term 'modernity' the author makes use of *civiltá*/civilisation. Her analysis centres on the view that 'civilisation' is an ideology about town life. According to her, elements of *civiltá*/civilisation describe élite behaviour and élite values that include: command of the written language; familiarity with the idiom of government; and appreciation of formal culture. *Civiltá* is based on an élite way of life (1975: 105), spreads from the centre to the periphery, and the people of the periphery might claim 'civilisation' and urbanity as cultural attributes of the centre to be yearned after. It is interpreted as a fluid ideology that is manipulated and often recast by certain groups in pursuit of their interests. In her analysis 'civilisation' is assumed to come from 'above' and to be developed from the local élite. However, unlike central Italy, in the Vanoi valley, as in most of the Italian Alps, there is no élite whose economic power is based on landownership, probably because agriculture has never been a business for profit to the same extent that it is in the nearby lowlands, and so it never attracted the interests of large landowners.

17. Rich people, large landowners. The dialect term is the equivalent of the Italian *signori*.
18. In fact this also applies to those who work in the power station outside Caoria. The opening of the power station in the 1960s was a chance for a few Caorians to undertake a manual job without working in the fields or looking after animals, and represented an opportunity for them to raise themselves above their covillagers.
19. As a rule these were families of politicians.
20. Rough and uncouth people. In Italy this term is normally used to refer to country people.
21. As in most communities, in Caoria and Ronco it is quite rare to address one another by one's own name, but it is instead customary to use one's nickname. This is especially true of the Mediterranean area, notably in villages with extensively shared surnames.
22. There is a local dictum that runs that the people of Castello Tesino are so smart, that one of them is tantamount to seven of Canal San Bovo.
23. Underlying Pratt's and Silverman's interpretations of *campanilismo* is their emphasis on the town as a centre of 'civilisation', and the view that 'civilisation' itself is an ideology about an urban way of life to be yearned after. Although this certainly applies to the situation they found in central Italy, it does not seem to hold up in the eastern Alps. In other words, the above scholars seem to imply that there is a hierarchy that is taken for granted, but do not take into account the social actors' views, nor do they allow for the fact that there may develop their own notion of 'civilisation', alternative and conceptually opposed to the 'official' one: while being 'rustic' may be a negative connotation, it may also be positive.
24. This is consistent with what Goffman (1968: 172) wrote about so-called 'social deviants', who 'often feel that they are not merely equal to but better than normals, and that the life they lead is better than that lived by the persons they would otherwise be'.
25. This would run counter to the idea of wildness and resistance to authority.
26. This holds up in a community such as Caoria that places very great emphasis on the achievement of manhood. However, although the church hierarchy in the valley is male, most of the religious activities (including church attendance on Sunday morning) are carried out by women, and give religious practice a 'feminine' cast. As Dubisch (1991: 42) noted, this has been found in other parts of the northern shore of the Mediterranean.
27. See, for a comparison, Sutton's study of a Greek island (1994: 247).
28. More on this in chapter 3.
29. The story was published in the magazine '*Voci di Primiero*' in 1966.
30. The term **bacán** refers to the owner of a large number of livestock. Nowadays it connotes backwardness.
31. I did not attend any of the performances, but I was able to get hold of the texts, and watch some of the videos and slides that were made while the plays were staged.
32. This is difficult to translate, for there is not any correspondent term in English. *Malghèr* is a herder appointed by the municipal authority on a contractual basis to supervise the activities in the upper pastures during the grazing season.
33. High pasture used during the grazing season.
34. This play was not targeted at outsiders in general, but only at those of the neighbouring regions.
35. Their analysis of the Trentine village is consistent with (and predates) Silverman's view that Italian society is organised around urban centres (1975: 227).
36. Interestingly, many of the Trentini who attended the huge gathering of Trentine autonomists on 29 October 1995, at the village of Borghetto, at the southern border between Trentino and Veneto, wore the clothes that function as ethnic symbols of South Tyrol.
37. As has been seen in chapter 3, in the valley respectability is still closely entwined with property and property relations, in spite of fragmentation of landed property.

38. This is also the case of Lombardy, where the Northern League received considerable support from the members of hunt clubs, who strive to keep exclusive control of territory and oppose the establishment of natural parks.

39. Ancient paramilitary Civil Militia identified by public opinion at large with German-speaking South Tyrolean nationalism.

40. It is not coincidental that one of the slogans of the Northern League is 'away from Rome, closer to Europe'.

41. The idea of 'hard work' aimed at acquiring property was also one of the central tenets of Catholic ideology (Guizzardi 1976: 199–202).

42. See Argyrou's Cypriot case study (1996) for a discussion of 'modernity' as a legitimising discourse.

43. The flexible, changeable and situationally adaptive nature of the 'ethnic' identity analysed is partly reminiscent of Barth's notion (1969) of ethnic identity (but see also Leach 1954), even though his notion would not do justice to the situation of the Vanoi valley and Trentino.

13. Electoral poster: Tyrol, pathway to Europe.

14. Electoral poster: 1945–1995, 50 years of Autonomy.

15. Memory of the Great War..

16. Men of Ronco wearing the Austro-Hungarian
uniform during the Great War.

17. Local pride: 'I am from Trentino.'

18. Bumper stickers: 'Yes, I am an Autonomist' and 'I am a hunter.'

6
NATURAL TIME, POLITICAL TIME: REPRESENTATIONS OF HISTORY

Introduction

This chapter is an attempt to illuminate the question of how the past is represented among the inhabitants of the valley, and sets out to explore the relationship between representations of history and local identity. The starting point of this investigation was the discovery of the existence of a conceptualisation of local history that seems at odds with 'official' views. I became interested in this issue when I realised that all narrations of the past of the valley dwell on the same events, that all the people I interacted with draw a clear-cut line between the past itself (*'sti ani*) and the present (*'ncói*), and seem to place very much emphasis on the former as a frame of reference.

My focus, in this chapter, is mainly on the articulation between local and national history, and on how the political changes of the 1990s affected the ways social actors represent their local history. Constructing a local history often implies symbolic confrontation with an encompassing state, for central to the definition of the state is the idea of a territory that contains citizens both physically and symbolically. The spatial discourse of citizenship is articulated with a temporal one, in that the state's being the embodiment of legitimate political power is also conditional on its management of historical narratives (Shapiro 2000: 80). Friedman (1992: 837) noted that

'The construction of a past …is a project that selectively organises events in a relation of continuity with a contemporary subject, thereby creating an appropriated representation of life leading up to the present, that is, a life history fashioned in the

act of self-definition. …The construction of a history is the construction of a meaningful universe of events and narratives for an individual or collectively defined subject'.

Thus, Nation-states locate themselves in identity-producing narratives by
imposing univocal models of temporality. If we take on board the idea that such
a model of temporality is a kind of 'commodity' produced by the powerful and
superimposed (Davis 1989: 116), we will also have to allow for the existence of
'other times' that may question the relation between the past and present state
of affairs that making national history involves: but how are these times represented, and how do they relate to the accounts purveyed by the nation-state?
Anthropologists' focus on 'other times' has a long story, and it is outside the
scope of this work to explore it in detail. Suffice it to say, for now, that anthropologists have continually emphasised the difference between 'modern' and 'traditional' societies by constructing an opposition between different their time
perceptions (Adam 1994: 504). They have been describing Western societies as
having a social reading of time, which means that it is perceived as linear and
irreversible. By contrast, non-Western and pre-industrial societies have been
associated with an idea of time as natural, which involves that it is perceived as
cyclical and repetitive. Central to Lévi-Strauss's (1973) distinction between
Western (hot) and non-Western (cold) societies, for example, was the view that
the former represent the past as being abstract, linear and driven by events,
whereas the latter emphasise the repetitiveness of time and abolish eventuality.[1]
The polarisation between cyclical and linear time has been criticised on various grounds,[2] and it has recently been argued that the continued characterisa-
tion of whole societies as having either linear or cyclical ideas about the past
'impoverishes our understanding of different attitudes toward the past that
occur cross-culturally' (Sutton 1998: 2). The postulated unsustainability of the
above polarisation went hand in hand with anthropologists' growing interest in
the content of disputed histories in an attempt to challenge official, dominant
versions of the past (Sutton 1998: 3); especially in the study of Europe, anthropologists have paid much attention to the way in which memories are constructed around political contests,[3] with the result that they have shied away
from an analysis of perceptions of 'time', and have instead focused on 'history'.
If I were to take the above critiques at face value, there would be grounds for
inferring that labelling a society as 'cyclical' is part of the process through which
a society is 'orientalised', in Said's terms (1978): in other words, if the distinction between natural and social time is not sustainable, we will have to assume
that societies' self-representation as 'cyclical' is purely a Western 'invention'. Yet
while this dichotomy may represent a Western construct, accepting its unsustainability would blind us to the meanings social actors attach to it, and to its
current uses in everyday life. That a social group talks about its past by placing
emphasis on the repetitiveness of events does not entail that time is perceived as

repetitive but, rather, raises the issue of whether this is the way time is represented. In my analysis I pursue instead the idea that a study on images of time should not so much focus on perception, as on representation, and on the multiple meanings that such representations convey to social actors. In suggesting this, I follow Thapar (1996: 44), who stresses the necessity of enquiring how a society uses a particular category of time, and what is being intended by that use.

Making Sense of a Sequence

The study of representations of history is a task of both reconstruction and translation: it is a reconstruction because informants draw selectively upon a shared storehouse of knowledge; it is a translation because the raw data the researcher ends up analysing is in fact constituted by a wide range of narratives and stories that had to be made sense of and contextualised within the social and cultural structures with which the researcher is concerned (Strathern 1984b: 7). In a sense, researchers have to draw attention 'both to the ways in which people assert control over the meanings of "local events" and to the embedding of the "local" in the wider, translocal context' (Roseman 1996: 852).

The considerations that follow are based on the recollection of informants born between 1904 and 1968. The construction of history is treated primarily as a social, rather than an individual, experience, and the focus is on the events nearly all informants recall or talk about. During my fieldwork I neither conducted a specific study of the perception of the past, nor did I make use of patterned questionnaires, mainly because in the conversations in which I engaged the past is constantly appealed to as a frame of reference. In this chapter I analyse the use of history as a set of narratives of localism, and I look at the meanings attached to significant events as a reflection of both 'partial accommodation and resistance to externally imposed material conditions and cultural meanings' (Roseman 1996: 836). The accounts of the past I solicited seem to provide an image of the community, rather than a simple historical account, in which the village becomes the locus of memory and a focus of identification, and ultimately a repository of moral values. The geographic space of the community, in particular, becomes symbolically opposed to the 'anonymous' one of the nation-state that lies around it.[4] This village-centred attitude suggests that 'the most powerful element is the memory of the community in opposition to the outside world, which is a reinforcement of its own social identity in opposition to that of others' (Fentress and Wickham 1992: 114).

In considering the symbolic construction of history at the local level, I was confronted with the ways in which narratives are constructed around events of different kinds. However, narratives have also produced the image of a society in which things 'have always been done this way'.[5] Zonabend's criticised view (1984) of Lévi-Straussian matrix, that in peasant society great value is placed upon the potential of the repetitiveness of time[6] instituted by a series of rituals of community was the starting point of my analysis. Although the idea that rural society has a notion of circular time and does not construct an image of history seems questionable, ideas of linear and circular time do not necessarily contradict each other.[7] Repetitive time in rural society, epitomised by the seasonal cycle, is not simply an abstract idea: in the case of the valley it is an objective truth. If anything, the issue is to disclose the kind of discourse that the idea of repetitive time implies.

In the case of Caoria I attempted to make sense of a sequence of events (both mythical and historical) that are recounted by virtually everyone in the village. Such recollections are personal, concerned with the person's own self, and are also social, as the overwhelming majority of the people I talked with recall or talk about the same historical events. If I were to reconstruct and summarise the history of Caoria as recounted by its inhabitants, it would be a relatively simple task. As Nives (b. 1957) once said, 'in the old days there were the bears' (*'sti ani ghe n'era i orsi*), until someone slew the last one;[8] then the First World War broke out; finally, the flood of 1966 put an end to the story (but somebody added 'Then came the "Italians", the *foresti*').[9]

The past as an ideal source of identity for a peasant (and even post-peasant) society is mirrored in the myth of origins. In the village of Caoria the killing of the last bear is doubtless a sort of myth of origins, a story that was told so many times that now there seems to be no 'true' version: its salient feature is timelessness, as it happened *'sti ani*, but nobody knows exactly when.[10] Suffice it to say, for now, that the event is relevant as it signified man's appropriation of nature. There is a significant narrative void between the above story and the First World War, even though there is evidence that the period between the mid-nineteenth century and the outbreak of the conflict was characterised by waves of emigration abroad. Nearly all the villagers I met vividly 'remember' the First World War, despite the obvious fact that most of them did not live through it. Their interest in it is also affected by the commemorative ceremonies that take place in the valley on a regular basis.

As already stated in chapter 2, Caoria, as the only village on the Front, remained evacuated for about three years after the arrival of the Italian army, whereas the evacuation of Ronco and of the other villages in the valley lasted about four months. Unlike the killing of the last bear, now a timeless event whose significance lies in the change that it brought about, the First World War marks the moment when experienced history begins, and when time reckoning becomes precise. It is also when locals acquired a sense of distinctiveness vis-à-vis the 'Italians'. As Domenica (b. 1913) said, 'The border was here... We have always been speaking Italian. I do not know why I cannot speak a word of German even though we were under the Germans.[11] They [the Italians] fought the war and conquered us'. The evacuation and the long-standing stay of the people of Caoria in camps for evacuees in Lower Austria and in northern and central Italy posed the problem of national identity very dramatically. As the above person put it, 'I was a foreigner in Italy: they used to call us *todéschi*... They talk so much about Austria. It was not that great, there was so much poverty'. The evacuation of Caoria, in particular, is remembered by the few who are still alive as a coerced division of the village (Palla 1994: 173), as a displacement of the community.[12]

The idea that 'We were between Italians and Austrians' or *tra 'taliáni e todéschi* (Margherita, 1904–2002) partly explains why nowadays several informants imply that while they may declare themselves Italians, they also descend from a *ratha austriaca*. This idea is shared not just by those who experienced the war and deportation, but also by the young people (especially men), and generally by those who did not live through it. Nowadays those who learned about Austria-Hungary from their parents or grandparents seem to share the opinion that it was good to be Austrians because education was compulsory.[13] Giuseppe (b. 1930), for example, made this point very clearly in the course of a conversation, and prided himself on the fact that his father had attended the local school under the sovereignty of the Dual Monarchy. According to him, however, it was not so much primary school attendance that mattered, as the fact that 'the more you know, the less likely you are to be given orders by someone else', which suggests an association between Austro-Hungarian times and freedom and self-determination (but not necessarily 'modernity'). This association is epitomised by the statement, 'This place used to be part of Austria (*qua l'era Austria 'sti ani*) until the Italians came', which is often heard in the valley. It is no accident that several households in the valley keep a collection of photographs of ancestors wearing the Austro-Hungarian uniform during the Great War.[14] The identification of Austro-Hungarian times with self-determination is highlighted by negative views about the arrival of the Italian mountain troops in 1916. Silvano (b. 1967) and his sister Anita (b. 1968), for example, pointed to this when they told me the story of how, at the end of the conflict, the villagers who fought in the army of the Dual Monarchy were deported to a concentration camp in Isernia, in central Italy, and remained there for two months for punishment.[15] Although their views in all likelihood reflected what they heard from their covillagers or read in books, the fact remains that they were depicting the advent of the Italians in the valley as an 'intrusion'.[16]

There are different views about the great divide between the Austrian past and the Italian present. The most relevant, as I said, is that the pre-1916 past seems associated with freedom (epitomised by the fact that nearly all villagers could read and write), whereas the post-1916 period seems associated with the idea of loss of freedom (as is the case of the villagers' deportation to Isernia), and with the enforcement of national laws. Taking a hint from Loizos's Cypriot case study (1975: 3), this suggests that the Austrian past (i.e. 'before' modern politics) is depicted as the period when villagers fought over things within their own local control, whereas after the arrival of the 'Italians' (i.e. 'after' modern politics) they had to fight over things beyond their control. Another important aspect is that the opposition between the Austrian past and the Italian present and between freedom and imposition of laws is usually emphasised by men, but very seldom by women. In the case of men the Austrian past is appealed to as a frame of identification, and the legitimacy of the Italian conquest is contested; in the case of women (especially the young ones), being Italian seems taken for granted, and the Austrian past is not invested with the same meaning. This distinction brings us back to a theme already discussed earlier in this work, and suggests that negative views about the Italian state mainly reflect men's attitudes vis-à-vis the larger society, and particularly gendered ideas about locality.

What is astonishing in the actors' representations of the past is their silence about the last world conflict (except that it was a time of poverty): for some informants it was a sort of nonevent, or had very little significance for the history of the valley, even though many people fought in the Italian army abroad, and war memorials in the valley commemorate the fallen. According to some villagers, the Second World War had no impact in Caoria. 'I do not even remember the other war, I do not think I have studied it (i.e. at school). ... They did nothing here'. If anything, there were fights in Canal San Bovo. In pointing to this Domenica (b. 1913) implied that partisans were in the nearby village (or in Castello Tesino), but not in Caoria.[17] What is astonishing in the scanty accounts on the fights between partisans and Nazis is that such fights are not talked about as part of local history, for they did not involve anybody of the village: as Agata (b. 1928) put it, 'partisans were outsiders' (*i l'era foresti*). This idea about the last war may also be functional to the ideology of *campanilismo* analysed in the previous chapter: in placing 'the other' out of the community, villagers define a moral order, and draw a boundary between insiders and outsiders. Remembered history legitimates this boundary: there was no Second World War in Caoria because it was in Canal San Bovo. So, historical narratives are not simply statements about the past, but are deployed to give historical foundation to the widely shared conviction that the other village is different and even morally inferior.

The other event that marked a dramatic change in the history of the village (and of the valley as a whole) was the flood of 1966, which levelled several houses. Now it is represented as the watershed between '*sti ani* (the old days) and '*ncói* (these days), between the past and the present. Caorians made it clear that the flood also signified the demise of agro-pastoralism and the last stage of the progressive erosion of the village's ideal autonomy. Now the history of the valley seems divided between 'before' and 'after' the flood. Obviously, everybody experienced the flood in a different way: in Ronco, for example, the flood brought about great damage to the cultivated area, but not to the dwellings.

Even Caorians' views about the flood revolve around the notion of a moral order. The most interesting of these, according to the villagers I talked with, is that they and their covillagers joined forces and worked hard to reconstruct their own community. 'In case of need, as during the flood, Caorians did not await someone else's help, but they did everything themselves' (*In caso di bisogno, come nell'alluvione, **no i a spetà l'aiuto dei altri, i a fat tut lori, i Caorióti***) (Bruna Z., b. 1923). That Caorians joined forces and worked hard to reconstruct their own village creates an opposition vis-à-vis Canal San Bovo, the nearby municipal seat, on the grounds that its inhabitants did little to rebuild the houses of their community. In inferring that the people of that village did not draw on their own forces, but needed the help of outsiders, the Caorians interviewed implied that such people were not able to rely on their own means, a denial of the self-sufficiency which is considered a constituent part of Caorian (and Trentine) identity. Narrative accounts of the flood, as this example suggests, are used to stress difference: the past is appealed to in claiming distinctiveness and cohesiveness of locality in spite of modernity and differences of power with respect to other communities.[18]

Repetitive Past

Nowadays people of all ages in the valley nostalgically evoke a better village 'of the old days'. There is a widespread perception that 'true' Caoria and 'true' Ronco disappeared with the demise of the agro-pastoral economy, and the customs and the way of life of these days are contrasted to those of the past. The elderly especially tend to portray the past as a better period, and depict the present as socially disordered (see, for a comparison, du Boulay 1974: 249). The contrast between past and present also carries a moral judgement on the nature of local society: the idea of a fallen present is in this case a rhetorical move to express the imperfection of social life as it is lived.

This idea permeates much of village thinking:

'In the old days it was necessary to work in the fields (***'sti ani ghe n'era de far i campi***), then to store firewood in the barn, to look after livestock… [one had to] plant potatoes in spring, make hay during the summer, and all that stuff, then mow wheat and barley… In May one had to take the livestock to the pastures, first to the *masi*, and then, in June, to the upper pastures, then pick raspberries in autumn, in the old days, I mean. There was nothing else (***no ghe n'era altro***). …Then all changed. …now everything can be purchased. In the old days there were meadows everywhere (***'sti ani l'era tuto prà***), not like these days, forest! …[now] nobody tills the fields, aside from the vegetable garden, as I do. …It's all changed. In the old days we were all equal (***eravene tuti uguali***), all identical. …we were gullible, everything was easier, …now you need a bit of cunning'. (Agata, b. 1928).

Assunta (b. 1931) expressed similar views: '[In the old days] there were fields in these villages (*de 'sti paesi ghe n'era la campagna*). Everybody used to have goats, sheep, hens, rabbits, hogs. ...we used to grow potatoes, beans, onions, wheat, barley, ...then the forest started encroaching [on the village], and now nothing can be grown. ...Now we have all become "lords",[19] and nobody does that job'. The idea of repetitive time was reflected in cooking habits too: 'Always *polenta* and cheese, cheese and *polenta*,[20] soup, ...rustic stuff!' (Bruna, b. 1923).

The idea of social inertness being attributed to harsh economic conditions stems from the predictability of economic and social careers on it: 'All men here used to be lumberjacks' (*i l'era tuti boschiéri qua*) (Francesca, b. 1926). Even these statements portray the village as a system that reproduced itself over time: the social configuration of the valley of *'sti ani* was described as fundamentally stable, as the only divide was between the common people (*la pora dènt*) and the few powerful families, alongside some individuals in high places such as the mayor (*sindico*), the village priest (*prete*), the schoolteacher (*maestro*), and even the clerk of the post office (*maestra de posta*). The stability with which the past is invested is partly illusory and, as already observed, serves to contrast the past itself with the present, and carries a moral judgement on the nature of local society. This idea coincides with Christian Democrat representations of local community recorded elsewhere (Filippucci 1992: 73), which is in turn a vision of the countryside as a repository of moral values that is largely of Catholic matrix (Guizzardi 1976). The idea of a fallen present is also epitomised by the view that these days there are too many 'Italians' in the village, especially in the summer,[21] thereby implying that the physical (and symbolic) boundary of the valley has become blurred.

Nowadays an idealised past, epitomised by the community of 'the old days', may provide moral coordinates to orient social practices. Images of the past, for example, present the community as extremely poor, as the context in which everybody had to be content with the few things they had. 'There was no money (*soldi no ghe n'era*). They used to sell their cow to survive, to pay the cooperative store'. (Bruna, b. 1923). Yet the presentation of the community to the outside as 'poor' and 'miserable' is also a common feature of most European villages: as has been observed in relation to a similar context (Bauer 1992: 573), in doing so people 'strategically manipulate their putative marginality and subordination' and 'accentuate the traces of a harshness and brutality that once pervaded older villagers' lives, but have all but disappeared in the present'. In a sense, they also present themselves as representatives of a dying way of life that is both disdained and admired.[22]

The idea that in 'the old days' all helped out (*'sti ani tuti se giutéva*), whereas these days are characterised by selfishness, is heard everywhere in the valley: this is echoed by a shared conviction that in the past all the people stayed together and knew each other very well. 'In the old days we were all friends, ...[and] we could trust each other' (Assunta, b. 1931). A similar view was expressed by Virginia (1910–2002): 'My son used to say: "I wish I had been born one hundred years ago because …there was so much friendship." [People] used to help each other, and after reciprocating a favour they used to chat. …Now there are few people'.[23] Nowadays the elderly complain that young people do not want to remain in the valley, that they require a car, and other expensive items not available in the past. Another complaint about the young is that they do not know about the past or genealogies, thereby implying that ancestors are no longer as important as they used to be.[24]

Community resistance to external authority, by contrast, is one of the favourite topics of the stories told by the men of the village, not so much in Ronco as in Caoria. So, for instance, stories abound as to how a villager succeeded in shooting game without a permit, and in defying the gamekeeper, as has been seen. Linked to this is the theme of an idealised past freedom that in a bureaucracy-ridden present nobody has (aside from the powerful), a time when there were no restrictions, and when the local people were the 'lords' (*paroni*), in other words a 'structural nostalgia' (Herzfeld 1997: 116). Although it is hard to state whether narratives about a putative past freedom are reliable, the fact remains that they reveal an acute awareness, on the part of the inhabitants of the valley, of the disparity between village-based institutions on which they have retained control, and the institutions of the state that have been imposed upon them.

That in the past the local people were the 'lords' and the valley was 'independent' was predicated upon their ability to sustain hard work. The idea of hard work as a repository of past morality is cast as a virtue, as has been seen in the preceding chapters: when talking about emigration to the Americas in the late nineteenth century, Domenica (b. 1913) said, 'They emigrated to work hard, to survive, and not to sell drugs as people do these days'. The past, albeit an expression of tradition, becomes a custodian of morality, as shown by the widespread perception that in the past villagers used to work much harder: 'We used to work as much as we could. …[we were] always busy, always, always'. (Margherita, 1904–2002). By contrast there is a shared conviction that nowadays nobody wants to work.[25] As Gino (b. 1929) wryly noted, 'There is no longer willingness to work' (*no ghe n'e pi chela voia de lavorar*). This is consistent with Caorians' self-portrait as hard workers, as opposed to the 'slack' workers of the other villages: 'Caorians are "bears", but hard workers too' (*i Caorióti l'e orsi, ma bravi de lavorar*) (Libera, b. 1932). Aside from the statements which express the ideology of *campanilismo*, the dichotomy between past and present workers, between hard and slack workers, is significant as it asserts the moral integrity of the community of the past: as Libera (b. 1932) said, 'If they [the young people] had to work as hard as we did, they would probably die'.

Hard work is usually associated with the rural origin of locals, and this emerged in the course of a conversation when Mario (b. 1948) said that he was born in the *masi*.[26] Although this does not seem to be the case, the fact remains that in saying so he wanted to stress that having been born there and having survived are signs of strength,[27] and his view, once again, reflects the widespread perception that social worth stems from hard work (i.e. engaging in agro-pastoral activities) and poverty. If I were to take his statements and other people's emphasis on having been born in the *masi* at face value I would be led to believe that this is an assertion of the worth of the past over the present and of 'tradition' over 'modernity' which, once again, expresses the idea of a fallen present contrasted to an ordered past. The positive value that having been born in the *masi* takes on stems from the fact that, as has been observed, the past was characterised by poverty and harshness; however, some villagers stressed that it was a time when the degree of child mortality was quite high, which implies that those who survived were of a 'stronger' breed. Therefore this idea is not simply related to that of villageness, but also, more or less explicitly, to that of strength and survival: *'sti ani* people were 'better' because stronger and more resistant, 'the result of a natural selection', as the above person put it. People of these days, he added, are not like that. So, the idea of strength is intimately associated with that of the past, with the ability to wrest a living from the land. In the past few could survive; nowadays everybody can. In Darwinian terms, in the past it was the survival of the fittest that mattered. Hence, the putative superiority of the past over the present is not simply predicated upon the latter's 'moral fall', but also upon 'objective' reasons. Mario's statement, however, conveyed another meaning: it is not just because he was born in the old days that he is stronger and more resistant than the young generations, but it is because he was born in the mountains that he is of a better 'breed' than those of the lowlands (and all urban dwellers). In his view, a harsh environment makes hard people.[28]

The idea of hard worker, it has been observed (Passerini 1987: 45), is also an integral part to the self-stereotype of northern Italians who look upon Southerners (those of 'lower' Italy, *la bassa Italia*) as slack workers to justify the disparity between the two areas. The identification of Southerners as slack workers has been found in the valley too.[29] What is interesting is that my informant's self-stereotype is not used vis-à-vis Southerners, but with respect to the younger generations on the one hand (who had not experienced the hardships of rural life) and outsiders on the other.[30] However, not only does social worth stem from hard work, but from poverty too, and is contrasted to the unwillingness to work of the wealthy. When the rich families of the 'old days' are talked about, mention is usually made of the fact that they did not work. As Aurelio (b. 1924) said, in the 1940s the 'boss' of Ronco was known as a person who used to go to church every morning, then to the bar for a chat, and finally back home for lunch, but not as a 'worker'. So, being stigmatised as backward, as has been shown in the previous chapter, may sometimes result in the manipulation of meanings to the advantage of the stigmatised, and particularly in the development of a counterdiscourse: it is tradition, and ultimately having endured hard conditions in a harsh environment, that legitimate local people's claims to moral superiority over the younger generations and urban dwellers in general. This is an interesting aspect that reveals an ability for manipulating cultural meanings and situations which is very common in rural communities (Reed-Danahay 1993: 223; Roseman 1996: 837), and further validates the view that not working hard is construed as a source of loss of personal dignity. As status and personal dignity are predicated upon hard work and self-sufficiency (which enable people to place their lives within moral coordinates), images of the past necessarily evoke ideas of autonomy and self-determination.

Museums and Monuments: a Celebration of the State?

Thus far, I have tried to assess how locals represent their past and construct histories. What unites such accounts (or images of the past) is a portrait of a social group that had to endure the hardships of rural life, and rely on its own means to make a livelihood. However, doing so also enables locals to achieve a sense of agency, as such narratives convey ideas of self-sufficiency and, more importantly, allow social actors to locate themselves within the frame of their place of origin. This means that local histories also enable them to place their lives outside the nation-state. But how is it possible to construct a local history without allowing for the impact of the Great War in the valley? In an attempt to answer this question, I focus on the articulation of Italian and local identities through the medium of museums and monuments, and analyse the relationship between the way in which state ideology is imposed on the local people, and the ways these reinterpret 'official' meanings through the prism of the 'local'. In using the term 'local', however, I am not oblivious to the problematic nature of its definition. Rather, following Green (n.d.), the 'local knowledge' alluded to involves local interaction with objects and ideological messages which, although they are located and have agency in a certain place, have agents elsewhere. In saying so, I am implying that the local and the nonlocal may be combined, and particularly that the nonlocal may be incorporated into 'local' knowledge construction.

In his seminal study on nationalism, Anderson (1991: 204–6) concentrates on the process that gives rise to the possibility of identification of individuals with an 'imagined community', the nation. One of the ways in which this is possible, the author observes, is the construction of the past as a historical narrative. National museums often serve this purpose: they do so by constructing the past as a narrative of national struggle.[31] So, the 'construction of community' takes place in national museums because they present a national history as a focus of identification. In the valley studied, as will be seen, museums also construct 'locality', and present the past as a narrative of the articulation between the 'national' and the 'local'.

As I said in an earlier chapter, between 1914 and 1918 most of the Province of Trent (then the southernmost part of the Austro-Hungarian province of Tyrol) was the theatre of military operations. Virtually every small village in the province in which a battle was fought during the Great War has one or more monuments dedicated to the Italian soldiers who perished during the fights. The valley under study (and particularly Caoria) is no exception: at the end of the war the valley became the heart of a monumental landscape connected with the arrival of the Italian army and the valley's annexation to Italy. Monumentalisation, by its very nature, forms part of the way spatial arrangements are invested with past associations (Herzfeld 2001: 78). The official, monumental time of the Italian nation-state, which inscribes onto the landscape, is physically expressed by the presence of monuments or 'timescapes', in Green's terms (n.d.), which celebrate the Italian victory in the First World War. Anyone visiting the village cannot help noticing the military cemetery, built by the Italian army in 1917, which lies by the road sign marking the village boundary. The cemetery, which used to house the coffins of about 200 Italian soldiers who perished in the valley, was built with the purpose of giving the area an aura of Italianness, and of marking the beginning of a new era after about 600 years of German and Austrian sovereignty. The corpses were then moved to the memorial military cemetery of Rovereto,[32] now a venue for commemorative ceremonies.

The military cemetery of Caoria was meant as a field of remembrance, as a place of commemoration of the events of the First World War. It is rarely visited, except when state-sponsored commemorative ceremonies take place, though in 1999 the provincial administration sponsored its restoration. Villagers are very seldom seen there, and the national flag flies during the summer only. The other monument dedicated to the fallen of that war, a big war memorial cross, lies at the very end of the valley, a few miles north of Caoria, in a hamlet called Refavaie, now a small tourist resort. This place is known for the battle fought between the two armies in 1916, shortly after the arrival of the Italian mountain troops. Nowadays the monument is difficult to reach, as there is no footpath going there. It is surrounded by fir trees, and can hardly be seen from the inhabited area. It is dedicated to the Alpini who perished during the fights in the Alps of Fassa,[33] but is neglected by the Caorians who own a *maso* there. Thus, while until a few years ago the Italian nation-state used to act as the dominant framework in the management of the historic landscape, nowadays its marks are hardly considered part of the 'local' landscape, or are looked upon as mere 'additions' to what is referred to as 'local': taking a hint from Herzfeld (1992), it may be suggested that they could be described as 'indifferent' to the people of the valley in the same way that the valley is 'indifferent' to the Italian nation-state.

Another place that has become a venue for commemorative ceremonies is doubtless Mount Cauriol, which marks the upper end of the valley. The emphasis placed on that mountain may be accounted for by the fact that during the

Great War mountains, as sacred mountains, symbolised the nation (Mosse 1990: 114), and this mystique came to the fore on the Alpine Front. In nationalist discourse the mountain represents the symbol of the Italian conquest of the valley, and Italian historical accounts of the 1910s depict the seizure of the mountain's peak as an heroic undertaking. More recently, however, there have been attempts to rethink this view, especially when the local group of the Alpini commissioned a book on local history from two historians of Trent to question the myth of the Italian heroic conquest. The book (Bettega and Girotto), published in 1996, relies on the written reports of the Austrian officials who witnessed the events, and aims to provide an alternative historical account of the Italian conquest. One of the interesting aspects is that it was the local group of the Alpini, the ones that are most strongly identified with the nation (at least nominally), who questioned the reliability of 'official' sources. As the valley remained evacuated for the duration of the fights, nobody in the village could state what happened there, and until a few years ago the few historical accounts available about the seizure of the mountain were only those written by Italian officials. This suggests that the meaning that Mount Cauriol has for the army officials is not the same as it has for the people whose forebears died in various parts of Europe in the course of fights. So, the 'Italianness' of the valley is contested, and is attached a different meaning by those who live there. It is worth noting that the brochure about the valley issued by the local tourist board in the mid-1990s stresses that '...the valley was *wisely ruled* by Austria until the First World War' (emphasis added). Taking a hint from Herzfeld (1991: 12), it may be argued that the different meanings that Mount Cauriol takes on reflect a contest over social (and national) identities: my place or national monument?

Alternative views of the First World War (and of local history in the broad sense) are expressed by the historical museum of Caoria. Museums, by their very nature, do not simply put history on display: they also create a particular knowledge for the public, and have the power to legitimate that knowledge (Macdonald 1998: 2). However, displaying knowledge cannot be divorced from politics, and the museum of Caoria is no exception. This is located at the very centre of the village, opposite the new church, and is a venue for the tourists who visit the valley at weekends. It was established under the sponsorship of the Italian armed forces, and was opened to the public in 1991. It is run by the National Association of the Alpini of Caoria and by volunteers,[34] and its main aim is to present a narrative of the events of the Great War in the valley. It displays original (and photocopies of) documents about the war, weapons, bombs, newspapers, photographs, and any kind of material related to it. It also sells various historical publications on the same subject. Given the link between the Association and the Italian armed forces, anyone visiting the museum would expect to associate it with the monumental time of the Italian nation-state. Apparently this is the case, as is suggested by the Italian flag which flies outside the building. Contrary to this expectation, the only thing to be seen displayed, on entering the museum, is a portrait, in the form of a poster, of the Austro-Hungarian emperor Franz Josef.

The museum consists of a big room divided into two wings: on the right side, on entering the hall, are displayed old photographs and printed material. At the centre one can see the flags of the Italian Kingdom and the Dual Monarchy. The left side displays different kinds of weapons used by the two armies, especially small bombs and rifles. There is no division between Italian and Austrian weapons, nor is there any special arrangement, although written explanations state where the displayed objects come from. Written sources on display (i.e. newspapers of the time), both in Italian and in German, provide different accounts of the fights in the valley. The most interesting part of the museum is the section of old photographs, some of which were taken by Italian officials after the conquest of the valley. Other photographs displayed there, taken from private collections in the village, portray Caorians wearing the Austro-Hungarian uniform.[35] Others show groups of villagers who migrated to South America in the late nineteenth century, even though these have little to do with the war. By contrast, not many pictures of Italian troops can be seen in the exhibition. It is surprising, for example, that the pictures of the Italian Alpini parading through the main street of Caoria in 1917, albeit displayed, are not thrown into relief. In spite of the presence of publications about the war in the valley, the exhibition seems to focus more on the people of the village than on the Italian conquest.

It is astonishing that what was designed as a museum of the Great War functioned instead as a museum of the village and of village identity. This is partly suggested by the absence of photographs of the same period of other villages (and people) of the valley. The section of pictures which partly contrasts with those described so far is the one devoted to Cesare Battisti, a leading Italian socialist, although a representative of the Trentino in the Vienna parliament, executed for treason by the Austrians in 1916, now one of the symbols of Italian nationalism. Such pictures portray the last moments of his life, when escorted by the Austrian platoon to the place of his execution. Although he is a central figure in the Trentine history of the early twentieth century, the presence of such pictures was contested by the some of the Alpini who run the museum. According to these people, the above pictures have been imposed by an outside agency, thereby implying that Battisti is not part of local history.[36] In a sense, by placing Battisti outside local history (at the level of discourse at least), these people challenged the legitimacy of the official narratives of the Great War, and particularly placed their own community outside Italian history.[37]

As a matter of fact, a significant aspect is that the narrative of the events of the Great War does not present the history of a national struggle. If it were not for the Italian flag at the entrance, and for the Association of the Alpini (which runs the museum itself), one would be led to think that it is just a local historical museum about the turn of the century, with very little or no emphasis on the glorification of the Italian nation-state. If the visitor knew nothing about the war, s/he would receive the impression that the war had neither winners nor losers, for there is no precise identification of a common enemy. Rather, there are grounds for suggesting that the points of view expressed are those of the villagers; there is no oppressor or oppressed, and neither Italy nor Austria-Hungary emerges victorious. In other words, the museum does not create a conceptual space of national time. What emerges instead is the image of a village contested between two nations, which shares a past history with one, and a language and a recent history with the other.

If I were to interpret the presence of the museum as an attempt, on the part of the Italian state, to legitimate a certain image of history and assert continuity with an Italian past, the history narrated by the museum of Caoria would probably contradict this view. As Gillis argued (1994: 17), 'The reality is that the nation is no longer the site or frame of memory for most people and therefore national history is no longer a proper measure of what people really know about their pasts'. In fact, as the same author suggests, people's knowledge 'is no longer confined to compulsory time frames and spaces of the old national historiography'. In Trentino this is hardly new. In the museum of Caoria 'global' history is turned into 'local' history; 'global' events are interpreted through the prism of the 'local'. Local history is not depicted as part of the global one: rather, it is a global event that becomes incorporated into local history. The museum, initially designed as the celebration of the attainment of Italianness of the valley, eventually presents the image of a village and the contradictions of local identity itself, and enables social actors to claim a 'history'.[38] In presenting such an image those who run the museum recast 'official' meanings to meet personal experiences and aspirations.

The ambivalences in the meanings of the museum raise the issue of what being Alpini actually means to its members. Given their involvement in local feasts and commemorative ceremonies, it would be tempting to infer that they represent the 'official' face of the village, the 'front', in Goffman's terms (1959). However, given their kin relations to those who fought in the army of the Dual Monarchy, it can hardly be inferred that all the Alpini of Caoria look upon themselves as representatives of the nation-state, at least at the local level. This became patent on various occasions, particularly when the Alpini of Caoria declined the invitation to participate in the commemoration of Cesare Battisti that took place in Trent in the summer of 1995, a ceremony that was sponsored by some right-wing groups of the province. While the Alpini are identified as 'people of the Alps', on account of the importance attached to the military service as a personal achievement (or, it is tempting to suggest, as the achievement of manhood), they may also be seen as representatives of the 'local' community, even though this does not imply loyalty and allegiance to the nation-state. What was intended as a national symbol was instead turned (and even manipulated) into a symbol of local identity, and attached a different meaning according to the viewpoint of the 'local'. Phrased differently, it represents an official ideology appropriated and reinterpreted in familiar terms.

Commemorative Ceremonies: Presenting Different Pasts

Having explored some aspects of the articulation between local and official accounts of the past, I now turn to an analysis of how different pasts are presented in commemorative ceremonies. Clearly, such ceremonies play a central role in the representation (and narration) of local history, as they establish a relationship of ideal continuity with a past by telling a story in the tense of a metaphysical present (Connerton 1989: 43). In this section I seek to highlight the relationship between the ceremonies that present an 'official' view of the past, and the local ones, which present a past which may be at odds with such a view. These include both national celebrations and local feasts held on set days, and ceremonies commemorating events that are 'remembered' but have not necessarily been lived through. I confine myself to the analysis of the events that took place during my fieldwork, which include, first of all, the commemoration of the arrival of the Italian army in the valley in 1916, held every ten years (as a rule in the years ending with –6) in Caoria. Religious celebrations, albeit not necessarily commemorative, include the feasts of the patron saint day, celebrated in mid-May in Caoria (St John Nepomucene) and in early September in Ronco (the Nativity of the Virgin Mary).[39] Another event worth mentioning is the celebration of the beginning of the new year, held in Caoria. Last, but not least, is the role of the theatre in Ronco in the narration of the past itself.

I start my analysis with a brief description of a state-sponsored celebration, the commemoration of the eightieth anniversary of the Great War in the valley, held in Caoria and its environs between 31 August and 1 September 1996. The choice of Caoria obviously stems from the fact that during the fight the village was on the Front between the mountain troops of Italy and those of the Dual Monarchy, and the ceremony was also meant as a celebration of Italianness. On the first day of the celebrations the battalion of the Alpini of Feltre (which conquered the valley during the Great War), which includes both officials and commoners doing military service in the Alpine infantry, came to Caoria to run a ceremony at the memorial cemetery, at the edge of the village, with the purpose of commemorating the fallen of the war. The event was also attended by the mayor and by the local priest, who blessed the graves and performed the sacred rites prescribed for such an occasion. The large crowd that was present included, for the most part, outsiders from the neighbouring province of Belluno who did their military service in the Alpine infantry, as well as the Alpini of Caoria and their kinsfolk. When the commemoration came to an end, all the uniformed Alpini who participated in it moved to the centre of the village and paraded through the main street, along which several national flags were flying for the special occasion. The parade was followed by a brief commemoration of the Caorians who perished during the Second World War.

The 'pilgrimage' to Mount Cauriol, held the day after, had the same huge attendance. However, only a group of uniformed Alpini, led by a general, reached the summit of the mountain (marked by a big stone cross), where another brief ceremony of commemoration was performed. About fifty people, mostly former Alpini from the nearby Veneto region, joined later. All these were wearing the typical Alpino hat, adorned with an eagle feather, that they used during military service in the Alpine infantry. None from the valley reached the top of the mountain to attend the commemoration. The ceremony was followed by a religious service on the mountainside and then, when it finished, the mayors of the three municipalities that have jurisdiction over that area delivered a speech. That of the mayor of Canal San Bovo was characterised by the rhetoric that is typical of speeches delivered on occasions of that kind. However, he took it as an opportunity to warn all the people who were present to bear in mind the terrible losses that the unification of Italy had entailed; more importantly, he advised the gathering to remember the bloodshed of the Great War on 15 September of that year,[40] the date on which the secession of northern Italy from the rest of the country was expected to occur, according to the plans of the Northern League's leader.

The commemoration ended in Caoria with refreshments offered by the Alpini of the village. That the celebration was designed as a celebration of Italianness in an area which became Italian only eighty years ago seems to validate the view that temporal and topographical memory sites emerge at those times and in those places where there is a perceived or constructed break with the past (Nora 1989: 7). However, assuming that the commemoration was perceived as a glorification of the valley's being part of the Italian nation-state would blind us to the relationship between the 'official' meaning and the meanings that actors attach to such ceremonies. As a ceremony run by an outside agency (the Italian armed forces) and as an expression of the nation-state it was contested, but not overtly. Those who did not approve of it simply did not take part in the events on the plea that they had work to do at home, or stated very clearly that because their forebears used to fight in the Austro-Hungarian army there were no reasons, for them, for going to Mount Cauriol. In a sense, by deciding not to attend the events on the mountainsides, they were implicitly contesting the idea of the mountain as a symbol of the nation.

The role of the Alpini as 'official' representatives of the community becomes manifest during other ceremonies as well, and especially during processions. That of the patron saint day, held in Caoria in mid-May, deserves special attention for its significance, as it is a celebration that many people, both from the village itself and from the outside, attend. The relevance of the procession as a commemorative ceremony partly lies in its 'local' character as an alternative to the official (or 'national') one just described. As other processions have been abolished or devalued, that of the patron saint day (and, to some extent, that of Corpus Christi as well) remains one of the few events that may be termed as a collective representation of the community. Obviously it is not possible to deal with all the meanings of the procession, and just some aspects will be focused on. Clearly, Catholic processions focus on the unity of the parish (Pratt 1984: 224; Destro 1984: 194). Now the procession route encompasses most of the inhabited area of the village of Caoria, although the route itself is growing shorter.[41]

Although such a procession should be conceived as a form of collective prayer, it may also be attached different meanings. It is not different from other Catholic processions, as it moves from the new church and heads for the upper side of the village, and then moves back to the church. The whole event lasts about twenty minutes. The most important aspects of the procession are the values that are expressed, though it must be borne in mind that many attend the procession only out of habit or convention. The division of the village along age and gender lines is one of its salient features.[42] The separation of women and men in the church is observed as it still is, to some extent, in daily life. In the procession men (usually the elders) go first, led by one carrying a banner.[43] Men usually go in twos, followed by the priest in the centre, by the statue of the patron saint (carried by four uniformed Alpini of the village), and then by all the women and children. What characterises the procession is also its ideally unchanging pattern, for the people who led the procession in 1995 were roughly the same that did so in the Corpus Christi procession in 1996: this suggests that even processions ideally reproduce themselves over time. Despite this ideal, there were complaints, among villagers, that nowadays processions are no longer as rigorous as they used to be 'in the old days'.

As a 'commemorative' ceremony, the procession just described is intended to establish a relationship of continuity with the past, as shown by the clear-cut division between men and women (even though this is no longer so sharp in everyday life). However, its being a religious event and the involvement of the Alpini in it suggest a rather strong association between the Catholic Church and the state, and particularly that the procession itself serves to cast the village as part of the nation-state. In spite of its apparently clear meaning such a ceremony is difficult to interpret, given the ways in which both the Church and the Alpini are perceived in the social context under study. It is unclear, for example, how far the Alpini themselves are looked upon as expressions of the state or simply men of the Alps, of 'national' or 'local' identity.[44] Similarly, processions, instead of expressing loyalty to the Church, may turn into vehicles of local sentiment: they may be perceived as secular, and not religious (see, for example, Boissevain 1965; Christian 1972; Davis 1984: 19), especially for the men who participate in them.[45]

While the processions of Caoria aim to recreate (at least to some extent) the community of the 'old days' through stressing divisions along gender and age lines, the analysis of similar events in Ronco, such as the patron saint day and some of the plays staged at the local theatre, reveals the existence of different views of the past. The celebration of the patron saint day in which I participated was held on 8 September 1996. Just like Caoria, on that occasion Ronco became crowded with natives of the village who came back just to participate in the event.[46] The procession which followed the end of the religious service was different from that of Caoria: firstly, it was the statue of the Virgin Mary, carried by four young men of the village, that led the procession; secondly, these four did not wear any uniform, nor did they act on behalf of any specific group or organisation; thirdly, no divisions of the village were evident in the procession. The separation between men and women that still remains clear-cut in the procession of Caoria could not be noticed in the procession of Ronco, in which men and women, irrespective of age, walked side by side. After the religious event, the organisers (two of whom wore a 'traditional' costume) invited all those who were present to participate in some games (which, for the sake of brevity, will not be described), those that the children of the village used to play in the 'old days'.[47] The whole feast ended in a game of bingo.

There are similarities and differences between the celebrations of Caoria and Ronco. Just like the procession of Caoria, the events of Ronco aimed at the recreation of an idealised community of the past. However, while the procession of Caoria sets out to establish an ideal continuity with the past through stressing hierarchy and division along age and gender lines, that of Ronco expressed different values. Although similar divisions were quite common in Ronco until recently, these were simply played down during the procession and the games. The community that was presented on the patron saint day was one of 'equals', and the feast itself was meant to stress equality and solidarity as the values which characterised the village of the 'old days'.

In spite of the emphasis attached to local 'commemorative' events, in Caoria, as well as in Ronco, many processions were abolished or devalued by the local priest (who used to perform religious rites in both communities); also there were some rumours that he was trying to cancel other religious traditions, which runs counter to the image of the village priest as an upholder of local traditions promoted by the Catholic Church. To cope with this loss, in the late 1980s the Alpini of Caoria created a local tradition. This 'invention' consists of the burning of a small straw bear on New Year's Eve, and apparently there had been no 'tradition' like this prior to its creation by the Alpini. Why I subsume it under the label of 'commemorative ceremony' will be explained briefly. Although it resembles a simple celebration of the new year, in fact it is something more complex. The event, which includes a procession, is held on 31 December around 9 p.m., and unlike other celebrations it does not have a religious character.

I attended such celebrations in Caoria in 1995, 1996 and 1997. Although they were not identical, they had a common pattern, which may be described as follows: a procession moves from the upper fringes of the village and heads for the new church. Participants include men and women in single file, and the procession is headed by an Alpino carrying a pelouche bear on his shoulders, which symbolises the new year. There is no division by gender, but children go in front. This is consistent with the 'spirit' of Christmas, as children are the focus of the celebration. Every participant holds a couple of lit torches, which have to be kept for the duration of the procession. The route encompasses all the centre of the village around the new church. Once the procession has reached the church grounds, all the participants circle around a pile of wood that supports a small straw bear.[48] Then the Alpino leading the procession sets fire to the bear, and afterwards all the participants, one by one, throw their torches at the puppet, and remain there until the bear is entirely 'consumed'. Once the ceremony is over, most of the people go back home to celebrate the beginning of the new year with their kinsfolk.

There may be different ways of interpreting the above ceremony. On the one hand it resembles what may be called a ritual of regeneration;[49] on the other, it would be similar to a religious procession, if it were not for the fact that the village priest plays no part. Some participants (notably the elderly) stated that the event was also meant as a commemoration of the killing of the last bear, even though few of the people who attended were aware of this (as was the case of the very young). Be that as it may, in burning the bear not only do Caorians celebrate their community, but also 'the beginning of the history' of their own village, marked by the killing of the last bear and by 'appropriation' of nature. Many Caorians stated that this was intended as a celebration of their being 'bears', although a few villagers stressed instead that it was a celebration of the local hunting tradition (even though the hunters of the village were not involved in the organisation). This mirrors some of the main concerns of the local people: on the one hand, the necessity to maintain a boundary between them and the outside, particularly between the village and the 'wild' at a time when this boundary has become blurred; on the other hand, this reveals an acute awareness that such recreations of the past are illusory, and that the world of *'sti ani* is gone. Clearly, this 'invented tradition' provides a contrast to the invented traditions and rituals in the past and at the national level focused on by Hobsbawm (1983), and supports instead the view that public celebrations in Europe are expanding as a response to the homogenising forces of modernity (Boissevain 1992: 15).

Concern with boundaries informs the bits of history of Ronco as known by its people. As has been said in the previous chapter, the myth of the origins of Ronco too may be described, to a certain extent, as a history of struggle for boundaries. This was shown by a play performed at the local theatre in 1978 and again in 1992. That staged in March of 1992, during Carnival, was aimed at presenting a narrative of the most significant events of the village's history.[50] The play is structured around three events central to village identity: the first one is the quarrel over the administrative boundary between Canal San Bovo and Castello Tesino that resulted in the loss of the cluster of Ronco Cainari; the second is the appearance of the first motor vehicle in the village, a red coach;[51] finally, the third is the introduction of the telephone in the 1980s. However obvious its meaning may seem, the above play presented the village's shift from a state of isolation to its opening to the outside world. Although it is the struggle for boundaries that marks the beginning of the village's history, it is the appearance of the coach and of the telephone that enabled the village people to communicate with the rest of the world and become part of it: in other words, these marked the end of their state of isolation. Therefore, if my interpretation is well founded, the village's story is portrayed as a sort of 'linear progress', a shift from *gemeinschaft* to *gesellschaft*, that frames the people's present 'identity' as both villagers and citizens of the Italian state.

The comparison between the images of history in the two villages reveals remarkable differences. Obviously what is conveyed by customs like those discussed so far is just a small part of a worldwiew. Yet customs of this kind reveal much about the social and historical context in which they occur (Bendix 1985: 73), and the events held in Caoria and Ronco are no exception: in both cases what is known about the villages' origins is placed in the mythical past (the killing of the last bear and the struggle for boundaries). However, in the case of Caoria the past event that is commemorated is a hunting foray, an assertion of control over nature and territory or a story of 'appropriation', while processions aim to establish a relationship of continuity with the past, and particularly to stress social boundaries; in the case of Ronco, it is the village's quest for modernisation, the opening of peasant society to history, and the beginning of widening horizons which inform the representations of its history. Obviously the different attitudes towards history which emerge reflect present-day concerns: as regards Ronco, it is the village itself that strives for a place in the larger society and in 'history'; in the case of Caoria, by contrast, claiming 'history' means constructing a local history outside the nation-state: national 'history' is regarded as an 'intrusion', as imposed from the outside, and as the cause of the progressive erosion of village autonomy. Phrased differently, while in the case of Caoria boundaries have to be 'defended', in the case of Ronco they have to be 'opened'. These attitudes inform different perceptions of landscape, as will be seen.

Social Involution: History and Perceptions of Landscape

Having tried to assess how 'local' histories may be deployed to challenge the legitimacy of the 'national' one, I now turn to a revisitation of the idea of circularity of time. The ethnographic information analysed so far obviously suggests that, especially in Caoria, social actors do not represent themselves as people without history. However, it seems clear that ideas of circularity of time, epitomised by the idea of the community as a system that reproduces itself over time, inform the ways actors represent and talk about history. But how do such ideas relate to that of history as a succession of political events? I concur with Pina-Cabral's idea (1987: 730) that 'time past' may be idealised as a condition in which the community succeeded in keeping under control the conflict-laden effects of irreversible time. This view, however, should also allow for the uses that are made of the idea of 'circular time' at present, and take into account the role of the idea of nature in local history. Phrased differently, it should acknowledge the role of the concept itself as a rhetorical weapon. I intend to pursue the idea that 'circular time' is not simply tantamount to 'repetition', but that in a post-peasant society it is also involved with the perception of landscape,[52] particularly of the natural environment. I will try to make the point that 'political time' as a succession of political events is not perceived in isolation from 'natural time' (the history of the transformations of the natural environment): on the contrary, in the context studied these seem to inform each other.

One useful point of departure is the notion of repetitive (natural) time analysed earlier in this chapter: if I were to take my informants' statements at face value, I would be led to argue that local history (and, implicitly, natural history) is considered repetitive, but only as far as *'sti ani* are concerned. If, on the other hand, the history of the valley after 1966 is looked at, the idea of circular time is no longer appealed to: time seems to be no longer repetitive, but irreversible. The information about this topic was collected on various occasions, but mostly when interviewing the local people about the past or when participating in various social events such as, for example, hunting forays. The story of the killing of the last bear was the starting point, not just because in local discourse it seems to mark the natural environment's shift from 'wild' to 'domesticated', but also because it is when 'history' begins.[53] The story is relevant not just as a symbol of appropriation of nature, but also because the event established a state of 'equilibrium', an ideal ecological balance predicated on the domestication of nature itself.

Most of the conversations I engaged in centred to a significant extent on the perception of the natural environment in the valley. Judging from what nonagricultural workers say about the economic transformations which occurred in the 1960s, proximity to nature is now seen as an expression of a past which has not simply to be forgotten, but also to be abhorred. Such people distance themselves from that past on the grounds that they have never had anything to do with agro-pastoral chores, thereby implying that the agricultural past is not their past. There are also opposite views (notably men's views) which place instead emphasis on the necessity to know more about this past and the relationship between humans and the natural environment. This became clear in the course of a conversation about pets in the 'old days', in which Federico (b. 1963) and noted that in Caoria there used to be plenty of cats.[54] This was accounted for by the presence of several stables in the village that were infested with mice. Cats used to have an important role as hunters, rather than pets, as 'domesticators'. It was not necessary to feed them, he added, as they were 'self-sufficient' owing to the incredible number of mice. Now, he said, there are no longer mice, and cats, in turn, have become spoiled. 'If a mouse came in, a cat would probably pay no attention to it', he said, and added jokingly 'or would be swallowed by the mouse itself'. Given that in the two villages a cat is usually referred to as an extension of its owner,[55] the domestic animal (and, implicitly, humans through the domestic animal) is no longer deemed able to exert its power over the natural environment.

The statements of the above person do not simply mirror ideas about spoiled cats, but also, and especially, about the human condition in the valley. That cats are no longer considered hunters, but spoiled animals, reveals another aspect: that man no longer knows and controls nature. Cats' lost self-sufficiency is a projection of a social transformation. This is suggested by another example: on a different occasion the above man told me some stories of when he was a child, and recounted tales of when he used to go to the forest to play alongside other boys of his village. This occurred very frequently, he said, because there was nothing else to do in the village, and at that time the forest represented the children's playground. Parents were unlikely to be worried about this, given that everybody, including teenagers, used to have a very good knowledge of the natural environment surrounding their community. It was 'their' place that they symbolically 'cultivated' until quite recently. The statement (to which I have already referred) 'I was born in the *masi*' is a case in point: although it does not necessarily mean that whoever speaks was actually born there, it serves to assert knowledge, possession and, ultimately, control of land and nature. Now, the informant wryly said, the young people of Caoria know very little or nothing about nature, and seldom go out of the village for a walk, and footpaths are becoming densely overgrown. Footpaths, in this case, create a relationship between man and the natural environment; taking a hint from Hastrup's Icelandic case study (1998: 119), it may be suggested that the more people have walked there, the greater the significance attached to this relationship.

This brings us back to the story of the killing of the last bear, the event that marked the beginning of a state of 'equilibrium' or of an ideal 'ecological balance'. My conversations with the local people suggested that this state was predicated upon two factors: humans' cultivation of the place they lived in (even in the form of hunting), and humans' appropriation of the environment. In a sense, this ecological balance coexisted with a social one as, according to the people I talked with, all were poor and equal (**eravene tuti uguali**). Domestication and appropriation of nature were predicated upon other factors: as long as humans cultivated their land, the 'wild' (and also outsiders) was kept at bay. This became patent during the initial stages of my fieldwork, when someone drew my attention to the forested stretches of land lying around Caoria and

Ronco, and complained that in the 'old days' the forested area used to be farther away. It came as a surprise to hear how much land (now forested) was under cultivation: every single piece of land on the mountainsides, irrespective of its size and exposure to sunlight, used to be tilled, given the scarcity of cultivable land around the dwellings.

While this ideal state of 'ecological balance' was symbolically established by the killing of the last bear, this condition faded some time ago. Now very little land is under cultivation, and nature is encroaching on the villages, as shown by the expanding forested area. 'É tutto selvatico qui adesso' ('Now it is all wild here') or 'It used to be cleared, open, now it is like a jail' (Noemi, b. 1926) are statements frequently heard both in Caoria and in Ronco. The dividing line between the village and the forest, between the domesticated and the wild, has become blurred: 'There were not the trees you see now. There used to be a foot-path along which you could walk'. (Virginia, 1910–2002). If I were to take these statements at face value, there would be grounds for suggesting that the people's failure to cultivate their land broke the ecological balance established by the domestication of nature. Nowadays the natural landscape's going wild is associated with the community's (and valley's) 'moral fall'. 'When the landscape becomes wild, humans too become wild and antisocial' (Daniele, b. 1930), is a statement that may be interpreted as a sort of environmental determinism. Depopulation and the demise of agro-pastoralism played a decisive role in accelerating this process, though social actors relate it to the fact that shooting animals and felling trees require a special permission.[56] This brings us back to the relationship between the history of the valley and ideas about the natural environment: history, from the actors' viewpoint, may be read as a process that starts in the mythical past, when the territory became 'domesticated', and ends in the present, when the area became wild again. Obviously, the association between knowledge of nature and freedom is not specific to the area studied: if anything, this is reminiscent of tales about communities that used to live in a harmonious relationship with nature, and were eventually displaced by ruthless capitalist aggressors (see, for example, Schama 1995: 13).

The other issue that views about landscape raised was the difference between categories of meanings associated with nature. Landscape became an issue of debate when a regional park was established in the area, and acquired jurisdiction over a substantial part of the territory surrounding the villages. Although it did not expropriate the land from its owners, the park's establishment had the effect of denying them control of some of the natural resources. Among the projects which were in the park's agenda was that of the creation of an open-air museum on land formerly cultivated or used for grazing. While this was intended to attract visitors to the valley, its creation also meant that a territory once accessed by locals only could become an object of enjoyment or a commodity to be consumed by outsiders. As in other places, the debate over access to the area under the park's jurisdiction mobilised cultural oppositions between work and leisure, which are expressed by contrasting ways of conceiving the countryside as either 'land' or 'landscape' (Milton 1997: 17). What the debate threw into relief was also a concern over who had knowledge of territory: the people who live on the land or an outside agency.

The portrait of the area in the tourist brochures published in 1995 was that of a 'natural' and 'untamed' valley, that is to say an image intended for the urban taste for 'wild' nature.[57] In local discourse, by contrast, what looks 'untamed' is interpreted as the result of environmental 'degradation': it looks untamed because few people fell trees, and even fewer cultivate the land. As we have seen, the history of the landscape expresses a moral judgement of the 'fallen' condition of the valley, and suggests an association between 'cultivation' and 'freedom'. The valley was under cultivation because it was 'free' and because, according to some informants, there were no restrictions: if humans no longer cultivate the land, this is because they are inhibited from doing so. Trees can no longer be felled freely, and even the animals that used to be hunted have become protected by law and by the park. This sense of discomfort is expressed by the statement 'Arriva il parco, e il bosco avanza' ('when the park was established the forest started advancing'). The moral implication is that it is no longer humans that have control over nature, but it is the other way round. If I were to take such statements at face value, I would be led to infer that landscape has become wild because of the bureaucracy of the nation-state and of environmentalists (usually referred to as *i verdi*) who impose certain rules and restrictions on the local people.[58] Be that as it may, this reveals that in local discourse control over nature through its cultivation legitimates ownership, whereas the urban idea of preservation of nature is interpreted as a device to deprive locals of their land. According to some informants, conservation laws are not necessary: '[Nature] was respected much more than it is now. They used to go hunting illegally, but they used to shoot the animals that it was necessary to kill' (Andrea, b. 1920).

By drawing an association between ownership and cultivation, social actors relate to landownership as achievement, as the result of hard work. Emphasis on this shows that landscape embeds not just concepts of nature and aesthetic meaning, but also social relations, history. In other words, it may entail a history of property relations (Abramson 2000: 5), which also casts territory as ancestral land. Conceiving of territory as ancestral land involves investing it with meaning, and particularly means that ownership of land is conditional on its cultivation by successive generations, that is to say by the same family group. This presupposes the existence of a territory connecting land, the ancestors and the owner. The presence of the same family group, in turn, evokes ideas of a territory as an extension of its owners, and the continued presence of that group means that territory, like the people owning it, reproduces itself over time. Although this cannot necessarily be considered mythical land, it seems arguable that land relations are influenced by cyclical readings of time. As Abramson observed (2000: 14), such property relations may be contrasted with those jurally instituted, which are embedded in the stream of linear time, the time of the nation-state, of bureaucracy, of officialdom.

Associating kinship and a successful stewardship often provides occasions for social actors to complain about environmental 'degradation' in the area, and stress instead that countries such as Austria have not experienced the same problem. In this regard, I happened to hear contrasting descriptions of local and 'Austrian' landscapes, particularly from those who had had a chance to visit Tyrol; what underlies such comparisons is the depiction of the latter as 'ordered' and 'clean' and, as an object of aesthetic contemplation. Perhaps it is reasonable to believe that these represent not so much the characteristics of Tyrolean landscapes, as those which are seen as lacking in the valley at present. In a sense, drawing a contrast between the two landscapes serves to express the view that in the past the valley used to have the characteristics now ascribed to an 'Austrian' landscape. In other words, that of the valley was an 'Austrian' landscape until it became Italian after the First World War, and with the demise of agro-pastoral economy. Implicit in this assertion is the view that although the valley has the potential to have the same landscape, it is the state's bureaucratic machinery and the enforcement of conservation laws that prevent the valley from looking as 'ordered' and 'clean' as it should be. However, reference to Tyrol/Austria does not simply serve to draw a comparison: Austria embeds kinship relations, as being of a ***ratha austriaca*** is a constituent part of local identity. Tyrol and Austria are associated with the system of impartible inheritance which enables farmers to remain on the land and prevent its alienation: they embed the ideal of freedom and independence. More importantly, associating Tyrol/Austria with continued ownership of land from the same family group enables social actors to establish a relationship between Tyrol/Austria and cyclical readings of time and, implicitly, with order and stability.

Nowadays the dichotomy between different ways of constructing landscape emerges as a political issue. In fact the struggle over landscape is mainly caught in the symbolism of power relations: the main issue was not simply environmentalism per se, but particularly *who* should talk about it. What caused uproar was the idea that conformity to an environmentalist directive entails the acceptance of rules imposed from the outside. In this case social actors were contesting the concern with the aesthetics of public space on the grounds that a public space cannot be an object of aesthetic contemplation. Paradoxically, land's becoming such an object is conditional on its being privately owned, as the comparison with Tyrol/Austria has suggested. On the one hand this debate reflected the dichotomy between an understanding of place as 'landscape' (i.e. an object of aesthetic contemplation) which all have the right to enjoy, and the idea of the countryside as 'land', that is to say private property, place of work (Milton 1993: 139; 1997: 21) and, more importantly, ancestral land; on the other hand, the debate revealed that an understanding of place as 'landscape' did not clash with the idea of private property: rather, these merge seamlessly.

Although the idea that the experience of cyclical time is dominant seems untenable within the social context under study, the data discussed suggest that the idea is better understood as a form of collective self-appraisal. It may also be read as a statement about the past to express the view that things were better on the grounds that 'we were the lords': in a sense, it represents a sort of lament for a lost virtue. However, if I were to read the history of landscape as a transformation from wild to domesticated, and then back to wild, I would be led to argue that even the natural history of the valley is perceived (and represented) as a struggle against outside forces, i.e. the 'wild' that preexists human presence, and the 'wild' that is brought by outsiders (*i verdi*, city dwellers, the 'Italians', and the Italian nation-state) with the enforcement of laws. In a sense, 'natural history' takes on the form of a rhetorical device to cast the nation-state as the 'outsider' and to advocate a social appropriation of the territory as opposed to a political/administrative one (Filippucci et al. 1997). Landscape (which may also be read as 'property') becomes the object of contention between insiders and outsiders. So, in the symbolic confrontation between the valley and the outside access to territory emerges as the main issue, and landscape becomes a powerful symbol: it may also represent the context where the signs of the state are weaker and fewer (particularly in the forest), and where men create a space for themselves and social agency.[59] In this case it is imagined as the embodiment not just of the community, but of the region as a whole. However, far from being an object to be consumed, it is described as a mosaic of individually owned lots or 'bounded fields', a 'clean' and 'ordered' landscape to which outsiders should not have access.

Conclusion

Representations of history seem to posit the past existence of a state of 'ecological balance' predicated upon the 'cultivation' of the territory, that coexisted alongside a situation of ideal 'equilibrium' in social relationships. Clearly, the fact of having lived close to nature, and having endured the hardships of rural life, is not deployed to acknowledge cultural degradation, but to assert instead the moral integrity and superiority of the locals over the outsiders who have not experienced the same hardships. The past (and especially its association with Austria and the idea of hard work) in this case acts as a device to challenge official views of 'modernity'. Perhaps the most intriguing aspect of this analysis is that social memory revolves to a significant extent around the idea of natural history. Accounts of the past may act as rhetorical weapons to question both official history, and the official understanding of economic development projects (or the establishment of the regional park) as delivered to the local community from the outside: in other words, they may be used for political ends. The 'other times' on which a local history is built represent a combination of 'natural' and 'political' history. They combine the relationship of continuity with an Austrian past advocated by autonomist political leaders with a vision of the past in which things used to be within local control.

The current use of memory for political ends brings us back to the distinction between natural (cyclical) and political (linear) time. Clearly, appealing to a time characterised by the repetitiveness of events does not entail that time is actually perceived as repetitive. In suggesting this, I am arguing that the issue surrounding the above distinction is not so much the perception of time, as its representations: in other words, the past is represented as repetitive, and is not necessarily perceived as such. If we were to subscribe to the view of cyclical/natural time as an unconscious process we would commit ourselves to a framework of interpretation that excludes individuality and human agency. I hope I have made it clear that appealing to such a time is not tantamount to a refusal to be part of history. At a time of political change emphasis on cyclical time should not be interpreted as an expression of the apolitical nature of village life, but should be contextualised in the wider worlds of power and meaning that gave it legitimacy: appealing to it represents a way of blending repetitive (or natural) time with political (or linear) time, and particularly of ascribing the former to a period of order. In the representations of local history cyclical time, reproduction, landscape, order, and Tyrol/Austria form part of the same set of ideas.

By yearning for a time characterised by an idealised order, when events used to repeat themselves and when all were equals, actors implicitly place themselves outside national history, and particularly question the univocal model of temporality of the Italian nation-state. Nature, in turn, expressed by ideas about landscape, turns into an objectifying discourse whereby actors make sense of political history, and make their claims against state bureaucracy. In suggesting this I argue that the issue surrounding the dichotomy between cyclical and linear time is not its sustainability, but its current meanings. Representing time as repetitive is part of a conscious process. Cyclical time forms part of people's self-representation in history. Thus, history does not blind to present realities; rather, it forms the background against which current political issues are debated and understood. This aspect is further explored in the following chapter.

NOTES

1. Bourdieu (1963) too made a very similar point in relation to Algerian peasants' attitudes toward time (see also Zonabend 1984).

2. In his seminal work Fabian (1983: ix) has suggested that representing peoples as dominated by a perception of time as cyclical is a political act through which these are cast as the 'other', and Bloch (1997) has pointed to the unsustainability of the view that one type of experience of the passage of time is dominant in one society.

3. See, for example, Roseman (1996).

4. See Collard's Greek case study (1989: 91) for a comparison.

5. See, for example, Minicuci's study of two southern Italian villages (1995: 71).

6. See, for a critique of this view, Pina-Cabral (1987: 721).

7. As Sahlins observed in this respect (1985: 151), 'in the nature of symbolic action, diachrony and synchrony coexist in an indissoluble synthesis'.

8. This aspect has been explored in chapter 4.

9. In the local dialect strangers are referred to as *foresti*, a dialect term derived from the Latin *foris* that accentuates their being nonmembers of the community.

10. There is documentary evidence that the bear was shot on 28 October 1840 (Fontana 1935).

11. This term is a translation of the all-including dialectal expression *todéschi*, which refers to all German-speaking peoples (Germans, Austrians, northern and southern Tyroleans, etc.) irrespective of their nationality. In this case *todéschi* should be read as 'Austrians'.

12. The image of Caoria as a divided village becomes obvious in everyday conversations. One day I came across two villagers, Mario (b. 1948) and Danilo (b. 1965), who were chatting in a bar near Caoria. All of a sudden the former jokingly addressed the latter with 'You, Italian!' (*ti, 'taliàn!*). This expression does not make any sense unless it is borne in mind that *'taliàn* usually conveys a pejorative meaning. In this circumstance that was not the case, since the two men have been very good friends for quite a long time. Asked why he addressed his fellow villager in that way (albeit jokingly), Mario explained that it was a reference to the time of the Italian conquest, when Caoria was on the Front between the two armies. Before withdrawing, he added, the Austrian troops destroyed the bridge that linked the two halves of the village, with the result that the upper side of the village was controlled by the Austrians, whereas the other one was controlled by the Italians. In all likelihood the allegation that Danilo was 'Italian' was related to the fact that he resides in the lower side of the village (*Caoria de fora*), that on the side of the 'Italians'. Later it became clear that the expression 'You, Italian!' was a way of making fun of the other man, by jokingly questioning his being a member of the community where he has always resided. At the same time, however, Mario's statement implied that the Austro-Hungarian legacy is a constituent part of local culture. Unlike Caoria, I did not find similar attitudes in Ronco, where the 'consciousness of the boundary' does not seem to have the same significance nowadays, probably because the Great War did not have the same impact.

13. A device frequently used by the local people to distinguish themselves from the 'Italians', who were not required to attend primary school until the end of the Great War.

14. These can be noticed in the living-rooms of most of the houses.

15. See for details Palla (1994: 337).

16. It is worth noting that until the 1970s schoolchildren in Caoria used to be assigned, by the native schoolteacher, the task of collecting information about local history, particularly about the rural past (for example about the dialect names of agricultural implements, how cheese used to be made, etc.), and also about German expressions present in the local dialect. This is likely to have given them a sense of the local past as distinct from that of the rest of Italy.

17. The perception of the partisans (*partigiani,* i.e. the guerrilla movement against the Fascists and Nazis in northern Italy in the last years of the Second World War) in the valley is ambivalent: whereas at the national level they are pointed to by left-wing party spokesmen as proof that a government of national unity is possible, their symbolic value at the local level is more complex. They are not necessarily perceived as heroes, but may be identified as outlaws and cowards (see for details Kertzer 1980: 162–3). The idea that partisans were not in Caoria but in the other village clearly aims to point out that the former was devoid of war whereas the latter was inhabited by outlaws, and serves to project positive moral values on one's own community and negative ones on the other.

18. Filippucci's considerations on the Italian town of Bassano (1992: 49) and Mitchell's on Malta (1998: 87) are very telling in this respect.

19. In this case 'lords' (*signori* or **siórì**) should be read as 'wealthy' rather than as 'owners'.

20. A maize-flour porridge that was part of the peasant diet.

21. Particularly those who have acquired landed property.

22. Pina-Cabral (1987: 725) and Bauer (1992: 574) made very similar considerations in relation to their Portuguese and Spanish case studies.

23. This stress on past unity reveals the ability of social actors to provide different (and sometimes contrasting) portraits of their community according to the situation in which they are asked to do so. While stress on unity may serve to contrast the past with the present, pride on self-reliance and on the capacity to solve one's own problems without asking others for help aims instead to establish a relationship of continuity between past and present.

24. See, for a comparison, Heady (1999: 190).

25. This view, however, is challenged by those (especially the elderly) who argue that the present is much better because of the pensions they earn from the state.

26. The temporary settlements located between the village and the upper pastures. The statement 'I was born in the *masi*' is heard from time to time, especially in Caoria, but does not mean that the person who makes the statement was actually born there; rather, it points to his/her being a 'true' villager born and bred in the community. One day, two villagers, Fabio (b. 1957) and Otello (b. 1957) jokingly engaged in a discussion about which of them was a 'true' Caorian. Each claimed to be 'more Caorian' than the other. Eventually one ended up claiming to be 'more Caorian' on the grounds that he was born in the *masi* (although there is no evidence of this), and the conversation shifted to another subject. In this and other cases, stressing birth in the *masi* serves to show to an outsider that he whoever is speaking is a 'true' villager.

27. This is related to the urban image of the countryside as backward and traditional. According to some Caorians who achieved a certain degree of wealth during the last few years, having been born in the *masi* is exactly the opposite of what Mario was implying, that is to say a sign of backwardness and narrowness of mind. This image is obviously related to a tendency, on the part of the better off, to distance themselves from the people of Caoria through what Fabian (1983) called the 'denial of coevalness', i.e. by placing the 'other' in another time. This caused instead some villagers to emphasise their rural origins to assert their identity in the face of a 'modernising' village. As Carla (b. 1936) said, 'I was born here [in the *masi*] and I am not ashamed of it'.

28. This theme has been explored in chapter 5, and has been defined as a sort of environmental determinism.

29. This is based on the interviews recorded by Renzo Grosselli in the valley in 1993 on behalf of the Emigration Office of the Province of Trent. These are about emigration in the aftermath of the Second World War to France, Germany, Switzerland and the United Kingdom. Each interview, which follows a fixed pattern, contains some questions about the relationship between the people of the valley and the other Italian immigrants. There is a shared convic-

tion, among the interviewees, that the Italians of the northern provinces are hard workers, whereas Southerners are described as slack.

30. The same point is made in chapter 5. The idea that the people of Canal San Bovo 'drag the sack' is a case in point.

31. See, for example, Papadakis (1994: 400).

32. A town a few kilometres south of Trent.

33. Both Italian and Austrian military maps place the valley in the Alps of Fassa, in spite of the fact that these are located further north.

34. The group of the Alpini was founded in the 1950s under the sponsorship of the battalion of the Alpini of Feltre, which conquered the valley in 1916. Caoria and Zortea are the only villages in the valley that have a branch of the National Association of the Alpini. These organise all the summer feasts that take place in these two villages, hold commemorative parades at war memorials or reunions high on the mountainsides. At the time of my fieldwork the group of Caoria numbered twenty members.

35. These photographs can also be seen displayed in the living-rooms of each house, usually pinned to the wall alongside hunting trophies.

36. In Caoria many regard him as a traitor.

37. This is an intriguing aspect that reveals the capacity of social actors to adapt to different situations in pursuit of their goal. As the above example shows, the presence of the pictures of Cesare Battisti was contested, but not overtly, and in the end the Alpini had to display them in order to benefit from the funding necessary to run the museum. This means that while certain aspects of nationhood such as encompassment and domination may be questioned, the image of the state as a funding body was not contested at all.

38. The inauguration of the new building in the summer of 1996 was meant as a commemoration of the war. On that occasion the mayor, wearing a scarf in the colours of the national flag, symbolically opened the building. It is worth noting that one of the sides of the museum displayed the Italian and the Austrian flags, whereas the opposite side showed those of Italy and of the Dual Monarchy.

39. Lesser religious celebrations are not taken into consideration in this section.

40. The warning of the mayor was primarily targeted at those who, just a few days before, went to Fiera di Primiero to hear the speech of the Northern League's leader, Umberto Bossi, who presented his project of creation of an independent northern Italy or Padania. It comes as no surprise that very few of the supporters of the autonomist parties attended the commemorative ceremony on Mount Cauriol.

41. In 1996 the procession was not held owing to the bad weather.

42. This is also the case of the Corpus Christi procession.

43. In Caoria this was a man who used to lead all religious processions (including funerals). For a long time a supporter of the Christian Democratic Party and a municipal councillor, he used to be the secretary of the local branch of the Catholic Association of Italian Workers (ACLI) and an active member of the Alpini Association in his village.

44. Patrick Heady, personal communication.

45. The different meanings attached to processions gave rise to arguments between the village priest and some of his parishioners: while for the former such events are occasions for collective prayer, for the latter they represent instead a celebration of local identity.

46. It should also be borne in mind that both in Caoria and in Ronco the religious aspect of the celebration was accompanied by a lay celebration, the *sagra*, in which the organisers sell food and drinks in stalls which are set up for that special occasion.

47. A device to contrast the 'genuine' village of **'sti ani** with the fallen one of a 'spoiled' present.

48. The bear, as already seen, symbolises the people of Caoria.

49. This is suggested by the fact that the Alpino carrying the bear 'burns' the old one.

50. Although I did not watch the play, I managed to get hold of its text.
51. In fact the coach that in the 1960s used to link the valley of Primiero with the city of Trent passed through the Vanoi valley and Ronco itself.
52. In this case landscape refers to the meanings imputed by social actors to their cultural and physical surroundings.
53. This is partly reminiscent of what Evans-Pritchard (1940: 104–8) wrote on the perception of history among the Nuer: there is a tale of first occupation of the territory; then there is a second period in which time is repetitive; finally there is what the author calls 'historical time', that is to say a period in which real events take place.
54. Even nowadays most of the households of Caoria and Ronco keep one or more cats.
55. This is suggested by the practice of naming cats after the nickname of the owner's family group.
56. In fact national and regional laws have been strictly enforced only for a few years.
57. See, for a comparison, Thomas (1983: 254–69).
58. The expression *i verdi* encompasses a wide range of environmentalist groups which include green political formations, the WWF, and the regional park as well.
59. See, for a comparison, Skultans's Latvian case study (1998: 83) and Heatherington's considerations on representations of time in a Sardinian village (1999: 323).

19. Alpini parading along the main street of Caoria.

20. Commemorative ceremony at the military cemetery of Caoria.

21. Alpini carrying the statue of the patron saint in Caoria.

22. Religious procession in Ronco on the patron saint day.

23. Religious procession in Caoria, 1954: men go first.

24. Religious procession in Caoria, 1995: men still go first.

7
LOCAL POLITICS IN
THEORY AND PRACTICE

Of Politics and Political Symbolism

The starting point of this analysis of local politics was the ethnographic information collected about representations of history and the construction of otherness, and particularly the idea that national history may be interpreted through the prism of the 'local'. This has suggested that there may be a difference between the meaning attached to historical events or commemorative ceremonies by the political establishment and the ways these are interpreted by individual social actors. If the same consideration holds true for political ideologies, then it may be asked what kind of effect the political changes of the 1990s had on the individual actors' views of politics, and whether the political messages propagated by party leaders necessarily mean the same thing to those who receive them. As I said at the beginning of this work, social scientists' focus on individual actors' capacity to interpret politics as a set of ideas is relatively new. Social theory's little interest in this aspect partly stems from a view of the nation (and of politics) as an 'objective' form existing over and above social relations (Thompson 2001: 31), which coexists with an image of the Subject as essentially political (Delanty 1999: 46). Especially at a time when the legitimacy of the social and political order is challenged, questions of social action and human agency come to the fore: social actors have access to knowledge which is no longer the exclusive domain of élites (Delanty 1999: 58), and their role of interpretants turns into a bind between the abstraction of political identity and the concreteness of the world they live in (Hedetoft 1998: 8–9).

Anthropological scholarship too has so far paid relatively little attention to the role of human agency in recasting political symbols and messages, its major focus having been political symbols and ideologies as 'objective' forms (see, for example, Cohen 1977: 121). Especially since the 1970s there has been a tendency to stress the compelling power of political symbols (Cohen 1977, 1979) and their dominant role in ritual and political life (Kertzer 1988; 1996, Abélès 1991), particularly the fact that they provide a certain view of the world, that they impel people to action (Gluckman 1965: 252), and that they integrate a group (Mach 1993: 265). Kertzer (1996: 155), for example, suggested that political symbols draw their strength by simultaneously representing individuals, thereby implying that they craft individual identity. In inferring that politics is expressed through symbolism (1988: 2), he echoes both Abner Cohen's emphasis on the obligatory character of political symbolism (1977, 1979), and a view of politics as 'ritual', inherited from Geertz (1980). While the anthropological analysis of political symbolism and official discourse has shown that ritual and symbols play a central role in the legitimation of the political establishment in Western society too, it may be asked how much an analysis of politics confined to 'representation' can tell us about the power of political symbols. So, for example, although Kertzer stresses the fact that symbols may be manipulated by power brokers for their own ends, in fact he ends up taking on a Durkheimian perspective, and reifying official discourse. Eventually he provides a top-down interpretation of politics, for his analysis of symbols leaves no room for human agency: that political symbols have a compelling power is taken for granted.

Establishing that political rituals involve symbolic discourse about legitimacy does not explain how these arouse emotions in the people, and how they achieve their appeal (Gledhill 1994: 145). The assumption that political parties or states simply impose their ideologies and values on the social actors conceals the complex relationship between political ideologies themselves and the individuals' perceptions of them and, as I said above, entails the risk of essentialising official discourse. The same holds true for the issue of identity:[1] Anthony Cohen (1996: 803–4) recently suggested that 'we should be alert to the difference between the regime's representations of the nation and individuals' interpretations of the representations'.[2]

If I were to take on board the above points there would be grounds for suggesting that whether political symbols and ideologies have a compelling power may be revealed by what individual social actors do and say (and think), and by the way they relate to politics. It would be rather simplistic to infer that people go to church because they believe in God: action does not always account for belief. This does not mean essentialising subjectivities, but rather involves acknowledging the fact that the role of social actors as interpretants may help make sense of collective action. In the area under study, as elsewhere, the analysis of the interpretation of political ideas, just like that of representations of history, is a task of translation: it is a translation because actors draw selectively on historical events and official discourse, and may interpret this in 'familiar' terms instead (Douglas 1986: 97; Herzfeld 1992: 10). However, while it has been argued that the nation and national identity (and, implicitly, the region, regional identity and politics in the broad sense) are sociological categories with which people work to make sense of the social world (Thompson 2001: 24), I will pursue the idea that it is instead the ways social actors make sense of their social world that help them understand concepts such as the nation, the region, and politics broadly defined. As is implied in the previous chapter, even the investigation of politics should not be confined to official ideologies or personal interpretations of these independently, but should rather focus on the ways in which they relate to each other. I will try to suggest that these two do not necessarily work independently towards forging a political identity, but may complement each other in a dialectical relationship.

This relationship emerged as a problem when I realised that, although most of the people I talked with have (or used to have) a clear political affiliation, in fact their interest in politics seems confined to the local domain: as a matter of fact during my fieldwork people tended to act as groups of hunters, of Alpini, or as members of a territorial unit, but rarely as a group with a political label, hence my contention that the compelling power of political symbolism needs to be assessed. The other problem, as I noted in the introductory chapter, is politics per se, notably what has been called 'the fragmentation of the political Subject': while talking about a Communist or Catholic identity presupposes the existence of political doctrines offering a programme to mobilise society, in late modernity it is increasingly difficult for social actors to conceive of society as a totality (Delanty 1998: 27), given the decoupling of nation from the state. So, how can a Trentine or northern Italian collective identity coexist with a vision of society as 'fragmented', in which individualism, self-help, and economic self-sufficiency inform so much of local discourse? What does a Trentine or northern Italian identity mean to the people involved? What is local politics about? Although social actors may declare themselves to be Catholics, ex-Communists, or supporters of the autonomist parties, in fact it is difficult to state what part of their lives is significantly shaped by that identity[3] and how much of a given political identity is actually part of the local one. This problem obviously emerged as a consequence of the dissolution of the two categories (Catholic and Communist) that used to keep political loyalties divided. The same issue emerged clearly in the course of a conversation, when a woman of Caoria, while talking about the men of her village involved in active politics (notably autonomists), said that 'they [her covillagers] do not understand anything about politics'. A similar thing happened when I visited a man in Caoria who was a Communist activist in the valley between the 1960s and the 1970s: during our chat he drew my attention to a box of books by Marx, which he received when he was attending the meetings of the Communist trade unions in Trent; he expressed his wish to get rid of such books through a donation to the municipal library because, he wryly confessed, even though he was advised to read them, he was not able to understand the theories expressed there. Clearly, party allegiance may simply mean drifting into doing what relatives and covillagers do, yet this also reflects a reading of political discourse which may not conceive of politics as a pure abstraction. As a result, an understanding of how social actors make sense of political discourse became possible chiefly by establishing a relationship with such discourse and what people say and do in their everyday lives.

The other starting points of this analysis were the 'classical' anthropological studies on Italian local politics, notably those by Silverman (1975), Kertzer (1980), White (1980) and Pratt (1986), which concentrated on the opposition between Catholics and Communists in social contexts in which politics used to pervade the actors' lives, yet took little account of social, economic and cultural transformation (Filippucci 1996: 58). As I said at the beginning of this work, the political situation I was confronted with was one of uncertainty and of shifting political allegiances, and the old political symbols did not necessarily play a crucial role. When I started my fieldwork in Caoria I soon realised that most of the considerations at the core of the above case studies had to be rediscussed in a new light, for the Catholic Church no longer plays as important a part as it used to, and being Communist does not have the same meaning that it had before the collapse of the Berlin Wall. Clearly, social actors had to come to terms with a changing political situation, for the new politics mainly seeks to mobilise society against the state (Delanty 1998: 31). More importantly, social actors had to negotiate the boundaries between an idealised image of politics, characterised by commitment to party ideologies, and a pragmatic vision. Yet although the Italian political scene underwent dramatic changes in that period, a political transformation can hardly obliterate the categories through which individual social actors make sense of the world they live in. Whatever the political context, village politics is expressed by contests between different factions for offices and resources (Gledhill 1994: 123). So, what is the relationship between a political past and a seemingly depoliticised present? To this issue I turn next.

Local Politics Over Time: From Christian Democrat to Autonomist

Perhaps the most appropriate way to start this analysis of local politics is with an historical account of the political situation in the valley. The political arena in the valley from the aftermath of the Second World War until the late 1980s was dominated by the Christian Democratic Party (hereafter referred to as DC) through the capillary infrastructure of the Catholic Church. The leadership of the DC (whose mass appeal was dependent on its identification with the

Church) was seldom questioned until the autonomist shift of the 1990s, and Ronco was the village in the valley in which the party was strongest until its demise.[4] Especially during the period between the 1950s and the 1960s the DC was so powerful in the valley (and in Trentino as a whole), that in some villages it succeeded in polling over 50 percent.[5] One of the factors that enabled the Church (and the DC through the Church) to achieve such a consensus was its role as the preeminent local institution. Yet another factor was its ability to create a system of meanings: as White (1980: 72) noted in relation to a similar social context, 'Catholicism offers a philosophy that accords particularly well with the experience of the peasant and small farmer'. 'The Italian Church has expressly constructed rural ideology, a result also of its cultural leadership on vast rural masses' (Guizzardi 1976: 199–202), and the rural people were idealised as repositories of authentic and uncorrupted traditions. That the local church magazine used to portray the families working in the *masi* as close to nature and God is a case in point.[6]

The elements that used to be central to Catholic ideology (which still permeate village thinking to a considerable extent) include the primacy of the family over society, the hard-work ethic, and private property. Private property (as opposed to the idea of collective property championed by Socialist thought) is probably the most interesting for, according to the Church's 'classic' doctrine, it represents a means of assuring a degree of freedom and independence for the family (Guizzardi 1976: 207). Above all, by means of the 'rural ideology', the Catholic Church gave legitimacy to the aspirations of the rural people, especially the interest in obtaining and maintaining property of land of small dimensions, of a 'domestic' nature (Guizzardi 1976: 213). It is no accident that the DC achieved its appeal in areas characterised by small private property, in which the family and the local community reproduce a work ethic and solidarity, and skills and practical knowledge (Diamanti 1996a: 30). This ideology is embedded in a context, that of the Vanoi valley and the Alps, in which private property is not simply an economic asset but, as noted in an earlier chapter, is also involved with the owner's personality, particularly nowadays.[7]

What secured the loyalty of the people to the Catholic Church in the valley (and in most of the Italian countryside as well) was also the authority of the village priest, on account of the fact that he would reside in the same community for many years and could be in touch with his parishioners on a daily basis.[8] In a valley in which the level of educational achievement has never been particularly high, the priest was not just an authority and model of behaviour, but also a sort of power broker whose statements could be taken at face value,[9] as shown by the fact that the people's (especially women's) views about outsiders were often affected by his opinions.[10] Also, the people who were publicly criticised by him (notably during the Sunday mass) were likely to become outcasts in their own village.

The priest's power to urge most of the villagers, men and women alike, to attend the holy mass on Sunday and the religious service held during the week is also a case in point. Most of my informants of Caoria recall that 'in the old days' there was always a long queue on Sunday morning to attend the holy mass, and that the old church was hardly sufficient to contain all parishioners. Yet it seems arguable that for many people attending the Sunday mass was more a way of submitting to the political power with which the priest was endowed (especially as a sort of power broker) than a matter of religious belief. This reflects a situation recorded in most of the Italian territory where the DC and the Church were particularly strong: voting for the DC did not entail loyalty to the party; people voted for the DC without being Christian Democrats (Diamanti 1996a: 33) and true believers. Another significant aspect was the priest's ability to call upon the villagers without close relatives to bequeath all or most of their patrimony (especially land and houses) to the Church. Both in Caoria and in Ronco there is a sizeable amount of land owned by the two parishes. A mountain, not far from Caoria, is jokingly alluded to as 'the mountain of the churchgoers', as most of the land is owned by the parish itself and by the families of devout churchgoers.[11]

What also contributed to the success of the Church in securing the allegiance of most of the people in the valley was its ability to monopolise the realm of ritual,[12] not just rites of passage, but also (and particularly) community rites such as the feast of the patron saint and processions.[13] As noted in the previous chapter, processions may symbolise the unity of the village (Destro 1984: 194; Pratt 1986: 203) and may be secular, not just religious (Boissevain 1965; Davis 1984: 19). Although emphasis on village processions seems at odds with the fact that most of the men I talked with see religion as degrading and for women (see for a comparison Christian 1972: 158),[14] processions may allow for the manifestation of a male narcissism and aggressiveness (Brandes 1980: 202–3). In other words, manifestations of religious practice are neither totally of the orthodox institution, nor totally of the people: rather, they seem an accommodation between the two (Brettell 1990).

The priest's capacity to affect electoral trends was shown by the fact that the Sunday mass often turned into an electoral campaign, especially when socialism and Communism were threatening Church supremacy. In the early 1960s the priest of Caoria led an anti-Communist crusade, and championed the construction of a new church in the centre of the village to accrue to the Church's power. The priest's role in maintaining village particularism,[15] and especially in heralding the ideology of the 'bounded village' (Le Bras 1976: 117–18), furthered the sense of attachment to the community that its inhabitants expressed on several occasions. In this regard the Christian Democrat use of a city-centric idiom in local propaganda[16] is reminiscent of that used by the Church in the countryside.[17] Catholicism itself used to affect ideas about locality, particularly as regards the 'symbolic construction' of a community with clear-cut boundaries between inside and outside, between *gemeinschaft* and *gesellschaft*.

Priests have long acted as repositories of village traditions and advocates of the maintenance of local traditions and dialects; it is not purely coincidence that those who emigrated abroad and came back to the community were looked at askance because of the unethical nature of the ideas that they were likely to bring into the villages. Likewise the idea of the indecency of life in the outside world, propounded by the Catholic doctrine, was used to legitimate ideas of distinctiveness and particularism (Christian 1972: 164). Ideas of local particularism were also legitimated by the DC, which did not create an image of the state with which citizens could identify; if anything, the state was portrayed as oppressive (Ginsborg 1990: 185). In the valley the idea that all men share an equality of rights in the social and economic fields is derived from the equality of man in the sight of God. This is epitomised by the statement, 'We are all equal here' (***Noi qua son tuti uguali***), and used in every village to oppose a 'moral' world of 'inside' to an 'immoral' one of 'outside'. This also expresses the division between state and civil society propounded by the DC (Ginsborg 1990: 167) as well as that between the local community and other communities (Diamanti 1996a: 34–35). However, when my fieldwork was under way the village priest[18] was considered neither a political leader nor an upholder of village traditions, much to the dismay of most villagers. More importantly, the village-centrism (and particularism) that had been advocated for such a long time by the Church was no longer at the core of Catholic doctrine,[19] even though this clashes with widely shared views on the role of the Church in the valley.

The contents of the ideological messages propagated by the DC in the past point to the issue of whether individual social actors were the passive recipients of a Catholic ideology. Obviously it is difficult to formulate hypotheses on the basis of second-hand information, though I think it is reasonable to postulate that the reception of such values had been selective: although most of such values were championed by the Catholic Church, other values, such as that of male dominance in the household (and also that of man's political responsibility for the community and women's concern with the spiritual welfare of their households), local particularism, the ethic of hard work and the emphasis on private property already informed 'lay' discourse, and were later appropriated by the Catholic Church: this means that support for the Christian Democratic Party was driven both by emotion and by calculation of personal interest, and the Church's and the DC's power in the area under study (and in the Italian countryside) was conditional on their ability to herald community identity and values and beliefs which were already firmly rooted.[20]

In the valley, as in other Italian municipalities, local interests were mediated through political parties, and the DC in particular acted as an 'ideological tissue' around clientelistic linkages (Tarrow 1977: 175).[21] The presence of wealthy families affiliated to the DC, both in Caoria and in Ronco, who had control over the means of production (i.e. timber trade) played a decisive role in the legitimation of the party's ideology. Their political and economic power was predicated upon control over the allocation of jobs at a time when, especially in the aftermath of the last world conflict, the demand for manual jobs in the valley was high, but their availability was limited. According to some people I talked with, those who did not provide electoral support for the powerful families of Caoria and Ronco had considerable difficulty in finding a job in their own village, and eventually had to emigrate abroad. These families' role as mediators in local people's dealings with officialdom, especially as regards personal recommendations to a prospective employer on behalf of those who were seeking a job in the public sector, also contributed to reinforcing the above party's power at the local level. As a matter of fact, in the ideology of the DC the relation between the local community and the state was not direct, but was mediated by someone (Diamanti 1996a: 34), both in the form of a sort of patron-client relationship, and through friends or friends-of-friends when valued scarce resources were at stake (Boissevain 1974: 232; see also Gellner 1977). However, the demise of the DC hardly affected the ways social actors deal with officialdom nowadays. During my fieldwork, for instance, I happened to hear several complaints about the fact that some people in the valley obtained a job thanks to the support of a powerful local politician, whereas others who did not get such support were unsuccessful. In spite of this complaint, what was contested was not the system per se, but the fact that the person who did not get the job did not have enough support. All the people of the valley turn to a mediator when they need to apply for a permission, funding, or something similar: they would not apply without making sure that someone supports their request. In other words, the need for mediators is not contested: it is simply taken for granted, and is part of the order of things.

Both in Ronco and in Caoria there used to be an interesting association between affiliation to the DC, loyalty to the Church, and allocation of jobs in the public sector: various members of the families affiliated to the DC, for example, have or used to have a job in the public sector as schoolteachers, clerks in the post office, or letter carriers. Thus, when competition for a job had to be advertised, those responsible for pinning the advertisement on a noticeboard in the village used to do so long after the deadline for applications; as a result, only those affiliated to the same political party were informed by the schoolteacher (usually a close relative) about the competition itself, and could enter it. In the valley political power was also interwoven with kinship and, as in most of Italy, the family was (and remains) the springboard for political values (Cento Bull 2000: 29). So, one of the conditions that contributed to the maintenance of the political system from the 1940s until recently was also the conviction that such a system could reproduce itself over time. However, the idea of reproduction was not simply central to the definition of the political system, but underlies the way the social world is perceived even these days, as has been noted.

The demise of Communism in eastern Europe, the subsequent transformation of the Italian Communist Party into two parties (Democratic Party of the Left and New Communist Party), the DC's lost control over its 'traditional' subculture of Catholics, and the economic crisis of the early 1990s prepared the ground for the ascendancy of the newly established autonomist parties, notably the Northern League and the Trentine-Tyrolean Autonomist Party (PATT, formerly Trentine-Tyrolean Popular Party or PPTT), which garnered the majority of the votes in the municipality in the 1990s. The former made big inroads in the southern fringes of the Alpine crescent (Diamanti 1996a: 39). These political formations replaced the traditional base of political identity and representation such as religion, class, and secularisation with elements revived from ancient contradictions in Italian society, which include contrasts between North and South, public and private, civil society and the traditional parties (Diamanti 1996b: 113).

That in 1996 45.3 percent of the inhabitants of the valley sympathised with autonomist political formations,[22] and no longer with those that governed Italy until recently, seems to substantiate the view that local boundaries are more important than national ones because related to the more intimate areas of the lives of the people involved (Cohen 1985: 13). In northern Italy the success of such political formations (hereafter referred to as *leghe*) lay in their ability to translate the people's grievances about political corruption and immigration from the South and the newly-developing countries, and also to give voice to territorial identity and intolerance for strangers under favourable circumstances, such as the end of the Cold War. During my fieldwork no political leader of the *Lega* came to the valley to deliver an electoral speech. Yet the people of the valley could become familiar with the contents of electoral speeches through the press and the media, and grass-roots politicians affiliated to the *leghe* played an important part too in affecting political allegiance in the valley. Along with other regionalist and separatist movements in Europe, what united the ideological messages propagated by the Northern League was a stress on cultural, political and economic self-determination (Ruzza and Schmidtke 1991: 58). Central to its rhetoric was particularly the idea of territory as a 'community of interests', and hard work as a crucial element that singles out a putative economically-independent northern Italy from a state-subsidised South (Diamanti 1994b: 672). In fact this myth of self-sufficiency was hardly new: it replicated a feature of separatist claims, notably the distinction between 'Europeans' as 'modern', 'prosperous', 'culturally distinct northerners' as opposed to the allegedly 'backward', 'lazy', 'subsidised' Mediterranean southerners (Judt 1997: 114), which in the 1990s was used to cast the Italian state as the 'other' (Dematteo 2001: 147). Overall the Northern League took over from the DC the representations of the interests of the local small-business model of development (especially in northeastern Italy). It was also able to translate the culture of the northern communities of small firms into the myth of northern Italian identity

(Cento Bull 1996: 171–85; see also Bagnasco and Oberti 1998), though its ascendancy has also been interpreted as the result of the secularisation of Christian Democrat areas (Cartocci 1994: 188).

What unites most of the interpretations of the success of such political parties is an emphasis placed on economy as a decisive factor. Yet the decline of village life has also been pointed to as an element that enhanced the advent of the *leghe* that promised the reconstruction of the local community through their appeal to regional identity (Messina 1997: 23). Against the background of the decline of the nation-state and the disintegration of community life, the Northern League's appeal to the region as a focus of identification was seen as a response to the changing political (and social) situation of the present, as it could meet the need for communal belonging that neither a putative anonymous and distant state nor even the disappearing rural community could provide. The Northern League created this community of values and meanings defined by regional 'ethnic' criteria. A curious aspect of northern 'ethnic' identity was that it was not defined by language, but by territory. The Northern League differentiated itself from most of the separatist movements of other parts of Europe, which stress language as a marker of differentiation, because it did not make use of language as a basis for the mobilisation of 'northern Italian consciousness'; more importantly, it succeeded in creating a myth of northern Italian identity even though being northern Italian had never been a problem before. As I said earlier, an intriguing aspect that underlies much of the Northern League's ideology is its appeal to 'European' values as opposed to the 'Mediterranean' ones expressed by the nation-state.[23] In Trentino this was echoed by the Trentine-Tyrolean Autonomist Party (PATT), with its emphasis on common customs and unbroken history with Tyrol and Austria, though it must be stressed that the *Lega* and the PATT had different political programmes. What also fostered the Northern League's success was its appeal to everyday life and values (Destro 1997: 371) and the use of a language that can be easily understood, that differentiated itself from the political jargon used by most politicians. The *Lega*, presenting itself as an opposition movement, chose a language 'usually sexist and phallocratic' (Allum and Diamanti 1996: 155), which sought to bring politics 'down to the level of common people', even at the risk of sounding vulgar (Ruzza and Schmidtke 1996: 65).

As I noted in the introductory chapter, in the 1990s Trentino, and the district of Primiero in particular, turned into strongholds of the Northern League and the PATT. In 1996 the majority of the voters in the valley supported the Northern League: in August of the same year its leader delivered a speech in Fiera di Primiero and presented his project of secession of northern Italy from the rest of the country, which was expected to occur on 15 September. Although both the Northern League and the PATT heralded autonomy from the nation-state, they had rather different political programmes, for the former had in its agenda the establishment of an independent Northern Italy (Padania), whereas the latter used to champion the creation of an Autonomous European Region of Tyrol (Euregio) between Italy and Austria, crosscutting national boundaries (Luverà 1996). However, despite different political programmes, both parties appealed to territory, instead of language, as a frame of identification. But did the notion of territory come to the fore just as a result of this political transformation?

'Practical' Politics

Although the part played by political ritual and symbols in forging local and regional identity cannot be denied (Abélès 1997: 247), seeing politics as mere *mise en représentation* obscures the role of social actors, notably the fact that it is not necessarily political ideologies which affect political behaviour: while localism can explain the Northern League, the Northern league cannot explain localism (Cento Bull 2000: 224). As a matter of fact, the huge gatherings which used to characterise the electoral champaigns of the Northern League in some parts of northern Italy were not held in the valley, except on one occasion in Fiera di Primiero.[24] However, the people of the valley were very familiar with these ideological messages, given the coverage of such news by the media. When I started my fieldwork I soon realised that social actors declare themselves supporters of the Northern League or of the PATT mainly when regional or national elections are about to be held. By contrast, when it comes to local (i.e. municipal) elections the symbols of such political formations are played down; candidates may instead form coalitions with supporters of other political formations, especially with those who live in the same village. Tyrolean identity, for instance, was stressed by political activists of the valley in 1996 before the national elections, but not during the 1995 campaigns for the election of the municipal government. In Caoria the PATT receives support mainly from the local hunters and their close relatives, as the DC did in the past. It must be stressed, however, that those who support the Northern League in one election may decide to vote for the PATT in another (and vice versa), particularly in Caoria: the fact that an individual prides himself on being a descendant of an Austro-Hungarian soldier does not mean that he will vote for the PATT in the following elections. In this respect, the electoral success that the Northern League has had in the valley during the last few years partly obscures the appeal that 'Tyrolean identity' has, especially in Caoria. More importantly, despite the different political programmes of the Northern League and of the PATT, very few in the valley seemed aware of such differences. What was appealing was instead a common conceptualisation of locality. Although individual social actors may shift from one political formation to another, such a shift hardly affects the ways they relate to locality: whereas a Tyrolean 'ethnic identity' may become patent in opposition to the 'Italians', when it comes to politics within the municipality it is played down, and becomes less significant than village identity.

The account that follows is largely anecdotal, and its main aim is to cast light on both the discrepancy and the congruence between political doctrines and messages and the multiple visions of politics expressed by what individual actors say and do, and the ways they perceive the social world they live in. Until the 1970s a study of local politics could be conducted through the attendance of the sessions of the municipal council, that is to say the open meetings of the representatives of the villages in the local government. At that time it was not so much commitment to political ideologies that mattered (given that only one political party governed the municipality), as the idea that politics was a form of defence of local (and often individual) interests, a fight over things within local control. Decision making in the sessions of the municipal council required a constant process of negotiation and bargaining, with the result that such sessions often became heated and sometimes even turned into brawls. On some occasions Caorians could not ask the municipal council for permission to build or improve a road running through their own village without first forming a temporary 'alliance' with the councillors of Prade or Ronco (or both), as they assumed that those of Canal San Bovo would not comply with their request. The councillors of Prade or Ronco, in turn, could rely on Caorians' support if, for example, they had to apply to the municipal government for permission to canalise the water of a stream to their own village. Therefore, as long as the municipal government was made up of councillors acting on behalf of their own villages, decisions could seldom be made without an informal agreement between the representatives of two or more communities. In other words, besides being a protection of local interests, local politics also took the form of 'exchange', which seems to accord very well with the nature of local government itself (Della Porta 1999: 19).

The necessity of reaching an agreement with opposing parties (i.e. representatives of different villages) used to affect the election of the mayor until quite recently, as he could not be elected directly by the voters, but only after an 'informal' agreement reached by the competing groups.[25] In 1985, when a Christian Democrat of Caoria took over the office of mayor of Canal San Bovo, his success was not only dependent on the votes he received, but also on the support of the group of local autonomists that he eventually managed to gain. The same happened in 1990 in the following election when, although the outgoing mayor received the majority of the votes, the candidate of the opposing slate (from Prade) succeeded in throwing him out of office; this was due to the timely support of another slate composed of the hunters of Caoria and their close relatives, who did not welcome the reelection of a mayor known for his opposition to hunting.

Nowadays, with the new electoral law[26] that decreed the abolition of village councillors in the municipal government, sessions are not as heated as they used to be; decisions are made by the leading coalition before open meetings are held, and very few people attend the sessions, unless relevant issues are debated. There is increasing awareness that politics as *mise en représentation* is no longer effective, and that important decisions are made behind closed doors. While this meant that the inhabitants of a given village could deal with the municipal government without turning to a mediator in their own community, the abolition of village councillors also meant that the village as a political unit no longer had a raison d'être. An example will illustrate this point. In the summer of 1996 the municipal government announced that works on the road linking Ronco to Canal San Bovo were necessary. This caused much uproar among the people of Ronco, as such works were expected to start in the autumn of the same year, and were going to cause much inconvenience to those commuting to other places on a daily basis. A few days after the announcement was made, the mayor was invited to Ronco to meet the people of the village, and give some clarifications on what was going to happen. Given the significance of the issue, the meeting was expected to be very heated. Despite this, only a few inhabitants turned up, and these included for the most part the people who were going to be affected by such works directly. After the mayor gave clarifications, the meeting did not turn into a debate, but turned instead into a verbal aggression against the mayor. So, the bartender complained that nobody would stop by her bar while works were in progress, and therefore she was going to lose several customers; the woman owning the store nearby expressed the same complaint; the hair-dresser said that because of such works she would have difficulty in getting to her workplace; finally, a man of the village expressed his concern about the damage that such works could cause to his brand-new car. Eventually such works were carried out as planned, and the people of Ronco had to accept the situation as it was. At the end of the meeting one of the organisers expressed his surprise and disappointment at the fact that no public gathering was held to discuss the problem before meeting the mayor. The obvious result was that the people involved failed to act as a group on behalf of their village, they did not pursue a common interest. It is not entirely clear whether this was simply due to lack of organisation. Be that as it may, each participant spoke for him- or herself, and the image of a village as a community of interests did not emerge. Clearly, the vanishing of this image affected perceptions of politics in a significant way.

A partial understanding of local politics as it is viewed by social actors became possible not so much through attendance of the meetings of the municipal council, as through engaging in informal conversations and attending gatherings such as the one just described. When elections draw near most of the local people, especially men, talk a great deal about politics, though they usually express pessimism about politicians' motives. This is epitomised by the statement *i politici l'e sporchi* ('politicians are dirty'), which reveals that politics, at whatever level, remains perceived as a form of protection of local (and private) interests. In fact the politics most people refer to is not represented by a set of abstract ideologies, but is a kind of 'practical politics', such as the policies of the provincial or national government that touch them directly. In the 1990s, for example, villagers used to complain that the taxes paid to the state were used to fund the South of Italy. Such complaints were hardly new, and the idea that in northern Italy people pay taxes, whereas in the South nobody does, has been commonplace for quite a long time. However, in the 1990s this grievance was taking on political significance, given that the function of the Italian state was shifting from being a provider of social goods and funding body to being a regulator and law-enforcing agent. This attitude, however, also reflects the fact that ideology plays a much lesser role in Italian politics nowadays (Cento Bull 2000: 227). So, for example, people complain about new taxes, or that they have to apply for permission to obtain something, and so forth.

Overall politics becomes an object of debate whenever there is something to complain about, usually the policies of the national government. When my fieldwork was in progress such complaints were also influenced by the propaganda of the Northern League, and by the stress it used to place on the necessity to free the hard-working northern Italy from a putative inefficient South. It was on such occasions that men used to state that 'This year we vote for the [Northern] League' (*'ncòi votòn per la Lega*), or stress that their valley has nothing to do with Italy because it used to be part of the Dual Monarchy (*qua l'era Austria*). When the Northern League was elected into the national government, in 1994, a woman of Caoria said 'Adesso le cose finalmente cambieranno' ('At last now things are going to change'), thereby implying that the state administration was about to undergo dramatic changes, for the presence of the Northern League in the government was expected to instil the hard-work ethic that is seen as missing in most of the country.[27]

Aside from a few exceptions, loyalty to a political party is rarely made explicit by actors, except when these are affiliated, though political allegiance can often be ascertained when villagers engage in a conversation about local politics. Such discussions very often arise from conversations about property, particularly landed property. So, for example, when local elections draw near villagers express a fear that the newly elected mayor might take advantage of his power and try to 'appropriate' their landholdings, especially the *masi* in the high meadows, as it is assumed that whoever participates in formal political activity does so to further personal interests and those of his family.[28] There is instead a widely shared conviction that the ideal politician should instead provide funds for the community, but should neither intervene to change the traditional order, nor threaten private property rights.

At the time of my fieldwork most of the men of the valley in their thirties and older were supporters of (but not necessarily affiliated to) the *leghe*. These mainly included manual workers (both the self-employed and those of the sawmill), the members of the local hunt club and their close relatives, and the very few small entrepreneurs. Discourse about politics used to pervade the lives of men, and was largely discourse about 'autonomy' or *autonomia*. Men in the bars had been claiming that they could defend their *autonomia* and that they would not submit to an external authority. In conversations they were assertive, declamatory, and some wanted to be known for their exploits such as, for example, going hunting without a licence. In a sense, such attitudes seem consistent with the idea of *grandezza* referred to earlier in this work. The issue of autonomy, and particularly the autonomy of the community, came to the fore in the summer of 1995, when the elections of the municipal government were drawing near. Apparently in Caoria there was a greater interest in them than there was in Ronco,[29] especially among those who wanted the mayor[30] thrown out of office. The two leading candidates who stood for election were the outgoing mayor and a retired geologist born in Caoria, now living in another valley. Each of these led a coalition that included, among its candidates and supporters, people of different political affiliations. A few days prior to the elections, the above candidates organised two parallel public gatherings (attended by men only) in two adjacent bars in Caoria, and presented their political programmes. Although they expressed different interests, they discussed common themes, among which the condition of the valley between tradition and modernity figured centrally.

The electoral speech delivered by the outgoing mayor is worth focusing on, not only because it addressed the economic and social problems of the valley, but because of the views of politics he expressed on such an occasion. His political programme was very explicit: it was necessary to open the valley to the outside world by encouraging entrepreneurs to invest money in the valley itself. This could be accomplished through the implementation of tourist structures, and the project of a chairlift linking the valley to the ski resort of San Martino di Castrozza. The other issue to which he pointed was that of local identity and relationships with outsiders: the preservation of valley identity emerged as a problem, given that the population of the valley was steadily decreasing. To cope with this process of depopulation he had two plans in his agenda: one was to grant to each married couple residing in the *comune* the sum of 1,000.000 Italian lire (scarcely £340)[31] for each newly born second child as a contribution towards expenses; the other one was to call migrants back to the valley to undertake an economic activity there. In a sense, with the slogan '2,000 residents in the 2000s'[32] he was championing the preservation of valley identity and the reconstruction of the 'community',[33] and in seeking to recall the natives of the municipality rather than to recruit new members he was championing a 'primordial' collective identity.

Perhaps the most interesting point of the mayor's speech was the view that in order to reconstruct the community it was also necessary to deny (or drastically reduce) access to land and houses to those not ordinarily resident in the municipality, i.e. to those who apply for a permanent address there but intend to live and work elsewhere.[34] In saying so, he was implying that valley identity could be preserved through preventing the land from being sold out to strangers. This point reflected both the inhabitants' discontent at the alienation of landed property to outsiders, and the policies in the agenda of the provincial government aimed at preventing fragmentation of property in Trentino. The mayor's stress upon landownership was very well received by the villagers who were present, given the strong identification of men with the land that they own and the symbolic value of land itself.[35] Clearly, the 'community' he was proposing to rebuild was that of the 'old days', that is to say a territorial unit ideally inaccessible to outsiders, a *gemeinschaft* vividly remembered (and yearned after) by most of the inhabitants of the valley. Obviously his emphasis on territory as a focus of identification was not new. However, a paradox is worth stressing: although the mayor was not affiliated to any of the autonomist parties, the content of his speech was clearly consistent both with the rhetoric of the *leghe* in the 1990s, and with Catholic ideology in the past.

In advocating a 'primordial' collective identity the mayor was also presenting himself as the politician who 'protects' the community from intruders, particularly those who appropriated land in the valley. Yet in doing so he was also heralding one of the values that figure prominently in local discourse, that is to say the idea of private property as 'inaccessible'.[36] Despite his emphasis upon these values, one can hardly find consistency between what was said and actual practice. His rhetoric was mainly aimed at achieving consensus among the people of the valley: as an estate agent, the mayor would have acted against his own economic interests in preventing the land from being sold to outsiders. He presented himself as the person acting on behalf of the community in the same way that he talked about the importance of national identity at the commemorative ceremony on Mount Cauriol one year later.[37] However, in heralding the community of the 'old days' he was not imposing his views: rather he was adjusting himself to local-level discourses through the use of the idiom of land, and especially private property, as foci of identification. In a sense, as Abélès noted in relation to a similar context (1991: 272), local political life provides a demonstration of the adaptability of the leading protagonists, 'who can combine elements of a distant past with the needs of the present as required'.[38]

The other significant aspect of the mayor's speech was the use of the local dialect with the people who attended the meeting, who were familiarly addressed with the informal *tu*. This reveals the existence of a vision of locality as a 'cosy' social field, in which politicians are in direct contact with the people (Filippucci 1992: 259), and entails the assimilation of locality to a family[39] or 'community' in which everybody knows each other very well. This agrees with Herzfeld's idea (1997: 4) that the rhetoric of domesticity in official discourse has a persuasive appeal: as has been seen, the mayor presented himself as the politician 'close to the people', the person who mediates between the community and the outside, that is to say the person who 'can get things done in Trent' (i.e. in the provincial government). This is the image of the 'transactional leader' that makes people believe that he can communicate with and manipulate officials in a way that the ordinary villager cannot. This rhetoric is hardly new: it used to loom large in the ideology of the DC, and reflects a perceived distance between the state and civil society. This distinction became patent shortly before the elections, as will be seen in the following section.

A Strange, Meaningful Event

Although the mayor eventually succeeded in being reelected, various people endeavoured to throw him out of office. The week preceding the elections, in particular, was the time when opposition between the two competing slates became rife on more than one occasion. During a session of the municipal council (which I did not attend), for example, a candidate of Caoria of the slate opposing the outgoing mayor launched a verbal attack against him; a few days later, an anonymous letter accusing the mayor of corruption and bribery was sent to the military police station of Canal San Bovo and to the provincial government in Trent.[40] Then a strange event happened: someone produced a derogatory poem, in the local dialect, targeted at the man who quarrelled with the mayor, made tens of photocopies, and one night dropped a copy in all mailboxes in Caoria. In all likelihood whoever wrote the poem was aware of the fact that the day after the above man[41] was expected to lead the procession of the funeral of his uncle. His participation in the event was an appropriate way of manifesting loyalty to the Church and attachment to the village and its people a few days before the municipal elections for which he was standing as a candidate, given that a number of people from all over the valley were expected to participate in the funeral. The poem (of which I give the original version followed by the English translation) was not merely aimed at denigrating him, but was meant as a device to discourage his fellow villagers from voting for him in the municipal elections. It reads as follows:

L'altra sera, davanti an quartin de vin / i Caorioti i a capì / chi che l'e Bepi Felín.

Saveven che el feva el finto santarel / fin che i forestai no lo ha ciapà / a far contrabandi par tut el Reganel.

L'era ani che i vecioti i diseva che el / Bepi el contrabanda piante qua e là / sempre fora del so prà;

A so modo el ghe spiega a tuti / quant la e granda la so proprietà / e intant ai boni censiti el ghe tol / entre e fora del tabià.

Ai Caorioti ghe dispias, che par colpa den coion / ghe rimete tuta la popolazion, / compresi i so parenti Felini / stimadi e onesti citadini.

Atenti cari Caorioti / che se votè el Bepi e i so soci / dal Reganel a la Fiamena / no resta gnanca i groti e a noi ne toca far fagoti.

[Last night, while having a glass of wine, / Caorians understood / who Bepi Felín[42] really is.

They were aware that he pretended to be a 'saint', / until the officials of the Forestry Department caught him / stealing timber on Mount Reganel.

Our elders have been saying for years / that Bepi is always chopping timber / outside his meadow.

In doing so he showed to everybody / how big his property is, / and meanwhile he stole from the stables of his fellow villagers.

Caorians are sorry that, because of a dickhead, / all the population, / including his respected and honest relatives Felini, / loses its reputation.

Beware dear Caorians! / If you vote for Bepi and his associates / not even the pebbles will remain / between Mount Reganel and Mount Fiamena, / and we will have to pack our things.]

In all likelihood the above poem was written by one of the supporters of the other coalition in light of the argument between Bepi Felín and the mayor of a few days earlier. The poem soon became the main topic of conversation in the bars of Caoria. Most villagers agreed that, although the above man is not known as an honest person, the poem was highly offensive, and that he did not deserve it. The poem referred to an event that happened a few years earlier not far from Caoria, when Bepi Felín was caught by the officials of the Forestry Department, chopping timber without permission in the municipal land adjacent to his landholding. Although the appropriation of timber was illegal, the case was not pursued, and the man was simply requested to pay for the timber he took.

However offensive, the poem throws into relief some of the themes analysed in earlier chapters; one of these is a moral evaluation of churchgoers: so, when it says that Bepi Felín 'pretended to be a saint', it refers to the fact that he was involved in the activities of the Catholic Association of Italian Workers (ACLI) in Caoria and to his commitment to the Church and to the DC in the past. The poem's emphasis on the illicit appropriation of timber from municipal land is deployed to prove that he is far from being an honest person (a *santarel*, that is to say a 'saint'), and to validate the widespread conviction that churchgoers are deceitful. In other words, it stresses that he is a 'saint' only for political reasons, and that he is not what he wants to appear, for example when he leads a procession and carries the cross. Perhaps the most interesting point is that Bepi Felín took timber *fora del so prà*, that is to say 'outside his meadow':[43] he trespassed across the boundaries of somebody else's property (even though it was land owned by the municipality), one of the worst offences in a social environment in which the identification between man and the land he owns is still very strong. That 'in doing so he showed to the other people how big his property is' (i.e. he put on airs) makes little sense unless it is borne in mind that one of the most important achievements in the life of a man in the valley is the acquisition of a large amount of land or its appropriation and 'domestication' through hard work. This means that in felling trees 'out of his meadow' Bepi Felín showed to all his fellow villagers that the land within which he was chopping timber is his (or that he was appropriating it). It seems arguable that the poem was intended as a warning for the Caorians who intended to vote for him and the other people of his slate: if Bepi Felín is elected the Caorians owning *masi* on mounts Reganel and Fiamena will have to leave because, once in power, he will seize the opportunity to get hold of all this, given that he has already tried to do so on another occasion.

The talk 'after the event', however, revealed other significant details about the contents and meanings of the poem, and particularly about Bepi Felín's unsuccessful attempt to appropriate timber from communal land. Everybody was aware of this, but nobody worried about it until the 1995 municipal elections, when Bepi was standing as a candidate for reelection. The problem was not so much that he tried to appropriate timber belonging to the municipality, but that in doing so he became a potential threat for privately owned land too. This is why, according to the author of the poem, Bepi did not deserve to be reelected.[44] The intriguing aspect of the poem is that although the author purports to speak on behalf of the people of Caoria, the poem's main emphasis is on private property: it is implied that if Bepi Felín were elected, people's private property rights would be undermined. Moreover, there is no reference to landed property in the villages, but only to that on the mountains, in the *masi*, which in the social context studied is considered more important, albeit more difficult to control. As one of the major concerns of the local people is landed property and its protection, it is implied that the election of this person could pose serious problems, as he had already tried to get hold of timber from land that is not his.[45] In stressing this, the poem throws into relief the putative 'intrusive' behaviour of Bepi Felín which, especially in Caoria, is ascribed to outsiders or even to the nation-state and its officials (i.e. the military police and the inland revenue). This is also a reference to the practice of moving into land that is either unused or never watched, which became quite common in the valley with depopulation and after the 1966 flood. Intererestingly, the poem in question echoes a rhyme, that was very popular in Caoria in the 1950s, which reads

Se ti voti Gino Favella / Dio salvi la Vallisella
[If you vote for Gino Favella[46] / God save Mount Vallisella [47]]

It is not necessary to go into details to suggest that the poem and the above rhyme convey the same ideas. Both Bepi Felín and Gino Favella are pointed to as potential threats because of their tendency to go 'out of place', to trespass across the others' boundaries. Their behaviour clashes with the rhetoric of the outgoing mayor who, during his speech, presented himself as the person who protects private property and, implicitly, remains 'in place'.

Nobody would have worried about Bepi Felín's appropriating timber from communal land if he had not pushed himself forward for election to the municipal council, simply because getting hold of timber from the land of the municipality or from the demesne is considered a moral entitlement, and should not require a formal permission. There is a dictum in the valley which runs *a rubàr al comùn no si ofende nisùn* ('You do not offend anybody if you steal from the municipality'): although this does not mean that illicit appropriations are customary, it implies that 'stealing' from the municipality is not conceived as a personal offence; and since it is not personal it is not an offence at all. For this reason in the valley the municipality (and public administration in general) is jokingly alluded to as the *laip*, i.e. an excavated log used to feed pigs. In local discourse the *laip* evokes the image of something from which everybody can 'eat', that is to say everybody can exploit. In a sense, both the poem and the talk after the event threw light on the moral evaluations attached to public and private domains. It seems arguable that the private domain, epitomised by the image of the 'bounded field' which should not be crossed by strangers, is seen as antithetical to the public one to which everybody has access, and which everybody feels entitled to exploit simply because it is open.

What emerged in the poem and in the talk after the event was the ideal inaccessibility of private property. One of the factors that enabled the outgoing mayor to be reelected was his promise to protect it, at least in Caoria. As a man stated, 'he does not stir up trouble' (*nol rompi i coioni*), which implies that he remains 'in place': social actors do not worry about the mayor's behaviour as long as he refrains from 'stealing' in the valley. By contrast, the policy of another mayor was resented because it was 'intrusive': nowadays he is remembered as a bureaucrat who used to get local people (including his covillagers) to abide by strict rules. The idea that whoever administers the municipality should remain 'in place' and refrain from 'crossing boundaries' (both physically and symbolically) is consistent with the Christian Democrat policy aimed at defending the traditional order and guaranteeing the autonomy of civil society instead of intervening to modify it (Filippucci et al. 1997), not to speak of that of the *leghe* in the 1990s. As has been noted, such an idea reflected both the Christian Democratic Party's and the Northern League's separation between society and politics that took the form of the defence of the private (family and private property) and of the traditions of the local community as opposed to the nation-state. Both in the poem and in the rhetoric of the above political formations territory emerges as a powerful symbol, as the embodiment of the local community, and private property comes to the fore as an 'extension' of its owner: in other words, it is a relationship loaded with meaning. However, the imagery of territory was not an 'invention' of political leaders: if anything, these legitimated a set of ideas which already informed local discourse.

The emergence of territory as a powerful symbol brings us back to the considerations made earlier in this work, particularly as regards the locals' (especially men's) obsession with property boundaries rather than politics per se: as the anecdote has shown, it is not abstract ideologies that are the focus of the actors' interest in politics, but making sure that whoever holds power remains 'in one's own place'. In other words, individual social actors may be sensitive to politics insofar as it touches them directly. The issue of the autonomy of the local community came to the fore again in the summer of 1997, when the mayor and the municipal council agreed to sue the official of the military police in Canal San Bovo for his 'intruding' into the administration of the municipality, i.e. for inquiring about what seemed an illicit issue of permits to renovate some buildings in the valley. The mayor was brought to trial at least twice because of this, but eventually he was acquitted. Social actors interpreted the event was in different ways. However, they did not express discomfort at the fact that there was something wrong in the issue of the permits. They expressed instead a complaint that an outsider, and particularly an official of the military police from the South, should not interfere with the running of the municipal government in that he is not a member of the community, and therefore he does not know what happens in the valley. So, the local people were ascribing to this official the same 'intrusive' character that is deemed typical of the nation-state of which he is a representative, and of the people such as Bepi Felín and Gino Favella who 'trespass' across property boundaries and behave like outsiders. The mayor, in turn, further legitimated his reputation as the person 'close to the people' who protects the community.

Shortly after the end of the inquiry the mayor wrote an article in the local magazine[48] to give some clarifications about what had happened. His main point was that there had been some mistakes when the aforementioned permits were issued because of some national laws that were difficult to interpret. So, he did not give a different version of what happened, but blamed instead the state administration for imposing laws that few or nobody can understand. This enabled him to place himself in the 'community', and further stress the distance between the community itself and the state. In the same article he added that the trials he was involved in cost the local government over 50,000.000 Italian lire (about £17,000); this sum, according to him, belonged to the community, and could be used in a better way. In saying so, he stressed the 'intrusive' character of the state, and implied that its 'intrusion' did not touch him only, but all the inhabitants of the municipality. The result of this, he added, was that the 'community' had to pay a considerable sum because of some putative incomprehensible national laws. Taking a hint from Rogers' French case study (1991: 210), it may be suggested that the mayor was eventually able to impose his vision of the community onto the local political landscape because he could do it in terms that were plausible to all the inhabitants of the valley, and because he could involve the 'community': phrased differently, if the state prosecutes him, eventually the 'community' will pay for it.

From the information discussed there emerge significant parallels between the mayor's views and the ideologies of the autonomist parties. Their emphasis upon the image of the community distinct from the state suggests that the autonomist parties such as the Northern League and the PATT managed to win the majority of the vote in the early 1990s because they were able to translate the grievances of the local people. However, they also succeeded in appropriating some of the values that were central to Catholic ideology, among which were support for local society and ideas that already informed local-level discourses. Thus, it does not really matter whether some ideas are championed by the Northern League or by the PATT as long as they guarantee the autonomy of the community.[49]

Conclusion

As pointed out in the previous chapter, the lament for a lost autonomy and 'independence' informs much of village thinking. That this lament may also be given political expression is suggested by the electoral success of the Northern League and the PATT in the 1990s. It seems clear that these found fertile ground in an area, such as the valley studied and Trentino, where various elements of their ideologies were not entirely new, and the promise of the reconstruction of the 'community' contributed to a significant extent to their electoral success. Many of the values that the Catholic Church no longer advocates were championed by these autonomist movements, whose ability to express few concepts in simple ways and in a language familiar to those who received such ideas has been crucial for their success. Their appeal to locality and local traditions (and, implicitly, to 'territory') is a case in point. If I were to infer that the political transformations which occurred in northern Italy in the 1990s had the effect of altering individual actors' perceptions of politics I would risk overlooking the social and structural frameworks which fostered such transformations at the local level.

That communities and local identities may be culturally constructed by means of language and symbols is a truism. However, as I have tried to show, this does not imply that these were arbitrary inventions of those in power. The construction of community does not entail the subject's applying his or her will to raw materials: 'The constructor is always forced to make use of the materials at hand' (Stråth 2000: 23), and so construction is never pure invention. So, issues of national concern such as northern Italian ethnic identity may acquire a specific meaning in certain settings. In Caoria and Ronco the autonomist parties' appeal to the 'community' was not so much perceived in terms of opposition vis-à-vis the South, as in contrast to the *'taliáni* who have acquired a substantial amount of land in the valley.[50] In Caoria the Northern League's appeal to hard work as a virtue which singles out the North of Italy from the South was instead associated with the perceived difference between a 'hardworking' Caoria and a 'slack' Canal San Bovo, and particularly as further evidence that those who hold political power do not do real work. The Northern

League's appeal to 'territory' (instead of language) and to 'locality' (as opposed to the nation-state) may translate ideas about private property which, in turn, reflect the villagers' obsession with property boundaries on the one hand, and those between the community and the outside on the other.

This brings us back to the considerations made at the beginning of this chapter, and especially to my critique of a reading of politics as *mise en représentation*. If an analysis of politics were confined to mere 'representation', we would have to assume that political symbols have a compelling power, and that the ideas expressed by the social actors mirror (and replicate) those propagated by party leaders or by those in high places. I hope I have made it clear that political ideologies played little part in the politicians' formulations of collective (and political) identity at the local level. The mayor of Canal San Bovo is a case in point: he did not 'invent' the communities he was addressing, but gave them legitimacy. During his electoral speech he did not address a group of people sharing the same political ideas or affiliated to the same political party, but a group of residents living in the same territory. In other words, he was addressing a 'territorial' community rather than a 'political' one. On the one hand, the emergence of a depoliticised social group is typical of a time when the Subject ceases to be political (Delanty 1999: 46–47); on the other hand, as we have seen, this emergence is hardly new: the image of the territorial community on which the mayor's speech centred should be seen in a relation of continuity with that of the 'old days'. What changed was its form, not its content, given the role that 'locality' played in the Italian political arena at the time of my fieldwork. Even the depoliticised Subject was not a creation of the mayor himself: rather, it was a widely shared view of the social order as largely depoliticised which helped make sense of the image of the 'community' advocated by the mayor. His rhetoric was effective as it rested on the concordance between his discourse and the meanings embodied in the people he addressed. So, the role of human agency in investing this image of the community with meaning had been decisive.

Behind the idea of the 'community' the mayor was heralding lay a complex image of the political landscape. In presenting himself as the person who remains 'in place' he implicitly legitimated the imagery of a community made up of 'bounded fields' or private properties ideally inaccessible. In doing so he did not simply impose his own view of the political landscape: rather, he expressed such a view in a way that enabled the audience to make sense of it, he accommodated it to local-level discourses. He did not appeal to abstract ideologies, but to what the inhabitants of the valley (especially men) are most eager to protect from the outside, private property as an extension of the self. It is largely the concreteness of territory as private property, as opposed to an 'abstract' nation-state[51] which helped to 'naturalise' the connection between politics and autonomy, and particularly the idea of politics as the formulation and achievement of private interests: the mayor had to take into account (not to say legitimate) the values shared by the people involved, and local society acted as a motive force. This seems to accord with Herzfeld's view (1992: 49) that nationalism imposed from above hardly allows for the role of individual social actors in recasting official meanings in familiar terms, all the more so at a time when access to knowledge is no longer restricted to the élites. In a sense, the success of the regionalist parties in that period could be interpreted as the outcome of the interplay of various social, cultural and political factors, of which the appeal to the local community as a 'private space' is probably the most significant. Although categories of 'region' and 'regional identity' (just like 'nation' and 'national identity') may affect the ways social actors conceptualise the social order (Thompson 2001: 25), it is instead ideas of social order and the experience of everyday life that help them make sense of such categories. Whereas the collective values of the region (or the nation) serve to shape human behaviour, social action and particularly everyday practices can also invest the region (and locality) with meaning.

NOTES

1. Bringa (1995: 230) observed that there is a key difference in the way identity (local, national, religious, political) is perceived by people locally and by the establishment. Handler (1988: 8) made this point even more strongly, and argued that 'it is only the subjective …perception of identity that launches a group on its career of collective action'.

2. See also Eriksen (1993: 116).

3. Pratt (1996: 129) made this point in his analysis of Catholic ideology.

4. It must be noted that, unlike other European countries, Italy had a pluralist party system with a plurality of parties represented in Parliament until the introduction of the majoritarian system in 1992 that brought about the consolidation of the power of the governing coalitions.

5. Source: Municipality of Canal San Bovo.

6. See '*Voci di Primiero*', 1, 4, 1941.

7. The custom of naming the land after the family that owns it is a case in point.

8. Ronco had a priest who lived there for about forty years, and Caoria had one who resided in the village from 1948 until 1966.

9. That families were very large in size, for example, was not only due to limited knowledge about contraception, but also to the fact that the ideal of a large household was central to the priest's teachings.

10. This is the case of the collective nickname 'bears' (*orsi*), that is attached to Caorians as a stigma. Although there is evidence that it acted as a stigma as early as the 1920s, all the people of the valley outside Caoria agree that Caorians are referred to as *orsi* because of a statement (which became famous in the valley) by the priest who resided there betweeen 1948 and 1966 ('You were "bears" when I came, you are still "bears" now that I am leaving this village'). That most Caorians refer to the inhabitants of Ronco as deceitful is due to another statement by the same priest.

11. Many stories in Caoria testify to the authority of priests in inheritance matters. A woman of Caoria, for example, told me that when her mother died, in 1985, she was visited by a priest who said that the night before he had dreamt of the deceased expressing her will to bequeath part of her patrimony to the Church. This person acknowledged that she had believed in what the priest had told her, until she was advised by her sister to ignore the whole thing.

12. See, for a comparison, Kertzer (1980: 133–5).

13. Aside from their religious meaning, processions are the 'traditions where the profane aspects are more strongly rooted …than are the religious aspects' (Schweizer 1988: 188).

14. It is not coincidental that some devout churchgoing men are accorded an aura of effeminacy.

15. Processions and the feast of the patron saint express this idea, as has been seen.

16. See, for an analysis of this idiom, Pratt's works on Tuscany (1980, 1984, 1986).

17. This idea of locality enabled the DC to stress shared interests, as opposed to the left-wing idiom of class conflict.

18. A native of the adjacent Valsugana who was the priest of Caoria and Ronco (then of the entire valley) from 1985 until 1996. He took no active part in party politics, and used to maintain a distance towards the families of supporters of the ex-DC. Moreover, he had little contact with villagers outside his official duties.

19. As Riegelhaupt (1973: 849) pointed out in relation to a different context, modern Catholicism is designed for individual salvation and 'does not see itself as the institution through which communal identity should be expressed and celebrated' (see also Brandes 1976).

20. Jeff Pratt, personal communication.

21. A factor that contributed to the persistence of local particularism in the valley until the late 1970s was the national law concerning the election of the municipal council, which entitled each village of the *comune* to elect its own representatives in the municipal government.

22. This information is based on the results of the 1996 national elections.

23. One of its slogans was 'away from Rome, closer to Europe', though 'Europe' did not mean 'Brussels', but a 'Europe of regions'.

24. See the previous section for details.

25. A new electoral law concerning municipal governments, based on the direct election of the mayor, was passed in 1993.

26. The new electoral law mandates that coalitions standing for election in the municipal council may be formed irrespective of where their candidates reside.

27. Although elected into the national government, the centre-right coalition of which the Northern League formed part had to resign at the end of 1994.

28. I use the possessive 'his' because all the mayors of Canal San Bovo so far have been men.

29. In 1995 there was only one candidate in Ronco, an industrialist affiliated to the Northern League. He was convinced by the mayor to side with him for he had a wide kin network on which he could rely for support. Notwithstanding the fact that the former was elected, he played no important political role in his village.

30. An estate agent, native of Prade, working outside the valley. Formerly the district secretary of the Italian Socialist Party and of the district section of the Catholic Association of Italian Workers (ACLI), currently affiliated to no political party. His role as estate agent gave him the opportunity to exercise his political power while at the same time controlling the transactions of sales of land and buildings in the valley, as most of the people who were in the process of acquiring land in the municipality had to turn to him.

31. When this book was in progress the pound sterling was exchanged at about 3,000 Italian lire.

32. When I did my fieldwork there were scarcely 1,700 people officially resident in the valley.

33. Aside from nostalgia for the community of the 'old days', it must be stressed that a *comune* of at least 2,000 inhabitants may enjoy financial benefits from the provincial administration.

34. He was referring to the alienation of land and houses to the people of the nearby Veneto which occurred during the last three decades.

35. See, for a comparison with southern Italy, Davis (1973: 161).

36. This is reminiscent of the protective landlord that was at the centre of Scott's analysis of the moral economy of the peasant (1976), even though the social and economic context studied by that author is different from that of the Italian Alps.

37. This accords with Bailey's argument (1991: xv) that words and other performances 'are messages that can be used to manipulate other people'.

38. This does not mean that those who attended the gathering were passive recipients of this message: on the contrary, most of these were aware that politicians keep only a few of the promises they make.

39. Pratt (1986: 149–52) found a very similar situation in Tuscany.

40. Eventually the accusation was not pursued by the police.

41. Formerly a supporter of the DC, he used to lead all the processions in the village.

42. A fictive nickname.

43. 'Meadow' should be read as 'property in the *masi*'.

44. In spite of this derogatory propaganda Bepi Felín managed to be reelected, thanks to his relatives of Canal San Bovo who gained him several votes.

45. The other implication of the poem is that he 'enlarges' his property through crossing its boundaries. This refers to the villagers who in the past moved their boundary markers in

order to get hold of a larger amount of hay for the livestock, which gave rise to many skirmishes between the people owning adjacent landholdings.

46. Another fictive nickname.

47. Another mountain where some Caorian families used to own *masi*. Now it is all forested.

48. See '*Vanoi Notizie*', 7, 1997.

49. Allegiance to autonomist parties does not mean that social actors necessarily see such political formations as expressions of local sentiment only: they may support a given political formation because of convenience. Such was the case of the 1994 national elections in Caoria, when a candidate from Castello Tesino (affiliated to the Northern League) gained the support of most Caorians despite the fact that the two adjacent municipalities are not on good terms. The main reason for this was that the new sawmill of Caoria, just taken over by the provincial government, was about to be sold to outsiders, much to the dismay of the local people. The above man promised that, if he were elected, he would endeavour to prevent the sawmill from being sold. In so doing, he acted as what Bailey (1969: 76) called a 'transactional leader'. Eventually, although he was elected, he did very little to keep his promise, and even now the future of the sawmill remains uncertain.

50. A survey made by the local rural credit institution in the early 1990s revealed that more than 50 percent of the houses in the valley are owned by people who do not ordinarily reside there.

51. See Abélès (1990: 82) for a discussion of the 'abstract' nature of the nation-state.

8
CONCLUSIONS:
LOCALISM REVISITED

Making Sense of the Data

I started this work by raising two main issues: that of the role of human agency in making sense of the constructions of locality made by the political establishment; and that of local identity at a time when the idea of collective identity is being deconstructed. The rather heterogeneous data discussed suggest that while there are multiple representations of locality, common themes emerge, particularly the idea of 'boundedness'. Clearly, the 'locality' which I investigated has not the same character that used to be ascribed to some Mediterranean villages until recently, but is undergoing a process of redefinition. However, although in anthropology the 'boundedness' of locality was interpreted as a reflection of a modernist theoretical analysis (Gupta and Ferguson 1997; Malkki 1997; Lovell 1998; Rapport and Dawson 1998), it seems clear that locality is described as 'bounded' by those who live there. Since the redefinition of locality was also related to the political and economic transformations that occurred in the 1990s at the national and supranational levels, I pointed to the different meanings the people involved attach to locality itself, and to the necessity of an analysis of how such transformations interweave with the experience of social actors' immediate world.

In this concluding chapter I intend to bring issues already discussed to bear on a theme that is central in local discourse. I argued that 'official' meanings, notably the regionalist ideologies championed by party leaders, are not always superimposed, but are often accommodated to local-level discourses. This led me to query the sustainability of a top-down reading of localism, and advocate instead both a theory of localism that allows for human agency, and a conceptualisation of localism as a defining feature of sociality. In saying so, I implied that the immediate issue is that of defining the nature of this process of accommodation: so, chapter 3 opened up the question of whether the description of locality as a 'private', 'bounded' space was simply the way social actors represent an intimate space or represents instead a conceptualisation of the social world. Then I pursued the idea that such a notion could be a useful analytical tool to describe the relationship with the encompassing society. That chapter was a starting point, for it set the background against which the issues discussed in the following chapters could be understood. The exploration of the idea of locality as a 'private space' is extended a step further in the analysis of hunting practices in chapter 4, where I pursue the idea that hunting is aimed at the 'protection' of nature and locality from strangers. So, it is by introducing distance between locality and the encompassing society, and by describing the community as a 'private' space that actors challenge the legitimacy of the nation-state, in the same manner that in 1844 Caorians appealed to distance to legitimate their claims to independence from Canal San Bovo.

The idea of locality as a 'private' space also informs the construction of otherness analysed in chapter 5: that the inhabitants of the nearby municipality are labelled as 'intrusive' (*invadenti*), and implicitly alluded to as 'matter out of place' throws into relief a conceptualisation of the regional and national territory as a space in which everyone should stay in one's own place. In that chapter I suggested that the stigmatisation of outsiders also reflects the ways in which the social order propagated by the state is questioned, and rests on a self-ascription of qualities such as the capacity to sustain hard work, which involves capacity to work one's own 'field' and protect it. The idea that locals partake of an Austrian or Tyrolean culture serves to give to local boundaries an 'ethnic' flavour, and defining oneself as 'Austrian' functions as a rhetorical device to stress (or invent) difference between locality and the state. Appealing to an Austrian culture does not entail claims to cosmopolitanism, but means instead self-ascription of the qualities which in local discourse are deemed to be typically Austrian: the capacity to work hard, and direct control over property which stems from hard work. More importantly, it is much easier for locals to relate to Austria by simply referring to a father or ancestor who was in the Austro-Hungarian army than by relating to a nation-state perceived as 'distant' and 'impersonal'.

That the notion of 'private' can be a useful analytical tool to describe distinctiveness was also thrown into relief (albeit not so explicitly) in chapter 6, in which I observed that representations of local history (particularly in Caoria) have to do not just with the interpretation of events which took place in the valley, but also serve to place locality outside national history. Whether or not the accounts of the past are accurate, they mark boundaries that exclude outsiders from the local pedigree. Representing the past as repetitive evokes the idea of a social group that reproduces itself over time, as has been seen; yet this is a reference to a group which reproduces itself on the same territory, on a territory which the group controls, that is to say a private property. This led me to suggest that local history is represented by a set of narratives of the ways in which locals seized and kept control of the territory: the landscape social actors allude to is not an object of aesthetic contemplation, but territory socially appropriated, namely, a mosaic of individually owned lots, a 'clean' and 'ordered' landscape to which outsiders should not have access. What emerged from that chapter was the idea, deployed throughout this work, that what is turned into 'property' (and particularly 'private property') becomes a focus of social identity and a site of resistance to the state: the image of a 'clean', 'bounded' landscape managed by locals evokes a counter-image of an 'open' one to which everybody has access. The nostalgia for a time when the community was 'free' is a reference to an idealised prepolitical past, when state agencies did not interfere with community affairs.

In the following chapter I looked at local politics, and suggested that it is not so much political symbols that impel people to action, as their ability to interpret political messages and ideologies in familiar terms. This is evidenced by the ways social actors combine the Northern League's emphasis on locality as a focus of attachment and hard work with the PATT's stress on Trentino's partaking of a Tyrolean culture. Particularly, the idea of local politics as a form of defence of local interests and territorial boundaries, which is central both to local discourse and to the rhetoric of autonomist politicians, suggests that although politics represents the achievement and sustained organisation of collective interests, its object may be the protection of the private. The idealised image of the politician who remains 'in place' (i.e. who does not cross boundaries, both materially and symbolically) and does not threaten private property rights represents the moral opposite of the 'intrusive' outsiders who trespass property boundaries to appropriate land and resources illicitly, the attitude ascribed to the state and its officials. It seems reasonable to suggest that in local discourse politics and hunting share similar aims: to avoid the intrusion of outsiders, and to keep the territory 'clean', that is to say to maintain the ideal order that now is attributed to the community of the 'old days'. I make no claims to novelty in emphasising the dichotomy between 'inside' and 'outside': if anything, what is unusual is that the appropriation of an environmentalist discourse serves to contest some aspects of nationhood, particularly domination.

In a sense, the range of information discussed tells us similar stories: it is the story of a human group that worked hard to create its spatial and social domain, and strives to ensure its reproduction and defend its physical and symbolic boundaries. It is a story of a group of people who occupy a definite space that becomes the context of interpersonal relationships and political action, whose boundaries should not be crossed. In sum, it is the story of the production and reproduction of a private domain, or 'bounded field'. So, when the villager yells at the *'talián* (or the covillager) who crosses the boundary of his field he expresses the same fear of 'intrusions' that was central to the rhetoric of the autonomist parties towards the state, an attitude which may be functional to integralist political engagements broadly defined. Similarly, the chit-chat that goes on in the bars or men's priding themselves ostentatiously on their ability to catch game without a licence also represent a concern with the protection of the 'private' from outside agents. Both hunting practices and, to a significant extent, representations of history reveal not simply ideas about what is local, but also about what is private. Hunting, as I observed, is part of the 'production of locality', the process through which landscape is symbolically turned into private property. The fear of the state is largely a fear that the latter's encroaching on the village would make the territory open to people who do not belong to the community. Opening the community would run counter to the ideal of keeping people and things 'in place' advocated by local politicians. Emphasis upon the 'private' also represents a rhetorical device to deny one of the main principles that defines the nation-state: that the nation-state itself is at the top of a set of nested levels that encompasses the periphery from an administrative standpoint, in terms of knowledge (Herzfeld 1987; see also Filippucci et al. 1997), and temporally: discourse about villageness, boundaries, landscape, the Austrian or Tyrolean legacy and the rhetoric of the DC and of the autonomist parties convey very similar meanings to the people involved, and have become constituent parts of the same mental schema. So, the spatial arrangement of peoples and cultures does not represent a conceptualisation of anthropologists, as Malkki (1997: 58) and others would have suggested, but may be an integral part of the way social actors represent and locate themselves in a changing world. Overemphasising rootedness would blind us to movement and displacement in the same way that stressing deterritorialisation and 'imagined' places would divert our attention from the range of meanings of the 'local' as the context for integralist political engagements. Although most of the locals experienced emigration abroad, eventually many came back, and now movement hardly forms part of their self-identity: being 'in place' (*a posto*) may give them that sense of security that the uncertainties which movement entails are unlikely to provide, and especially a 'private place' conjures up a notion of a social context in which those who are not the owners are not allowed. So, movement and fluidity can hardly obliterate the associations social actors make between persons and localities, and such associations continue to inform the ways these people conceptualise the social world.

It seems arguable that in the area under study discourse about localism is largely discourse about private property. In suggesting this, I subscribe to Herzfeld's view (1985a: 29–30) that a local, antistatist ideology is not necessarily articulated in terms of grand political theories. If anything, it is the highly charged symbols that belong to everyday life that are the most powerful, because of their connection with ideas about something 'familiar', hence their potential for manipulation (Herzfeld 1992: 10–11). They might be what Douglas (1970) called 'natural symbols', which include blood and kinship. In this case the natural symbol that is more familiar is privately-owned land: as Hann suggested (1998: 7), focus on property should not be limited to formal legal codes, but should include the cultural contexts within which such codes operate. A local-level notion of private property has to do with a social appropriation of the territory, and is consistent with Godelier's view (1986: 81) that property exists 'when it is rendered effective in and through a process of concrete appropriation'. Thus associating locality with private property accords to the 'local' the concreteness that is denied by a conceptualisation of locality itself as a mere 'structure of feeling' or as an 'imagined place'.

There are grounds for suggesting that the notion of the 'bounded field' epitomised by the image of a meadow high on the mountainside, surrounded by the forest, comes to represent the embodiment of this idea of locality: it is land named after its owner with very clear boundaries. While this is the characteristic attributed to a 'clean', natural landscape, it is also that ascribed to a 'political landscape'. It is local-level practices such as turning territory into private property, both materially and symbolically, that carry a sense of historical continuity for the local people. These practices help to naturalise the connection among the Austrian past, autonomy, and private property. The imagery of the bounded field and the ideas that it conveys bring us back to one of the main issues explored by this work, that of human agency and its role in making sense of the élites' constructions of locality. There are different levels of identity, the common one being the protection of the private. What emerges is the idea of order, epitomised by the bounded field. Boundedness, in turn, holds together political expression. I hope I have made it clear, in the course of this work, that the idea of the nation or the region as an entity existing over and above social relations needs to be rediscussed: although categories of 'nation' and 'national identity' (and, implicitly, the region, regional identity, locality, and local identity) affect to a significant extent the ways individuals conceptualise social order and perceive the difference between their society and others (Thompson 2001: 25), it seems arguable that it is instead perceptions of social order which enable actors to make sense of the above categories. A region which needs to be defended from outsiders may be conceptualised as an extension of a village in the same manner that locality may be imagined as an extension of the 'bounded field'. So, the distinction between 'us' and 'them' is not a creation of politicians, but is part of the way actors experience the world they live in. In this case it is the experience of village and private property boundaries that forms the background against which national and regional boundaries are perceived and understood. The ideology of the bounded field and its association with private property is functional to integralist political engagements, as has been observed, for it shapes a dissociative relation: a property comes into being with the exclusion of others (Abramson 2000: 13).

The above considerations leave a question unanswered: how can the imagery of the bounded field, which conveys ideas of exclusive control, coexist with that of local/regional identity, which presupposes the existence of a collectivity or 'imagined community'? I do not think there are any contradictions underlying their coexistence. If anything, this coexistence rests on the conceptualisation of a community made up of a mosaic of 'bounded fields'. Territory, the social world and the political arena are described (and, I would add, thought of) as projections of this imagery. This imagery is linked to the issue of the interpretation of political messages: I make no claims to novelty in saying that individuals reinterpret culture in their own ways instead of simply enacting it. On the one hand, this construction of locality as a private space is affected by a political rhetoric that casts property and territory as an extension of those who work it and live there; on the other hand, these ideas already informed social actors' views at the time of my fieldwork, and were not a product of a political rhetoric of late modernity. So, while the politician draws on the idea of hard work, and constructs locality (and the region) as a 'bounded field', he appeals to values that already permeate local discourse. However, social actors look to the politician for legitimation of such ideas: one draws upon the other one in a circular fashion. In this regard, there is a dialectical relationship between the images evoked by the élites and the social actors' understandings of such images (Smith 1999: 45). Yet the construction of locality as a private space not only legitimates claims to distinctiveness, but also accords very well with the values of late capitalism.

The Place of 'Place' in the New Millennium

When this work was close to completion, I had the opportunity to go back to Trentino to assess the impact of social and political changes between the late 1990s and the turn of the millennium. The project of the establishment of a European Region of Tyrol, undertaken in 1993, was dropped in 1996. Although the Euregio has kept an office in Brussels since the inception of the project, such a region now exists on paper rather than in the minds of the people, and it has no economic and political significance (Pallaver 2000: 273). The PATT, which championed the project in the early 1990s, ceased to be the leading party in Trentino, and although it allied with the Northern League in the provincial elections of 1998 and the national ones of 2001 it was defeated in both occasions. Moreover, the Northern League no longer has the appeal that it had in the 1990s, as other centre-right political formations gained most of the vote that the *Lega* used to garner. However, the fact that locality is not given political expression does not mean that it has ceased to be a context for political action. The distinctiveness of locality vis-à-vis the encompassing state continues to loom large in local discourse, and recent developments suggest that the situation is unlikely to change in the near future. Despite the decreasing significance of the PATT in the regional political arena, the Austro-Hungarian legacy is still appealing in the valley, as shown by the recent creation of a group of Schützen. In other words, for many people 'Austrian culture' remains a banner to fly proudly.

The fact that in 2001 locality figured prominently in local discourse reveals that the decline of regionalist political formations has hardly affected the ways a sense of belonging was expressed in the mid-1990s. This became patent after the national elections, held in May of the same year, which saw the victory of the centre-right coalition led by Silvio Berlusconi, the media tycoon of Milan, over the centre-left coalition led by Francesco Rutelli, formerly the mayor of Rome. The eve of the elections found the people of the area caught between a longing for 'order' which only autonomist and regionalist parties were believed to provide, and the awareness that their choice was in fact limited to either the centre-left or the centre-right coalition. It was clear, from what villagers said after hearing the results, that one of the factors that enhanced Berlusconi's success, aside from his promise to protect the interests of entrepreneurs, was his ability to make his speeches understandable. On the other hand, they stated explicitly that the political messages of the other candidate were difficult to understand. More importantly, the people I talked with said that they preferred to give their vote to a northern entrepreneur, that is to say, to a hard worker. According to them, his opponent, a Roman, has never worked in his life, and so he was not considered fit to lead the national government. So, the North/South dichotomy still affects the way actors understand the political arena at the national level, and is a transposition of the ideas that inform the distinction between the community and the outside.

Although it is difficult to predict how the situation will evolve in the future, the changes of the last few years seem to suggest that the valley is witnessing a decline of social life, which is due to depopulation on the one hand, and to the presence of an ageing population spending more time at home on the other. The able-bodied, in turn, spend most of the day at work, and do not socialise in the bars as much as they used to in the past, and nowadays meeting people on the streets does not occur very frequently. In a sense, what the valley is facing is an almost irreversible withdrawal of its inhabitants from public life. While part of the population leaves the valley to join close relatives living in urban centres, for those committed to remaining there locality, the household and the *maso* built by the ancestors are likely to remain the main foci of attachment. Emphasis on the private domain is patent in most of the conversations in the bars, which still centre on the boundaries of so-and-so's landholding. During the last few years such attitudes are expressed by the growing number of landholdings being fenced, and by the presence of 'private property' signs. So, the bounded field is not necessarily in the minds of the people only, but is materalising. The imaginary fence that used to be around the village in the 'old days' now criss-crosses the village itself. Retreat into private life and separation are becoming the strategies to cope with a changing situation. Paradoxically, the ideology of the bounded field now accords very well with the ideology of the self-reliant individual recorded in a very similar context (Bendix 1985: 77–9), with political engagements which are deemed typical of late modernity, and even with a retreat from politics itself.

The persistence of the bounded field as an ideological basis of local identity accounts for the emergence of specific political engagements in areas characterised by a strong Catholic subculture, and reflects a situation recorded elsewhere (Pine 1996), especially when and where the state and public administration threaten to undermine private property. Anthropological scholarship has focused extensively on this aspect, though it concentrated mainly on nationalist movements that have not achieved statehood, particularly linguistic minorities. The role of territory has scarcely been acknowledged by the substantial body of anthropological literature focusing on nationalism. Instead, there has been a tendency to concentrate on the degree of the people's attachment to language and traditions championed by nationalist or regionalist parties. The Trentine case illustrated here doubtless shares some similarities with case studies on nationalism, yet the lack of importance of language in forging a local/regional identity contrasts sharply with them. Localism, as has been seen, reflects a concern with territory. Although I agree that one of the tasks of the researcher is that of assessing the extent of match or mismatch between the ideas imposed 'from above' and those shared by the actors, I also contend that actors draw selectively upon such ideas, and tend to choose the elements of these that are more 'familiar' and more intelligible; as I have shown, this holds true both for political ideas and for those of regional or ethnic identity. That local-level practices and understandings may make sense of such ideas is a case in point. What emerged from this study is the interdependence between the two or, I would say, a dialectical relationship. Ideas about autonomy may already be part of a set of shared values, albeit in a different form, to which political leaders give legitimacy. This would resonate with Anthony Cohen's idea (1987) that local identities are formed primarily from within, if it were not for the fact that the role of the state (and of political parties as well) is downplayed in his analysis.

Aside from throwing into relief the significance of property in the understanding of local identity, this study has suggested that distinctiveness vis-à-vis the nation-state does not always stem from linguistic or 'ethnic' differences: rather, such differences are likely to arise from a set of ideas that pervade local discourse. Actors draw upon the experience of 'material' things, as is the case of the boundary of a field that has to be protected from the neighbour who attempts to 'enlarge' his landholding or to appropriate timber illicitly. The mere assumption that differences are created or 'invented' by the political establishment, that is to say 'imposed' on the actors, would prevent us from acknowledging the potential that 'natural' symbols assume in recasting official symbols and meanings in familiar terms. In the case of the area studied 'place', and particularly the imagery of the bounded field, need to be both deconstructed and understood as powerful meaning-giving systems, and not as products or 'inventions' of intellectuals. 'Locality' may be a construct of politicians and urban intellectuals at the same time that actors filter such a construct through local-level practices and understandings. Overstressing the role of official discourse would entail the risk of attaching to local identity the label of 'hollow category', in Ardener's terms (1989a: 69–71), at the same time that emphasising local identity as formed 'from within' would mean downplaying the role of the former. In either case we would risk reifying one at the expense of the other. In this work I have tried to analyse both the political leaders' representations of local identity and the actors' readings of these representations, so as to avoid reducing all social experience to a single model. In introducing the imagery of the bounded field between the two I hope I have done justice to the dialectical nature of this relationship.

APPENDIX I:
POPULATION OF CAORIA
AND RONCO, 1996

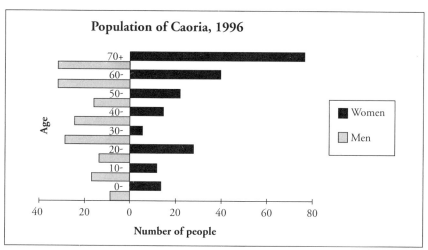

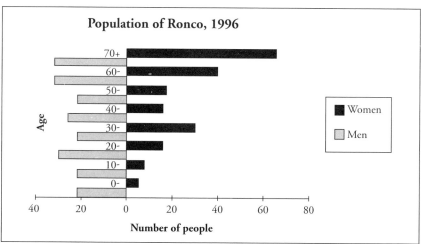

Appendix II:
Population in the Vanoi
Valley, 1826–1996

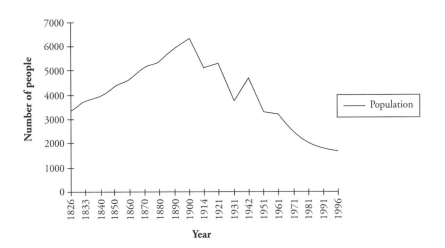

APPENDIX III: 1996 VOTING PATTERNS IN THE COMUNE OF CANAL SAN BOVO

	San Bovo	Caoria	Prade	Ronco	Total
PATT	29	54	24	19	126
Centre-Left	96	56	61	20	233
Green Party	1	2	5	1	9
Northern League	136	59	80	41	316
Centre-Right	110	59	92	30	291

Source: Commune of Canal San Bovo.

APPENDIX IV: EDUCATIONAL LEVEL OF THE POPULATION OF CAORIA AND RONCO, 1996

Level of educational achievement of the population of Caoria, 1996.

Level	Number	%
No degree (under 10)	28	6.91
No degree (adults)	4	0.98
Primary school	233	57.53
Secondary school	94	23.20
High school	40	9.87
University	6	1.48
Total	**405**	**99.97**

Source: Commune of Canal San Bovo.

Level of educational achievement of the population of Ronco, 1996.

Level	Number	%
No degree (under 10)	17	8.33
No degree (adults)	1	0.49
Primary school	114	55.88
Secondary school	65	31.86
High school	7	3.43
University	–	–
Total	**204**	**99.99**

Source: Commune of Canal San Bovo.

APPENDIX V: LAND USE IN THE COMUNE OF CANAL SAN BOVO (15 APRIL 1996)

	Amount of land (square kilometres)	%
Arable	1.802251	01.43
Meadow	14.583080	11.62
Vegetable garden	0.002519	>0.01
Pasture	4.041478	03.22
Alp	30.449032	24.28
Woodland	63.669616	50.77
River	1.677369	01.33
Road	1.065393	00.84
Barren	7.527143	06.00
Other	0.584257	00.46
Total	**125.402138**	**99.95**

Source: Land Registry Office of Fiera di Primiero.

Appendix VI: Occupations in Caoria and Ronco, 1996 (%)

	Caoria		Ronco	
	M	**F**	**M**	**F**
Civil servants, police, teachers, clerks, etc.	3.7	1.5	2.4	1.4
Manual workers	14.5	5.4	22.5	4.9
Shop owners, retailers	1.0	1.5	–	2.4
Students (school age)	2.2	2.2	3.4	2.4
Students (high school, etc.)	3.2	1.9	3.9	1.4
Working at home (unwaged)	–	9.8	–	8.3
Under school age	1.9	2.4	2.9	0.5
Retired	17.7	29.1	14.7	26.9
Unemployed	0.7	0.7	1.4	–

References

Abélès, M. 1990. *Anthropologie de l'état.* Paris: Armand Colin.

_____, 1991. *Quiet Days in Burgundy: A Study of Local Politics.* Cambridge: Cambridge University Press.

_____, 1997. 'La mise en represéntation du politique'. In *Anthropologie du politique,* ed. M. Abélès and H. Jeudy. Paris: Armand Colin.

Abrahams, R. 1991. *A Place of their Own. Family Farming in Eastern Finland.* Cambridge: Cambridge University Press.

Abramson, A. 2000. 'Mythical land, legal boundaries: wondering about landscape and other tracts'. In *Land, Law and Environment. Mythical Land, Legal Boundaries,* ed. A. Abramson and D. Theodossopoulos. London: Pluto Press.

Adam, B. 1994. 'Perceptions of time'. In *Companion Encyclopedia of Anthropology, Humanity, Culture and Social Life,* ed. T. Ingold. London: Routledge.

Alcock, A. 1970. *The History of the South Tyrol Question.* London: Michael Joseph.

_____, 1996. 'Trentino and South Tyrol. From Austrian Crownland to European Region'. In *Europe and Ethnicity. The First World War and Contemporary Ethnic Conflict,* ed. S. Dunn and T. Fraser. London: Routledge.

Allum, P. and I. Diamanti. 1996. 'The autonomous leagues in the Veneto'. In *Italian Regionalism. History, Identity and Politics,* ed. C. Levy. Oxford: Berg.

Anderson, B. 1991. *Imagined Communities.* London: Verso.

Anderson, D. 1998. 'Property as a way of knowing on Evenki lands in Arctic Siberia'. In *Property Relations: Renewing the Anthropological Tradition,* ed. C. Hann. Cambridge: Cambridge University Press.

Antonelli, Q. 1981. *Fede e lavoro. Ideologia e linguaggio di un universo simbolico.* Rovereto: Materiali di Lavoro.

Appadurai, A. 1995. 'The production of locality'. In *Counterworks,* ed. R. Fardon. London: Routledge.

Ardener, E. 1989a. 'Language, ethnicity and population'. In *Edwin Ardener: the Voice of Prophecy,* ed. M. Chapman. Oxford: Blackwell.

_____, 1989b. 'The "problem" revisited'. In *Edwin Ardener: the vVoice of Prophecy*, ed. M. Chapman. Oxford: Blackwell.

Argyrou, V. 1996. *Tradition and Modernity in the Mediterranean. The Wedding as a Symbolic Struggle*. Cambridge: Cambridge University Press.

_____, 1997: '"Keep Cyprus clean": littering, pollution, and otherness'. *Cultural Anthropology* 12:2, 159–78.

Bagnasco, A. and M. Oberti. 1998. 'Italy. "Le trompe-l'œil" of regions'. In *Regions in Europe*, ed. P. Le Galès and C. Lequesne. London: Routledge.

Bailey, F.G. 1969. *Stratagems and spoils*. Oxford: Blackwell.

_____, 1971. 'Gifts and poison'. In *Gifts and Poison. The Politics of Reputation*, ed. F.G. Bailey. Oxford: Blackwell.

_____, 1991. *The Prevalence of Deceit*. Ithaca, NY: Cornell University Press.

Banfield, E. 1958. *The Moral Basis of a Backward Society*. Glencoe, IL: Free Press.

Barozzi, M. 1996. 'L'Euregio Tirolo, un passo verso la Mitteleuropa'. *Limes* 1, 37–45.

Barth, F. 1969. 'Introduction'. In *Ethnic Groups and Boundaries*, ed. F. Barth. London: Allen & Unwin.

Battisti, C. 1912. *Guida di Primiero*. Trent.

Bauer, R. 1992. 'Changing representations of place, community and character in the Spanish Sierra del Caurel'. *American Ethnologist* 19:3, 571–88.

Bauman, Z. 1995. *Life in Fragments: Essays in Postmodern Morality*. Oxford: Blackwell.

_____, 1998. *Globalization: The Human Consequences*. Cambridge: Polity.

Baumann, G. 1996. *Contesting Culture: Discourses of Identity in Multi-ethnic London*. Cambridge: Cambridge University Press.

Bender, B. 1993. 'Introduction: landscape – meaning and action'. In *Landscape: Politics and Perspectives*, ed. B. Bender. Oxford: Berg.

Bendix, R. 1985. *Progress and Nostalgia. Silvesterklausen in Urnäsch, Switzerland*. Berkeley: University of California Press.

Berthoud, G. 2001. 'The "spirit of the Alps" and the making of political and economic modernity in Switzerland'. *Social Anthropology* 9:1, 81–94.

Bettega, A. and L. Girotto. 1996. *1914–1918: tra le rocce, il vento e la neve. Storia ed immagini della Grande Guerra sui monti del Vanoi e di Fiemme*. Tricesimo: Aviani.

Bhabha, H. 1994. *The Location of Culture*. London: Routledge.

Bloch, M. 1997. 'Time, narratives and the multiplicity of representations of the past'. In *How We Think They Think*, ed. M. Bloch. Boulder, CO: Westview Press.

Blok, A. 1974. *The Mafia of a Sicilian Village*. New York: Harper & Row.

_____, 1981. 'Rams and billy-goats: a key to the Mediterranean code of honour'. *Man* (N.S.) 16:3, 427–40.

Blok, A. and H. Driessen. 1984. 'Mediterranean agro-towns as a form of cultural dominance'. *Ethnologia Europæa* 14:2, 111–24.

Boissevain, J. 1965. *Saints and Fireworks*. London: Athlone.

_____, 1974. *Friends of Friends*. Oxford: Blackwell.

_____, 1975. 'Towards a social anthropology of Europe'. In *Beyond the Community. Social Process in Europe*, ed. J. Boissevain and J. Friedl. The Hague: Department of Education and Science.

_____, 1992. 'Introduction. Revitalizing European rituals'. In *Revitalizing European Rituals*, ed. J. Boissevain. London: Routledge.

_____, 1994. 'Towards an anthropology of European communities?' In *The Anthropology of Europe*, ed. V. Goddard et al. Oxford: Berg.

du Boulay, J. 1974. *Portrait of a Greek Mountain Village*. Oxford: Oxford University Press.

Bourdieu, P. 1963. 'The attitude of the Algerian peasant toward time'. In *Mediterranean countrymen. Essays in the Social Anthropology of the Mediterranean*, ed. J. Pitt-Rivers. Paris: Mouton.

_____, 1976. 'Marriage strategies as stratagems of social reproduction'. In *Family and Society*, ed. R. Forster and O. Ranum. Baltimore, MD: Johns Hopkins University Press.

_____, 1977: *Outline of a Theory of Practice*. Cambridge: Cambridge University Press.

Brandes, S. 1976. 'The priest as agent of secularization in rural Spain'. In *Economic Transformation and Steady-state Values: Essays in the Ethnography of Spain*, ed. J. Aceves et al. Flushing, NY: Queens College Press.

_____, 1980. *Metaphors of Masculinity. Sex and Status in Andalusian Folklore*. Philadelphia: University of Pennsylvania Press.

Brettell, C. 1990. 'The priest and his people: the contractual basis for religious practice in rural Portugal'. In *Religious Orthodoxy and Popular Faith in European Society*, ed. E. Badone. Princeton: Princeton University Press.

Bringa, T. 1995. *Being Muslim the Bosnian way*. Princeton: Princeton University Press.

Burns, R. 1963. 'The circum-Alpine area. A preliminary view'. *Anthropological Quarterly* 36:3, 130–55.

Calì, V. 1988. 'Il caso trentino'. In *L'autonomia e l'amministrazione locale nell'area alpina*, ed. P. Schiera et al. Milan: Jaca.

Campbell, J. 1964. *Honour, Family and Patronage*. Oxford: Oxford University Press.

Capuzzo, E. 1985. 'Carte di regola e usi civici in Trentino'. *Studi Trentini di Scienze Storiche* 64:4, 371–421.

Cartmill, M. 1995. 'Hunting and humanity in western thought'. *Social Research* 62:3, 773–86.

Cartocci, R. 1994. *Fra Lega e Chiesa. L'Italia in cerca di integrazione*. Bologna: Il Mulino.

Castells, M. and J. Henderson. 1987. 'Techno-economic restructuring, sociopolitical process and spatial transformation: a global prespective'. In *Global*

Restructuring and Territorial Development, ed. M. Castells and J. Henderson. London: Sage.

Cento Bull, A. 1996. 'Ethnicity, racism and the Northern League'. In *Italian Regionalism. History, Identity and Politics*, ed. C. Levy. Oxford: Berg.

_____, 2000. *Social Identities and Political Cultures in Italy. Catholic, Communist and Leghist Communities Between Civicness and Localism*. Oxford: Berghahn.

de Certeau, M. 1984: *The Practice of Everyday Life*. Berkeley: University of California Press.

Chapman, M. 1978. *The Gaelic Vision in Scottish Culture*. London: Croom Helm.

dei Chechi, T. 1930. *Raccolta Dialettale Primierotta*. Trent: Artigianelli.

Ching, B. and G. Creed. 1997. 'Recognizing rusticity. Identity and the power of place'. In *Knowing Your Place: Rural Identity and Cultural Hierarchy*, ed. B. Ching and G. Creed. London: Routledge.

Christian, W. 1972. *Person and God in a Spanish Valley*. New York: Seminar Press.

Cohen, A. 1977. 'Symbolic action and the structure of the self'. In *Symbols and Sentiments*, ed. I. Lewis. New York: Academic Press.

_____, 1979. 'Political symbolism'. *Annual Review of Anthropology* 8, 87–113.

Cohen, A.P. 1982. 'Belonging. The experience of culture'. In *Belonging. Identity and Social Organisation in British Rural Cultures*, ed. A.P. Cohen. Manchester: Manchester University Press.

_____, 1985. *The Symbolic Construction of Community*. London: Tavistock.

_____, 1986. 'Of symbols and boundaries, or, does Ertie's greatcoat hold the key?' In *Symbolising Boundaries. Identity and Diversity in British Cultures*, ed. A.P. Cohen. Manchester: Manchester University Press.

_____, 1987. *Whalsay. Symbol, Segment and Boundary in a Shetland Island Community*. Manchester: Manchester University Press.

_____, 1996. 'Personal nationalism: a Scottish view of some rites, rights, and wrongs'. *American Ethnologist* 23:4, 802–15.

Cohen, E. 1977. 'Nicknames, social boundaries and community in an Italian village'. *International Journal of Contemporary Sociology* 14:1–2, 102–13.

Cole, J. 1985. 'Culture and economy in peripheral Europe'. *Ethnologia Europæa* 15:1, 3–26.

Cole, J. and E. Wolf. 1974. *The Hidden Frontier. Ecology and Ethnicity in an Alpine Valley*. New York: Academic Press.

Cole, L. 2000. 'Nation, anti-Enlightenment, and religious revival in Austria: Tyrol in the 1790s'. *The Historical Journal* 43:2, 475–97.

Cole, S. 1991. *Women of the Praia. Work and Lives in a Portuguese Coastal Community*. Princeton: Princeton University Press.

Collard, A. 1989. 'Investigating "social memory" in a Greek context'. In *History and Ethnicity*, ed. E. Tonkin et al. London: Routledge.

Collier, J. 1997. *From Duty to Desire. Remaking Families in a Spanish Village.* Princeton: Princeton University Press.

Collier, J. and S. Yanagisako. 1987. 'Toward a unified analysis of gender and kinship'. In *Gender and Kinship*, ed. J. Collier and S. Yanagisako. Stanford, CA: Stanford University Press.

Connerton, P. 1989. *How Societies Remember.* Cambridge: Cambridge University Press.

Corbin, J. and M. Corbin. 1987. *Urbane Thought: Culture and Class in an Andalusian City.* Aldershot: Gower.

Dalla Bernardina, S. 1993. 'Approccio ecologico? Approccio economico? Per un'antropologia delle frontiere in ambiente alpino'. *S.M. Annali di San Michele* 6, 35–53.

Davis, J. 1969. 'Town and country'. *Anthropological Quarterly* 42:3, 171–85.

_____, 1973. *Land and Family in Pisticci.* London: Athlone.

_____, 1977. *People of the Mediterranean: An Essay in Comparative Social Anthropology.* London: Routledge.

_____, 1984. 'The sexual division of labour in the Mediterranean'. In *Religion, Power and Protest in Local Communities*, ed. E. Wolf. Berlin: Mouton.

_____, 1989. 'The social relations of the production of history'. In *History and Ethnicity*, ed. E. Tonkin et al. London: Routledge.

Delanty, G. 1996. 'The resonance of Mitteleuropa. A Habsburg myth or antipolitics?' *Theory, Culture & Society* 13:4, 93–108.

_____, 1998. 'Redefining political culture in Europe today: from ideology to the politics of identity and beyond'. In *Political Symbols, Symbolic Politics. European Identities in Transformation*, ed. U. Hedetoft. Aldershot: Ashgate.

_____, 1999. *Social Theory in a Changing World. Conceptions of Modernity.* Cambridge: Polity.

Della Porta, D. 1999. *La politica locale. Potere, istituzioni e attori tra centro e periferia.* Bologna: Il Mulino.

Dematteo, L. 2001. 'La Lega Nord: entre volonté de subversion et désir de légitimité'. *Ethnologie Française* 31:1, 143–52.

Destro, A. 1984. *L'ultima generazione. Confini materiali e simbolici di una comunità delle Alpi Marittime.* Milan: Angeli.

_____, 1997. 'A new era and new themes in Italian politics: the case of Padania'. *Journal of Modern Italian Studies* 2:3, 358–77.

De Winter, L. and H. Türsan. 1998. 'Les partis ethno-régionalistes en Europe'. *Revue Internationale de Politique Comparée* 5:1, 151–63.

Diamanti, I. 1994a. 'Localismo'. *Rassegna Italiana di Sociologia* 35:3, 403–24.

_____, 1994b. 'Lega Nord: un partito per le periferie'. In *Stato dell'Italia*, ed. P. Ginsborg. Milan: Il Saggiatore.

_____, 1996a. *Il male del Nord. Lega, localismo, secessione.* Rome: Donzelli.

_____, 1996b. 'The Northern League. From regional party to party of government'. In *The New Italian Republic*, ed. S. Gundle and S. Parker. London: Routledge.

_____, 1999. 'Ha ancora senso discutere di nazione?' *Rassegna Italiana di Sociologia* 40:2, 293–321.

Dobrowolski, K. 1971. 'Peasant traditional culture'. In *Peasants and Peasant Society*, ed. T. Shanin. Harmondsworth: Penguin.

Donnan, H. and T. Wilson. 1994. 'Introduction'. In *Border Approaches: Anthropological Perspectives on Frontiers*, ed. H. Donnan and T. Wilson. Lanham, NY: University Press of America.

Douglas, M. 1966. *Purity and Danger*. London: Routledge.

_____, 1970. *Natural Symbols*. Harmondsworth: Penguin.

_____, 1986. *How Institutions Think*. London: Routledge.

Driessen, H. 1983. 'Male sociability and rituals of masculinity in rural Andalusia'. *Anthropological Quarterly* 56:3, 125–32.

Dubisch, J. 1991. 'Gender, kinship, and religion: "reconstructing" the anthropology of Greece'. In *Contested Identities*, ed. P. Loizos and E. Papataxiarchis. Princeton: Princeton University Press.

_____, 1993. '"Foreign chickens" and other outsiders: gender and community in Greece'. *American Ethnologist* 20:2, 272–87.

Eriksen, T.H. 1993. *Ethnicity and Nationalism: Anthropological Perspectives*. London: Pluto Press.

Evans-Pritchard, E. 1940. *The Nuer*. Oxford: Oxford University Press.

Fabian, J. 1983. *Time and the Other*. New York: Columbia University Press.

Fedel, D. 1980. *Storia dell'ASAR e delle radici storiche dell'Autonomia*. Villalagarina: Pezzini.

Fentress, J. and C. Wickham. 1992. *Social Memory. New Perspectives on the Past*. Oxford: Blackwell.

Filippucci, P. 1992. *Presenting the Past in Bassano: Locality and Localism in a Northern Italian Town*. Unpublished Ph.D. dissertation, University of Cambridge.

_____, 1996. 'Anthropological perspectives on culture in Italy'. In *Italian Cultural Studies. An Introduction*, ed. D. Forgacs and R. Lumley. Oxford: Oxford University Press.

Filippucci, P., C. Grasseni, P. Messina and J. Stacul, 1997. *Knowing the Territory: Territory, Identity, and Local Culture in Northern Italy*. Paper delivered at the Annual Conference of the Association for the Study of Modern Italy (London, 21 November 1997).

Fontana, S. 1935. 'Una memorabile caccia all'orso in Caoria'. *Strenna Trentina*.

Fortes, M. 1969. *Kinship and the Social Order*. London: Routledge.

Fox, R. 1990. Introduction. In *Nationalist Ideologies and the Production of National Cultures*, ed. R. Fox. Washington DC: American Anthropological Association.

Friedman, J. 1992. 'The past in the future: history and the politics of identity'. *American Anthropologist* 94:4, 837–59.

Frykman, J. 1999. 'Belonging in Europe. Modern identities in minds and places'. *Ethnologia Europæa* 29:2, 13–23.

Geertz, C. 1980. *Negara. The Theatre State in Nineteenth-century Bali.* Princeton: Princeton University Press.

Gefou-Madianou, D. 1999. 'Cultural poliphony and identity formation: negotiating tradition in Attica'. *American Ethnologist* 26:2, 412–39.

Gellner, E. 1977. 'Patrons and clients'. In *Patrons and Clients in Mediterranean Societies*, ed. E. Gellner and J. Waterbury. London: Duckworth.

――――, 1983. *Nations and Nationalism.* Oxford: Blackwell.

Gillis, J. 1994. 'Introduction'. In *Commemorations*, ed. J. Gillis. Princeton: Princeton University Press.

Gilmore, D. 1980. *The People of the Plain.* New York: Columbia University Press.

――――, 1982. 'Some notes on community nicknaming in Spain'. *Man* (N.S.) 17:4, 686–700.

――――, 1987. *Aggression and Community.* New Haven, CT: Yale University Press.

Ginsborg, P. 1990. *A History of Contemporary Italy.* Harmondsworth: Penguin.

――――, 1998. *L'Italia del tempo presente: famiglia, società civile, stato 1980–1996.* Turin: Einaudi.

Gledhill, J. 1994. *Power and its Disguises. Anthropological Perspectives on Politics.* London: Pluto Press.

Gluckman, M. 1965. *Politics, Law and Ritual in Tribal Society.* Oxford: Blackwell.

Goddard, V. 1994. 'From the Mediterranean to Europe. Honour, kinship and gender'. In *The Anthropology of Europe*, ed. V. Goddard et al. Oxford: Berg.

Godelier, M. 1986. *The Mental and the Material.* London: Verso.

Goffman, E. 1959. *The Presentation of Self in Everyday Life.* Harmondsworth: Penguin.

――――, 1968. *Stigma. Notes on the Management of Spoiled Identity.* Harmondsworth: Penguin.

Green, S. n.d. *Timescapes: Greek-Albanian Border Peoples and the Generation of Temporal Fracture Lines.* Paper submitted for consideration to 'American Ethnologist'.

Grillo, R. 1980. 'Introduction'. In *Nation and State in Europe*, ed. R. Grillo. New York: Academic Press.

Grosselli, R. 1987. *Colonie imperiali nella terra del caffè.* Trent: Provincia Autonoma.

――――, 1989. *Dove cresce l'araucaria. Dal Primiero a Novo Tyrol.* Trent: Provincia Autonoma.

Gubert, R. 1997. 'La percezione dell'identità culturale trentina e delle ragioni dell'autonomia'. In *Specificità culturale di una regione alpina nel contesto europeo; indagine sociologica sui valori dei trentini,* ed. R. Gubert. Milan: Angeli.

Guizzardi, G. 1976. 'The "rural civilization". Structure of an ideology of consent'. *Social Compass* 23:2–3, 197–220.

Gupta, A. and J. Ferguson. 1997. 'Beyond "culture": space, identity, and the politics of difference'. In *Culture, Power, Place. Explorations in Critical Anthropology,* ed. A. Gupta and J. Ferguson. Durham, NC: Duke University Press.

Handler, R. 1988. *Nationalism and the Politics of Culture in Quebec.* Madison: University of Wisconsin Press.

Hann, C. 1998. 'Introduction: the embeddedness of property'. In *Property Relations: Renewing the Anthropological Tradition,* ed. C. Hann. Cambridge: Cambridge University Press.

Harvey, D. 1989. *The Condition of Postmodernity. An Enquiry into the Origins of Cultural Change.* Oxford: Blackwell.

Harvie, C. 1994. *The Rise of Regional Europe.* London: Routledge.

Hastrup, K. 1992. 'Introduction'. In *Other Histories,* ed. K. Hastrup. London: Routledge.

_____, 1998. *A Place Apart. An Anthropological Study of the Icelandic World.* Oxford: Oxford University Press.

Heady, P. 1999. *The Hard People. Rivalry, Sympathy and Social Structure in an Alpine Valley.* Amsterdam: Harwood Academic Publishers.

Heatherington, T. 1999. 'Street tactics: Catholic ritual and the senses of the past in central Sardinia'. *Ethnology* 38:4, 315–34.

Hedetoft, U. 1998. 'On nationalisers and Europeanisers in contemporary Europe – an introduction'. In *Political Symbols, Symbolic Politics. European Identities in Transformation,* ed. U. Hedetoft. Aldershot: Ashgate.

Hell, B. 1996. 'Enraged hunters. The domain of the wild in north-western Europe'. In *Nature and Society,* ed. P. Descola and G. Pálsson. London: Routledge.

Herzfeld, M. 1985a. *The Poetics of Manhood.* Princeton: Princeton University Press.

_____, 1985b. '"Law" and "custom": ethnography *of* and *in* Greek national identity'. *Journal of Modern Greek Studies* 3:2, 167–85.

_____, 1987. *Anthropology through the Looking-glass.* Cambridge: Cambridge University Press.

_____, 1991. *A Place in History. Social and Monumental Time in a Cretan Town.* Princeton: Princeton University Press.

_____, 1992. *The Social Production of Indifference: Exploring the Symbolic Roots of Western Bureaucracy.* Oxford: Berg.

_____, 1997. *Cultural Intimacy. Social Poetics in the Nation-state.* London: Routledge.

_____, 2001. *Anthropology. Theoretical Practice in Culture and Society.* Oxford: Blackwell.

Hirsch, E. 1995. 'Introduction. Landscape: between place and space'. In *The Anthropology of Landscape*, ed. E. Hirsch and M. O'Hanlon. Oxford: Oxford University Press.

Hirschon, R. 1984. 'Introduction: property, power and gender relations'. In *Women and Property, Women as Property*, ed. R. Hirschon. London: Croom Helm.

Hirschon, R. and J. Gold. 1982. 'Territoriality and the home environment in a Greek urban community'. *Anthropological Quarterly* 55:2, 63–73.

Hobsbawm, E. 1983. 'Introduction: inventing traditions'. In *The Invention of Tradition*, ed. E. Hobsbawm and T. Ranger. Cambridge: Cambridge University Press.

_____, 1992. 'Ethnicity and nationalism in Europe today'. *Anthropology Today* 8:1, 3–8.

_____, 1996. 'Identity politics and the Left'. *New Left Review* 217, 38–47.

Holmes, D.R. 2000. *Integral Europe. Fast-capitalism, Multiculturalism, Neo-fascism*. Princeton: Princeton University Press.

Howe, J. 1981. 'Fox hunting as ritual'. *American Ethnologist* 8:2, 278–300.

Hroch, M. 1985. *Social Preconditions of National Revival in Europe*. Cambridge: Cambridge University Press.

Hurwitz Nadel, J. 1984. 'Stigma and separation: pariah status and community persistence in a Scottish fishing village'. *Ethnology* 23:2, 101–15.

Ingold, T. 1986. *The Appropriation of Nature*. Manchester: Manchester University Press.

_____, 1993. 'The temporality of the landscape'. *World Archaeology* 25:2, 152–74.

_____, 1994. 'From trust to domination. An alternative history of human-animal relations'. In *Animals and Human Society. Changing Perspectives*, ed. A. Manning and J. Serpell. London: Routledge.

_____, 1995. 'Building, dwelling, living. How animals and people make themselves at home in the world'. In *Shifting Contexts*, ed. M. Strathern. London: Routledge.

Judt, T. 1997. *A Grand Illusion? An Essay on Europe*. Harmondsworth: Penguin.

Kapferer, B. 1995. 'Bureaucratic erasure. Identity, resistance and violence'. In *Worlds Apart*, ed. D. Miller. London: Routledge.

Kayser Nielsen, N. 2000. 'Food, hunting, and taboo. Cultural heritage in practice'. *Ethnologia Scandinavica* 30, 62–75.

Keith, M. and S. Pile. 1993. 'Conclusion: towards new radical geographies'. In *Place and the Politics of Identity*, ed. M. Keith and S. Pile. London: Routledge.

Kertzer, D. 1980. *Comrades and Christians*. Cambridge: Cambridge University Press.

_____, 1988. *Ritual, Politics and Power*. New Haven, CT: Yale University Press.

_____, 1996. *Politics and Symbols. The Italian Communist Party and the Fall of Communism*. New Haven, CT: Yale University Press.

Knight, J. 1994. 'Questioning local boundaries. A critique of the "Anthropology of locality"'. *Ethnos* 59:3–4, 213–31.

Kroes, R. 2000. *Them and us. Questions of Citizenship in a Globalizing World.* Urbana: University of Illinois Press.

Lampland, M. 1995. *The Object of Labor. Commodification in Socialist Hungary.* Chicago: University of Chicago Press.

Leach, E. 1954. *Political Systems of Highland Burma.* London: Athlone.

Le Bras, G. 1976. *L'église et le village.* Paris: Flammarion.

Leoni, D. 1995. *Il popolo invisibile. Guerra e identità nazionale: il caso trentino.* MS

Lévi-Strauss, C. 1969. *The Elementary Structures of Kinship.* London: Eyre & Spottiswoode.

_____, 1973. *Structural Anthropology Two.* Harmondsworth: Penguin.

Levy, C. 1996. 'Introduction: Italian regionalism in context'. In *Italian Regionalism. History, Identity and Politics,* ed. C. Levy. Oxford: Berg.

Levy, M. 1988. *Governance and Grievance. Habsburg Policy and Italian Tyrol in the Eighteenth Century.* West Lafayette: Purdue University Press.

Llobera, J. 1986. 'Fieldwork in Southwestern Europe: anthropological panacea or epistemological straitjacket?' *Critique of Anthropology* 6:2, 25–33.

Löfgren, O. 1996. 'Linking the local, the national and the global. Past and present trends in European ethnology'. *Ethnologia Europæa* 26:2, 157–68.

Loizos, P. 1975. *The Greek Gift.* Oxford: Blackwell.

Loizos, P. and E. Papataxiarchis. 1991. 'Introduction. Gender and kinship in marriage and alternative contexts'. In *Contested Identities,* ed. P. Loizos and E. Papataxiarchis. Princeton: Princeton University Press.

Lovell, N. 1998. 'Introduction. Belonging in need of emplacement?' In *Locality and Belonging,* ed. N. Lovell. London: Routledge.

Luverà, B. 1996. *Oltre il confine. Euregio e conflitto etnico: tra regionalismo europeo e nuovi nazionalismi in Trentino-Alto Adige.* Bologna: Il Mulino.

Lüdtke, A. 1985. 'Organizational order or "Eigensinn"? Workers' privacy and workers' politics in imperial Germany'. In *Rites of Power. Symbolism, Ritual and Politics since the Middle Ages,* ed. S. Wilentz. Philadelphia: University of Pennsylvania Press.

Mabileau, A. 1993. 'Variations sur le local'. In *A la recherche du 'local',* ed. A. Mabileau. Paris: L'Harmattan.

MacClancy, J. 1993. 'At play with identity in the Basque arena'. In *Inside European Identities,* ed. S. Macdonald. Oxford: Berg.

McDonald, M. 1986. 'Celtic kinship and the problem of being English'. *Current Anthropology* 27:4, 333–47.

_____, 1989. *We are not French! Language, Culture and Identity in Brittany.* London: Routledge.

_____, 1993. 'The construction of difference: an anthropological approach to stereotypes'. In *Inside European Identities,* ed. S. Macdonald. Oxford: Berg.

_____, 1996. '"Unity in diversity". Some tensions in the construction of Europe'. *Social Anthropology* 4:1, 47–60.

Macdonald, S. 1993. 'Identity complexes in Western Europe: social anthropological perspectives'. In *Inside European Identities*, ed. S. Macdonald. Oxford: Berg.

_____, 1997. *Reimagining Culture. Histories, Identities and the Gaelic Renaissance*. Oxford: Berg.

_____, 1998. 'Exhibitions of power and powers of exhibition. An introduction to the politics of display'. In *The Politics of Display. Museums, Science, Culture*, ed. S. Macdonald. London: Routledge.

MacFarlane, A. 1978. *The Origins of English Individualism*. Oxford: Blackwell.

Mach, Z. 1993. *Symbols, Conflict, and Identity*. Albany, NY: SUNY Press.

Macnaghten, P., and J. Urry. 1998. *Contested Natures*. London: Sage.

Malkki, L. 1997. 'National geographic: the rooting of peoples and the territorialization of national identity among scholars and refugees'. In *Culture, Power, Place. Explorations in Critical Anthropology*, ed. A. Gupta and J. Ferguson. Durham, NC: Duke University Press.

Marks, S. 1991. *Southern Hunting in Black and White*. Princeton: Princeton University Press.

Meriggi, M. 1991. 'Dal tramonto del Principato alla I guerra mondiale: percorsi e contraddizioni del regionalismo trentino'. In *Autonomia e regionalismo nell'arco alpino*, ed. V. Calì. Trent: Museo del Risorgimento.

Messina, P. 1997. *Persistenza e mutamento nelle subculture politiche territoriali*. MS

Milton, K. 1993. 'Land or landscape – Rural planning policy and the symbolic construction of the countryside'. In *Rural Development in Ireland. A Challenge for the 1990s*, ed. M. Murray and J. Greer. Aldershot: Avebury.

_____, 1997. 'Modernity and postmodernity in the Northern Irish countryside'. In *Culture and Policy in Northern Ireland. Anthropology in the Public Arena*, ed. H. Donnan and G. McFarlane. Belfast: Institute of Irish Studies.

Minicuci, M. 1995. 'Time and memory: two villages in Calabria'. In *Time. Histories and Ethnologies*, ed. D. Owen Hughes and T. Trautmann. Ann Arbor: University of Michigan Press.

Minnich, R. 1998. *Homesteaders and Citizens. Collective Identity Formation on the Austro-Italian-Slovene Frontier*. Bergen: Norse.

Mitchell, J. 1998. 'The nostalgic construction of community: memory and social identity in urban Malta'. *Ethnos* 63:1, 81–101.

Moore, H. 1988. *Feminism and Anthropology*. Cambridge: Polity.

Mosse, G. 1990. *Fallen Soldiers*. Oxford: Oxford University Press.

Nadel-Klein, J. 1991. 'Reweaving the fringe: localism, tradition and representation in British ethnography'. *American Ethnologist* 18:3, 500–17.

Netting, R. 1981. *Balancing on an Alp. Ecological Change and Continuity in a Swiss Mountain Community*. Cambridge: Cambridge University Press.

Nora, P. 1989. 'Between memory and history: "les lieux de mémoire"'. *Representations* 26, 7–25.

Ortolani, M. 1932. *Il bacino del Cismon. Saggio di geografia antropica.* Trent: Società di Studi per la Venezia Tridentina.

Osti, G. 1989. 'La marginalità sociale in bassa Valsugana e nel Vanoi'. In *Ruralità e marginalità. Tre aree alpine a confronto,* ed. R. Gubert. Milan: Angeli.

Palla, L. 1994. *Il Trentino orientale e la Grande Guerra.* Trent: Museo del Risorgimento.

Pallaver, G. 2000. 'Euroregione Tirolo. Genesi e sviluppo di un progetto politico'. *Storia & Regione* 9, 261–73.

Papadakis, Y. 1994. 'The national struggle museums of a divided city'. *Ethnic and Racial Studies* 17:3, 400–19.

Passerini, L. 1987. *Fascism in Popular Memory: the Cultural Experience of the Turin Working Class.* Cambridge: Cambridge University Press.

———, 2000. 'The last identification: why some of us would like to call themselves Europeans and what we mean by this'. In *Europe and the Other and Europe as the Other,* ed. B. Stråth. Brussels: PIE-Peter Lang.

Peres, H. 1998. 'Entre désenchantement et réenchantement: chasser en Chalosse'. *Études Rurales* 147–148, 99–113.

Peters, E. 1972. 'Aspects of the control of moral ambiguities'. In *The Allocation of Responsibility,* ed. M. Gluckman. Manchester: Manchester University Press.

Piccoli, P. 1978. 'Nello stato totalitario'. In *Storia del Trentino contemporaneo,* ed. O. Barbié. Trent: Verifiche.

Pina-Cabral, J. de 1987. 'Paved roads and enchanted mooresses: the perception of the past among the peasant population of the Alto Minho'. *Man* (N.S.) 22:4, 715–35.

———, 1989. 'The Mediterranean as a category of regional comparison. A critical review'. *Current Anthropology* 30:3, 399–406.

Pine, F. 1996. 'Naming the house and naming the land: kinship and social group in highland Poland'. *Journal of the Royal Anthropological Institute* (N.S.) 2:3, 443–59.

Pistoia, U. 1992. *La Valle di Primiero nel Medioevo.* Venice: Deputazione.

———, 1996. *Per la storia di Caoria. Alcune ipotesi e qualche punto fermo.* Comune di Canal San Bovo.

Pitt-Rivers, J. 1954. *The People of the Sierra.* Chicago: University of Chicago Press.

Poppi, C. 1980. 'Kinship and social organization among the Ladins of the Val di Fassa (Northern Italy)'. *Cambridge Anthropology* 6:1–2, 60–88.

———, 1991. 'The contention of tradition: legitimacy, culture and ethnicity in Southern Tyrol'. In *Per Frumenzio Ghetta.* Trent: Biblioteca Comunale.

Pratt, J. 1980. 'A sense of place'. In *Nation and State in Europe,* ed. R. Grillo. New York: Academic Press.

_____, 1984. 'Christian-Democrat ideology in the Cold War period'. In *Religion, Power and Protest in Local Communities*, ed. E. Wolf. Berlin: Mouton.

_____, 1986. *The Walled City.* Göttingen: Herodot.

_____, 1996. 'Catholic culture'. In *Italian Cultural Studies. An Introduction*, ed. D. Forgacs and R. Lumley. Oxford: Oxford University Press.

Rapport, N. and A. Dawson. 1998. 'Home and movement: a polemic'. In *Migrants of Identity. Perceptions of Home in a World of Movement*, ed. N. Rapport and A. Dawson. Oxford: Berg.

Reed, J. 1982. *One South: an Ethnic Approach to Regional Culture.* Baton Rouge: Louisiana State University Press.

Reed-Danahay, D. 1993. 'Talking about resistance: ethnography and theory in rural France'. *Anthropological Quarterly* 66:4, 221–9.

Reiter, R. 1975. 'Men and women in the South of France: public and private domains'. In *Toward an Anthropology of Women*, ed. R. Reiter. New York: Monthly Review Press.

Revelli, M. 1995. 'Economia e modello sociale nel passaggio tra Fordismo e Toyotismo'. In *Appuntamenti di fine secolo*, ed. P. Ingrao and R. Rossanda. Rome: Manifestolibri.

Rhoades, R. and S. Thompson. 1975. 'Adaptive strategies in Alpine environments: beyond ecological particularism'. *American Ethnologist* 2:3, 535–51.

Riegelhaupt, J. 1973. 'Festas and padres: the organization of religious action in a Portuguese parish'. *American Anthropologist* 75:3, 835–52.

Roberts, F. 1989. 'The Finnish coffee ceremony and notions of self'. *Arctic Anthropology* 26:1, 20–33.

Rogers, S. 1975. 'Female forms of power and the myth of male dominance: model of female/male interaction in peasant society'. *American Ethnologist* 2:4, 727–56.

_____, 1991. *Shaping Modern Times in Rural France.* Princeton: Princeton University Press.

Romagna, F. 1992. *La valle del Vanoi.* Trent: Alcione.

Romanelli, R. 1991. 'Le radici storiche del localismo italiano'. *Il Mulino* 40:4, 711–20.

Roseman, S. 1996. '"How we built the road": the politics of memory in rural Galicia'. *American Ethnologist* 23:4, 836–60.

Ruzza, C. and O. Schmidtke, 1991. 'The making of the Lombard League'. *Telos* 90, 57–70.

_____, 1996. 'The Northern League. Changing friends and foes, and its political opportunity structure'. In *Citizenship, Nationality and Migration in Europe*, ed. D. Cesarani and M. Fulbrook. London: Routledge.

Sahlins, M. 1985. *Islands of History.* Chicago: University of Chicago Press.

Sahlins, P. 1989. *Boundaries: the Making of France and Spain in the Pyrenees.* Berkeley: University of California Press.

Said, E. 1978. *Orientalism. Western Conceptions of the Orient.* Harmondsworth: Penguin.

Sanguanini, B. 1992. *Fare cultura. Attori e processi della modernizzazione culturale: il Trentino.* Milan: Angeli.

Schama, S. 1995. *Landscape and Memory.* London: Harper Collins.

Schneider, D.M. 1980. *American Kinship. A cultural account.* Chicago: University of Chicago Press.

Schneider, J. 1971. 'Of vigilance and virgins: honour, shame and access to resources in Mediterranean societies'. *Ethnology* 10:1, 1–24.

Schweizer, P. 1988. *Shepherds, Workers, Intellectuals. Culture and Centre-periphery Relationships in a Sardinian Village.* Stockholm: Stockholm Studies in Social Anthropology.

Scott, J. 1976. *The Moral Economy of the Peasant.* New Haven, CT: Yale University Press.

_____, 1985. *Weapons of the Weak: Everyday Forms of Peasant Resistance.* New Haven, CT: Yale University Press.

Shapiro, M.J. 2000. 'National time and other times: re-thinking citizenship'. *Cultural Studies* 14:1, 79–98.

Shore, C. 2000. *Building Europe. The cultural politics of European integration.* London: Routledge.

Shore, C. and A. Black. 1994. 'Citizens' Europe and the construction of European identity'. In *The Anthropology of Europe*, ed. V. Goddard et al. Oxford: Berg.

Silverman, S. 1975. *Three Bells of Civilization. The Life of an Italian Hill Town.* New York: Columbia University Press.

Skultans, V. 1998. *The Testimony of Lives. Narrative and Memory in Post-Soviet Latvia.* London: Routledge.

Smith, A.D. 1991. *National Identity.* Harmondsworth: Penguin.

Smith, G. 1999. *Confronting the Present. Towards a Politically Engaged Anthropology.* Oxford: Berg.

Stewart, C. 1991. *Demons and the Devil. Moral Imagination in Modern Greek Culture.* Princeton: Princeton University Press.

Stolcke, V. 1995. 'Talking culture. New boundaries, new rhetorics of exclusion in Europe'. *Current Anthropology* 36:1, 1–13.

Strassoldo, R. 1996. 'Ethnic regionalism versus the state: the case of Italy's Northern Leagues'. In *Borders, Nations and States*, ed. L. O'Dowd and T. Wilson. Aldershot: Avebury.

Strathern, M. 1980. 'No nature, no culture: the Hagen case'. In *Nature, Culture and Gender*, ed. C. MacCormack and M. Strathern. Cambridge: Cambridge University Press.

_____, 1981. *Kinship at the Core: an Anthropology of Elmdon, a Village in Northwest Essex in the Nineteen-sixties.* Cambridge: Cambridge University Press.

_____, 1984a. 'Localism displaced: a "vanishing village" in rural England'. *Ethnos* 49:1–2, 43–61.

_____, 1984b. *No Culture, no History.* MS

_____, 1987. 'The limits of auto-anthropology'. In *Anthropology at Home*, ed. A. Jackson. London: Tavistock.

_____, 1988. *The Gender of the Gift.* Berkeley: University of California Press.

Stråth, B. 2000. 'Introduction. Europe as a discourse'. In *Europe and the Other and Europe as the Other*, ed. B. Stråth. Brussels: PIE-Peter Lang.

Sutton, D. 1994. '"Tradition" and "modernity": Kalymnian constructions of identity and otherness'. *Journal of Modern Greek Studies* 12:2, 239–60.

_____, 1997. 'Local names, foreign claims: family inheritance and national heritage on a Greek island'. *American Ethnologist* 24:2, 415–37.

_____, 1998. *Memories Cast in Stone. The Relevance of the Past in Everyday Life.* Oxford: Berg.

Tak, H. 1990. 'Longing for local identity: intervillage relations in an Italian mountain area'. *Anthropological Quarterly* 63:2, 90–100.

Tarrow, S. 1977. *Between Center and Periphery: Grassroots Politicians in Italy and France.* New Haven, CT: Yale University Press.

Thapar, R. 1996. *Time as a Metaphor of History: Early India.* Delhi: Oxford University Press.

Thomas, K. 1983. *Man and the Natural World: Changing Attitudes in England 1500–1800.* Harmondsworth: Penguin.

Thompson, A. 2001. 'Nations, national identities and human agency: putting people back into nations'. *The Sociological Review* 49:1, 18–32.

Tilly, C. 1992. 'Futures of European states'. *Social Research* 59:4, 705–17.

Tissot, L. 1996. *Dizionario Primierotto.* Calliano: Manfrini.

Tonkin, E., M. McDonald and M. Chapman. 1989. 'Introduction'. In *History and Ethnicity*, ed. E. Tonkin et al. London: Routledge.

Turato, F. 1998. 'Il Trentino Alto Adige'. In *Idee del Nordest. Mappe, rappresentazioni, progetti*, ed. I. Diamanti. Turin: Edizioni Fondazione Giovanni Agnelli.

Vale de Almeida, M. 1996. *The Hegemonic Male. Masculinity in a Portuguese Town.* Oxford: Berghahn.

Viazzo, P.P. 1989. *Upland Communities: Environment, Population and Social Structure in the Alps since the Sixteenth Century.* Cambridge: Cambridge University Press.

Vincze, L. 1980. 'Peasant animal husbandry: a dialectic model of techno-environmental integration in agro-pastoral societies'. *Ethnology* 19:4, 387–403.

Waldren, J. 1996. *Insiders and Outsiders: Paradise and Reality in Mallorca.* Oxford: Berghahn.

White, C. 1980. *Patrons and Partisans: a Study of Politics in Two Southern Italian Comuni.* Cambridge: Cambridge University Press.

Wright, S. 1998. 'The politicization of "culture"'. *Anthropology Today* 14:1, 7–15.

Zaninelli, S. 1978. *Un'agricoltura di montagna nell'ottocento: il Trentino.* Trent: Società di Studi Trentini di Scienze Storiche.

Zieger, A. 1975. *Primiero e la sua storia.* Trent: Accademia del Buonconsiglio.

Zonabend, F. 1984. *The Enduring Memory: Time and History in a French Village.* Manchester: Manchester University Press.

Zorzi, A. 1966. *Monte Cauriol 1916.* Trent: Reverdito.

INDEX